ΩΨΩΨΩΨΩΨΩΨΩΨΩ

A DICTIONARY

OF OPPRESSION

IN THE WORKPLACE

by

GODFREY HOLMES

ΩΨΩΨΩΨΩΨΩΨΩΨΩΨΩΨΩΨΩΨΩ

© **Godfrey Holmes**
MARCH   2015

ISBN : 978-0-9536016-5-3

All rights reserved. No part of this publication may be reproduced or transmitted in any form or by any means: electronic or mechanical, including photocopying, recording - or entered into any information storage and retrieval system -
nor may its content be incorporated into staff training programmes, without the prior permission, in writing, from the publisher.
A catalogue record of this Dictionary is available from
the British Library

NETHERMOOR BOOKS
"St. Elphin"
12 North Promenade
Withernsea
East Riding of Yorkshire
HU19 2DP

Telephone : 01964-615258
Contact the Author :
godfrey.holmes@btinternet.com

*DEDICATED   TO
THE   UNK̫OWN   WORKER
SUFFERING   IN   SILENCE
YET   STILL   STANDING   AT   5*

CONTENTS

INTRODUCTION........1

A NOTE ABOUT TEXT LAYOUT......8

THE DIRECTION OF ENTRIES......9

WHY CAST THE NET SO WIDE ?......10

AN "A" TO "Z" OF OPPRESSION IN THE WORKPLACE......11

WHERE TO PROGRESS FROM HERE ? A Ten Point Plan......237

KEY REPLIES TO A BULLYING MANAGER......238

STILL STANDING AT 5 : Strategies for Getting Through 239

<< THE TRIADIC PERSONALITY >> 240

SELECT BIBLIOGRAPHY......241

STEAMROLLER

Image courtesy of Colin Lowson
The Scottish Traction Engine Society

A DICTIONARY OF OPPRESSION IN THE WORKPLACE

INTRODUCTION

Oppression in the workplace is best defined as : " any action or omission that prevents an employee enjoying a happy and productive experience whilst engaged in paid or unpaid employment."

Usually Oppression happens with the desire, or the leave, or the negligence, or the collusion, of an owner, a junior or senior manager, a section head or team leader, a foreman, or a charge hand - or not uncommonly, a colleague or co-worker.

Alternatively, *wider* society organizes itself, passes legislation, makes its decisions and its choices, to the end that workers are devalued, exploited, underpaid, trampled upon.

And *not being aware* that Oppression is happening is both a perennial and a totally specious excuse.

Nor are families - nuclear or amalgamated families - insignificant. It is partners and loved ones who say "Goodbye!" to their Breadwinner in a morning, "Hello!" in the evening.... or the end of each shift or outside assignment.

The term *Oppression* in the Workplace *includes* ever-present Workplace *Bullying* - but then reaches out much further : to those

unpleasant undertones, demands or expectations that may go undetected and unchallenged for years on end.

Each worker is possibly engaged in voluntary, self-, or remunerated employment for only a fifth, tenth or fifteenth of his or her life. Yet the repercussions, alienation, *havoc*, **of negative experience in factory, office, school, hospital, agency, shop or call-centre can never be underestimated, never overestimated either.**

ΩΨΩΨΩΨΩΨΩΨΩ

This Dictionary is to be found in the Human Resources' or Personnel Department of every workplace large enough to have such a specialized office.

It is also a Dictionary intended to encourage debate and reflection amongst Managers who manage at every level, whatever their job-description, day-to-day responsibility, seniority, or outposting.

Then I want this Dictionary to be dipped into by *employees* who have been to Hell and back ; or who *fear* oppression in the workplace and how it might impact upon their families or their leisure pursuits.

A *Dictionary* format has been chosen deliberately for ease identifying what is happening : where, by whom and why. And it is, of course, quite possible to extract or extrapolate the processes of Oppression in the workplace from the accounts of those who have suffered it.

Or Oppression can be *inferred* from office procedures or guidance, from job recruitment adverts or reports of industrial action.

Many books start with the assumption that because Oppression - because it is happening already - is somehow *inevitable* ; therefore we should only think of methods to combat or redress it. I am not quite so fatalistic. Change - and people hate change ! - *is* possible.

Simply *detailing* bad cases, notoriously, does not make good law. The problem with Oppression Tourism is that reading more than half a dozen Diaries or Life Histories - so-called Misery Memoirs - actually *immunizes* the reader from shock ; stultifying, reassuring - maybe even *gratifying* - the offending boss or colleague. Thus ground is *lost* rather than gained.

By contrast, a Dictionary goes *beyond* description - heart-rending as that often is - to *analysis* ; to the links that unite oppressed ones when factors come into play across different shops, different offices, different conveyor belts ; where sufferers have never actually met each other !

That universality is the key to *all* Oppression. Oppression boasts the same characteristics, the same language, the same devastating consequences, whether in John O'Groats or Land's End. So a tyrannical father in Edinburgh offers the same excuses as a tyrannical father in Southampton- though their paths have never crossed. And a Roman Catholic priest is persecuted by his congregants to the same degree as a Methodist Minister. Children are isolated and ostracized by their classmates as much in a Welsh public school as in an Inner London comp. Oppression is everywhere practised; everywhere learnt; everywhere *taught* ; everywhere endured ; everywhere tolerated.

This particular Dictionary sprang from three sources of inspiration : a railway journey, a lecture, and a story : a story of years of anguish - each faithfully recounted to me by a close work colleague ; a story so unbelievable, so memorable, so instructive, *so destructive*, as to make an abiding - and disturbing - impression upon me as compiler.

First, the train. I boarded the train at Sheffield. Not a new train. Not a posh train. More like a bus on railway wheels : with seating set at odd angles. It was a Saturday morning, in Spring. Whereupon one fellow-traveller : a mature, well-presented, woman, became so animated, so enlivened, so knocked backwards, by the Oppression she had been subject to in her workplace [a University Department no less !] that she only temporarily interrupted her arresting account, alerting the rest of us *and* her two chastened friends, so she could get off the train at Scunthorpe !

Her Story came out like a torrent, a cascade, a flood. There was no pause for breath, let alone interjection. She - I only knew her as "she" - had held onto her anxieties for 40 hours, 400, 4000 ; had slept or stayed awake with them ; had walked round the block with them ; had been on holiday with them ; had ridden Sheffield's tramways with them ; had eaten and drunk with them ; perhaps withholding many work secrets them a devoted husband, daughters too, until... until that moment she started her day's outing out to Scunthorpe, accompanied by two ladies whom she knew - instinctively knew - would listen to her and sympathize with her.

Second, the Lecture. Seated in a Nottingham lecture theatre, and ready to nod off for 15 minutes, I was suddenly alerted to this formula :

If someone has a negative view of you, each new piece of information gleaned - whether by gossip, encounter, letter or report [or, years later, trawl of the Web] is filtered, and refined, to conform with that held opinion.

In other words, whatever a person does or says, she can never improve another person's attitude or assessment, if her number is up. *Because* any positive feedback is totally discounted as a fluke, an aberration ; whilst *negative* feedback merely confirms how bad she always was.

Conversely, *if someone holds a positive view of you, each new piece of information gleaned - whether from casual conversation, formal interview, group discussion, or work submitted - is swiftly filtered, and enhanced, to verify that affirmative view.*

In this case, any *negative* feedback or adverse customer response is automatically discounted as a red herring ; whilst positive feedback reassures the assessor he or she was correct in their judgment from the beginning.

Thus the *favoured* one never faces criticism - nor even implied disapproval - provided she stays loyal and true to that boss, that Department or that shift. Each Tuesday brings a glow: the glow of acceptance ; also her employer's investment in a promising career. As does each Wednesday and each Thursday. At the other end of the corridor, the u*nfavoured* one reaches each Friday afternoon having received *no* praise, no recognition, no uplift, whatsoever. And Monday activates that cycle all over again.

Is this perhaps *the key* to the phenomenon known as Workplace Oppression ?

Third, my own colleague. That colleague had had a whole score, *twenty*, Team Leaders within Local Government over a 25-year career : only 3 of these Leaders drafted in at my colleague's direct request. Yet by any standard, six Leaders out of the twenty - six in harness over my colleague's most crucial, most debilitating, years - were incorrigible bullies, ably bolstered, garlanded indeed, by devotees who probably knew just how their bread was buttered; who had no investment in upsetting the apple-cart ; also exalted by *their* inert, inept, managers.

And, as you'd expect with a sequence, the worst Oppression was history repeating itself cyclically : giving my colleague a perpetual sense of *déjà vu*. Every January, this hard-working colleague hoped fortune would change. And, miraculously, there *were* some seasons when (s)he did gain full acceptance, and was able to relax.

Some Springs, some Summers, my colleague would seek to get his or her career back on course, untroubled - by trying harder to placate and to satisfy each newly appointed - or drafted in - bully....often to no avail. Thrice, perhaps more times than that, (s)he activated the Grievance Procedure - which caused even more angst.

That's because stated time limits were never adhered to ; "independent" managers were nobbled ; secret alliances were stitched up ; and my colleague was bombarded with new complaints; counter-claims ; counter-offences, new damning evidence concerning his or her performance.

ΩΨΩΨΩΨΩΨΩ

Deliberately, I speak of *Oppression* in the Workplace rather than "workplace bullying" because the word "bullying" is often used too indiscriminately these days. "Bullying," as such, evokes and reawakens in us early sibling rivalry, neighbourhood spats, and the Playground.

Whereas "Oppression" points to the *broader* canvas : a perplexing panorama or amalgam of grossly unsatisfactory working relationships.

"Oppression" leaves the oppressor with no comfort or escape. For "Oppression" means exactly what the oppressed one experiences Oppression to be: mental, physical and social degradation. No more. No less.

And although I refer in this DICTIONARY to the "Workplace" : most of the interactions, also responses, outlined here extend to Home, School, Charity, Church, Club, Court, Green, Stadium, Hospital...wherever. Wherever people congregate and are subject to power rather than empowerment.

Paying the oppressor, or the oppressed one, is not the sole qualification for facing Oppression. Very many partners : domestic and business partners ; very many attendees ; very many onlookers ; very many prisoners ; very many hapless patients ; very many participants; very many *Volunteers* face daily, weekly, continual, Oppression - regardless of formal remuneration or monetary reward.

And *if* this DICTIONARY makes any reader feel better about himself, herself: permitted to see the oppressor more clearly as *tyrant*, culprit, menace ; and if more organizations take active steps to challenge, and then minimize, oppression; its compilation will have been worth every moment**.**

G.H.H.
Withernsea, January 2015

ΩΨΩΨΩΨΩΨΩΨΩ

** A NOTE ABOUT TEXT LAYOUT **

Normally, capitals are used only for the *central subject* of any entry, and only for as long as that entry is explored ; where a proper name like McKenzie is employed ; where only one in that position exists : eg. the Prime Minister; or where Personnel is shorthand for the Personnel Department.

A ° means that one or two particular words need to be *cross-referred*. That suggestion, to cross-refer, is not made explicit - simply because all important words in every entry DO have an entry of their own.

Where 2 terms are vaguely similar : eg. "Strike" and "Industrial Action," the *more common* word heads that special entry - in block capitals - with up to two extra terms for the same event bracketed, using smaller capitals.

All entries are given a score between 1 and 10 for *overall relevance* in the debate surrounding oppression in the workplace.. That does not make 1, 2, 3, 4 or 5 *trivial* ; just slightly less weighty where the weight placed on the employee or volunteer - *any worker* - is crucial.

ΩΨΩΨΩΨΩΨΩΨΩ

THE DIRECTION OF PARTICULAR ENTRIES

Each Entry ends with a word, or words, to sum up its contribution to the phenomenon known as oppression in the workplace.

CAUSE : **A Cause of Oppression in the Workplace** is a contributor that fairly directly causes oppression and repeat oppression. Of significance, that Cause can be real *or* imagined.

RESULT : **A Result of Oppression in the Workplace** is an outcome - usually a negative outcome - of that oppression, its magnification, and its (usually unsuccessful) resolution. Of regret, many Results are invisible to, or disregarded by, the oppressor.

FACTOR : **A Factor in Oppression within the Workplace** is a contributor that matters ; but so also that Factor would matter in alternative behaviours and Responses.

ASSOCIATION : **An Association with Oppression in the Workplace** is slightly more tenuous than a Factor. Yet that Association cannot be overlooked in the total scheme of things.

MOTIVATION : **A Motivation for Oppression in the Workplace** is a detected circumstance or desire. Such determination might be keenly *disputed* by one or both parties in the oppressive cycle.

RESPONSE : **A Response to Oppression in the Workplace** is whatever relieves - or exacerbates - it once it has taken place. That Response might be proactive, by Personnel or management, or merely *reactive*. Some Responses prove more effective than others.

Dividing lines are inherently blurred, and slightly artificial ; nonetheless worth the attempt....even where Entries have up to three directions or interpretations.

W H Y CAST THE NET SO WIDE ?

The temptation when writing a Dictionary of this sort is to include *everything*. One newspaper used to advertise itself with the slogan: "All Human Life is There !"

Down that particular lane, the *over-assiduous* compiler would start with a concept like "Meal" and make separate Entries for : Meal Breaks, Meals Provided, Meals Delayed, Meals Cancelled, Halal Meals, Special Dietary Requirements, Canteens, Executive Dining Rooms, Plans Made Over Meals, Mealtime Humour....etc.

And that over-indulgence would be as ridiculous as it would be self-defeating. Doubtless Oppression sometime, somewhere, impacts upon *all* correlatives from Adrenaline to Zest.

So the guillotine had to be lowered, in order to chop off those headings that would clutter whatever forum or atrium or corridor Oppression in the Workplace is.

Which leads, inevitably, to thousands of *vaguely relevant* Entries being axed ; never given space in the office or the chance of attention in the assembly plant. It is therefore the Author's hope that any "new" subjects of merit will gain admittance at a later date - depending on inter-disciplinary discussion aroused by factors that *did* get in under the wire.

On a very positive note, the *Spider's Web of Oppression* that I adopted allowed numerous, *and disparate*, worries to find here, below, inter-connection and association (far beyond the captive *"Bullying"* at its centre); and has certainly shown itself resilient ; thus rewarding all effort expended on its mapping.

ΩΨΩΨΩΨΩΨΩΨΩΨΩΨΩ

AN "A" TO "Z" OF OPPRESSION IN THE WORKPLACE :
===

ABRASION   [ABRASIVENESS] 8
The Abrasive style of management° gets its name from two surfaces rubbing against each other : to the usual detriment, occasional benefit, of one of those surfaces : glass paper on wood, bleach on porcelain, grater on cheese, potato-peeler on potato. And it is not a compliment to any organization that it allows, or rewards, Abrasion. A possible outcome of the Abrasive approach is for raw recruits, underlings,° and powerless machine operatives to be rubbed up, literally, the wrong way. Abrasion is the direct opposite of collegiate management,° trust,° generosity. Of course, certain managers would not think themselves "robust" ° - or effective enough - *without* abrasion.   *CAUSE*

ABSENCE OF EMPATHY 5
Employers desperately need Empathy with their staff : able to imagine them at home, at leisure, making their wages stretch, bringing up children, arriving at work upset or overburdened. Where an employer *does* display Empathy, this yields an immediate dividend. Furthermore, status differentials are, thereby, usefully eroded.   *CAUSE / FACTOR*

ABSENTEEISM 5
Absenteeism, the opposite of Presenteeism,° is frequently quite innocent : the result of sickness,° a hospital operation, job interview elsewhere - or family responsibility.° Management should however always bear in mind the possibility, sometimes probability, that Absenteeism is both an indicator and early warning of workplace oppression. Predictably, sickness monitoring° might not uncover cleverly-disguised stress.° Many employees are simply too embarrassed - or too guilty - to cite bullying° as the primary reason they fell ill.   *CAUSE / RESULT*

ACCEPT ME AS I AM 4
This laudable sentiment : " Accept Me As I Am," is not quite as innocent as it sounds. Most oppressors cherish the *status quo*. They are in their own minds completely blameless. It is *the other* party who is to blame, and needs not only to change but also express suitable gratitude for their manager's forbearance ! Maybe the other party should never have been appointed. It is expressly *the other* party who is spoiling the show and dragging everyone down with her. Thus the oppressor becomes quite defensive,° even hostile, when his target° employee in rejoinder says : "Then Accept ME As I am !"   *MOTIVATION*

ACCEPTANCE 6
The best employers provide a safe, comfortable and welcoming environment for their staff. Moreover, Acceptance. That Acceptance embraces the nervous employee whatever his or her background, ethnicity, self-presentation or sexual orientation. Acceptance is as important *at home* as at work.   *RESPONSE*

ACCOMMODATION OF THE BULLY 7
Where everyone gives free rein to the practised bully : feeding him a diet of new - more quiescent - victims , devastation follows. Accommodating the Bully is an attractive option because "it gets the job done," and "keeps him on board;" but - as in the setting of domestic violence° - Accommodation also *widens* the Bully's influence. Ensuing complaints are more determinedly disregarded than earlier ones. Soon the Bully° pretends nothing's wrong - as does Personnel.
     CAUSE / RESULT

ACTOR IN ONE'S OWN STAGE SCRIPT 4

Oppressed ones often liken their predicament to the drama of a stage : "If ever folk got to know what I'm going through, they'd find it beyond belief !" All human interaction unfolds on as *drama* : at work, machine, meeting, office or site. The problem with bullying° - under whatever guise or disguise - is that it seizes the script from the main player (self) and misrepresents other Actor(s) by means of rival scripting.   *FACTOR*

ADMINISTRATIVE FAILINGS 6

Not everybody is a gifted administrator. A new employee's strength might be sales, or negotiation,° service delivery, or agenda-setting - not necessarily paperwork. The word "paperwork" covers everything from filing and photocopying to letters, logs and phone calls. Many oppressors cannot bring themselves to express satisfaction with overall performance, so jump in to express *dissatisfaction* with Administrative Failings. Defensively, certain employers appear more dedicated to administration than any of their operation's *superior* objectives : how and why the outfit was once set up. And the trouble with paperwork is that it is so repetitive and reproductive. Give an hour to admin and it takes three hours, three days !   *CAUSE / ASSOCIATION*

ADVICE 4

Giving and receiving Advice sounds remarkably innocuous. Who wouldn't welcome a bit of guidance° ? Better to know what's required; and which pitfalls to avoid. However the newer meaning of Management "Advice" is *correction°* : in ham-fisted hands, *reprimand.°* " It will go on your record, you know!" *Following* the oppressor's Advice, however, may well result in your being troubled again in the future : on a different pretext.   *FACTOR / RESULT*

[THE] AFFAIR 3

Far from protecting a new or junior employee from oppression, the Affair actually opens the floodgate to *further* oppression and more sexual gratification for the Oppressor and his willing accomplices. Workplace Affairs, it can be argued, are almost always *oppressive of themselves*. Rarely will they be entered into through a perfect balance of power or the sharing of responsibility.

And once the Affair is ongoing / recommenced / ended, there are numerous extra openings for blackmail, jealousy,° innuendo, scapegoating.° In fact, ending the Affair might be justification for someone coming down *harder* on a former lover. Even if no money or gifts change hands, the office philanderer benefits nine tenths of the time: cushioned from any adverse consequences. *ASSOCIATION / MOTIVATION*

AGENCY STAFFING 4

Good Agencies give an established worker more freedom : particularly the freedom to move Workplace, fresh challenges, and an escape route from sites where there was oppression. Good Agencies also do the hard spadework of job-finding, vacancy-filling.

Agencies do, however, provide less job-security,° curtailed job continuity, fewer emoluments° and a smaller pension than direct employment. Not unknown is for a workplace to exploit Agency Staff, expecting them to produce far more in a lesser time span than the establishment. Additionally, some Agency Staff are marginalized.° Hospitals° and Care Homes° have a particularly dim view of the Agency Staff on whom they are so dependent. In other words, Agency Staff risk being taken for granted, worse, bullied. *FACTOR*

AGENDA SETTING 4
Whoever sets the Agenda holds the power. It can be argued, indeed, that Agendas are inherently authoritarian.° The Agenda is not usually open to challenge : especially when dictated at a higher level. Furthermore, in Supervision, °the supervisor holds on to the Agenda in order to retain an element of surprise. And after the formal meeting or session comes the *un*scheduled meetings : some reassuring, others quite the opposite. In the circumstances, what better than *to share* the Agenda with supervisee, or across a team or department ?   *ASSOCIATION*

AGGRESSION 8
Aggression is alive and well in far too many workshops, offices, hospitals, schools and stores. And Aggression is nearly always deleterious to harmonious work relationships, also impacting on the total work experience. Besides, Aggression in the workplace is very likely to be an extension of [man's?] Aggression on the road, at the stadium ; pushing the supermarket trolley ; crucially, *in the home.*
Possibly a zero tolerance° of Aggression should be management's automatic response : thus isolating, , marginalizing,° or expelling the alleged Aggressor.   Where Aggression becomes widespread, by definition condoned, *all* staff relations° will be harmed. And, unsurprisingly, the *oppressed* one will hear or feel or get wind of that Aggression first, and worst, of all. Any manifestation of Aggression should be recorded and reported upwards immediately.   *CAUSE*

ALCOHOL 3
Whatever a company's or a local authority's Alcohol Policy, Alcohol is a significant factor in engendering, then aggravating, workplace oppression. Take secret, before-work, even *at-work*, drinking - or

hospitality in order to win a contract. Or take the Staff Christmas Party as an obvious tinderbox. Refusal to drink to excess there and then; reluctance, or enthusiasm for, joining in jokes, drinking games, food-throwing and rowdyism, may count as reason to be sent to Coventry,° or a blot on an otherwise unblemished employment records.°

Is arriving at work under the influence of Alcohol tolerated ? What about those with a hangover ringing in "sick"? Or the position of an *oppressor* drowning his sorrows as compensation for a damaged world view ? To make matters worse, there is colloquial evidence that those stressed or oppressed in the workplace drink more in quantity or strength in their overshadowed leisure hours. *ASSOCIATION / RESULT*

ALLIANCES 5
Alliances can be quite empowering : four or five oppressed ones fighting the system together. In solidarity. A proto trades union. Most Alliances in the workplace, particularly *in the office*, are however quite *destructive*. Hostile co-workers° can easily form an Alliance against the oppressed one : not uncommonly an Alliance formed *before her first day in work*. Meanwhile, *the oppressor* forms his Alliance either with a reliable cohort of co-workers,° or with his own supervisors and senior managers. This latter Alliance is particularly indestructible because it circumvents or undermines every single level of the best-written grievance procedure.°   *FACTOR   / RESPONSE*

ALLIES 5
The oppressed one desperately needs friends and Allies in the workplace. Even a solitary Ally can be taken to one side, invited out for lunch, for a confessional. And those employees *not* oppressed tend to have far more Allies than does the (problematical ?) oppressed one.

The oppressor has Allies too : both in management,° and among co-workers.° Management° routinely listens to the highest-status Ally. Not unknown is for the oppressor *to plant* an "Ally" in a work setting : someone who will obediently report back on the oppressed one.

Even the *faithful* Ally must be watched - in case she is Ally only on a single issue ; so once that single issue is resolved, she is off and away. Ideally, the victim progresses further if she attracts an Ally too : typically a school friend or sympathetic partner *outside* the workplace. Or if she goes *so* high up the management ladder, in search of an Ally, that no oppressor can offer resistance.   *ASSOCIATION   / RESULT*

ANGER MANAGEMENT 4

Anger Management strategies or training courses are the valuable complement to those promoting assertiveness.° Needless to say, the manager or overseer displaying unreasonable anger in the workplace - *probably at home too* - must *consent to* adjustments concerning, or transformation of, his learnt behaviour. Obtaining this consent is the duty of a sensitive Personnel Department. Hopefully, any existing victim(s) will soon see the difference.   *RESPONSE*

ANSWERING QUESTIONS 5

Most people find Answering Questions easy : simply lay out all the facts as understood, until your questioners are satisfied. But what about *diverging* perceptions and ambiguities ? Where there is no single truth, the manager can question an underling° for 50 minutes or more - and *still* not get the answer he is looking for. That is because the interrogated one, intent on self-preservation,° tries to explain her position, or point of view, *from a completely different angle.* A wise and generous manager picks up this perspective straightway. *FACTOR*

APPEASEMENT 7
The stated or unstated policy of Appeasement, in the face of one or more bullies° in the board-room or round the water-cooler, is self-defeating. The initial rewards of Appeasement are immediately cancelled out by lower staff morale,° reduced productivity,° also the instigation of lengthier, and costlier, grievance procedures.°   *RESULT*

APPRAISAL   [ANNUAL APPRAISAL] 7
Across the armed services and the professions, Appraisal is a relatively new buzz-word. Wherever, it is best done by someone *unfamiliar* with a candidate's day-to-day work. Even then, any Appraisal is heavily dependent on a line-manager's mood,° his prejudice,° and his subsequent report.° No line manager will supply the best employee feedback or leg-up if he has taken an active dislike to that employee. And in any formal Appraisal Interview the oppressed one will not come over at her best if she is aware her line-manager has scores to settle - ironically, scores out of 100 . Tallies to threaten a career . *FACTOR / MOTIVATION*

APPRECIATION 7
Most workers yearn for Appreciation. For when they are Appreciated by their employers, encouraged along the way, miraculously they act in a more committed and productive way. So it is that Appreciation brings its own rich dividend. A virtuous circle surprisingly *not* achieved through artifice. Appreciation is additionally free of charge to the insightful employer, yet worth its weight in gold.   *ASSOCIATION*

APPRENTICESHIP 3
Modern Apprenticeships are very unlikely to be indentured for 5 years! Even so, young Apprentices are easily marginalized° ; more readily - and disguisedly - oppressed. After all, Apprentices are often engaged

only on fragile, sale-or-return, terms and conditions. And, as if that were not enough, Apprentices are extremely likely to look youthful, thus arousing yet more negative instincts in their mentors whose job it is to confront sloth, carelessness, insolence and inexperience. *FACTOR*

APPROVAL [WITHHOLDING APPROVAL] 7

The word Approval is absolutely crucial to good - or poor - workplace relations.° Because self-esteem,° and self-image,° rests so heavily on Approval freely granted - more usually, grudgingly *withheld* - this is a marvellous tool for keeping the oppressed one in her place. We sometimes talk of *a thirst* for Approval, so recalling our early childhoods. *CAUSE / RESPONSE*

ARBITRATION 5

Arbitration is a bit different from mediation.° The best Arbiters in a work dispute - particularly one where the balance of power is tilted - are respected figures from another department, even another industry. Arbiters might well be former employees with time to spare to intervene when their successors are in difficulty. It can be very useful for the oppressed one to request Arbitration in place of ongoing discussion. The very request might surprise her line manager° as much as it does Personnel.° And there is absolutely no requirement for Arbitration to have been used in that workplace before. The person under stress has incentive to ask for anything at all : any switch, any re-designation, any reward, *any recourse to justice.* Personnel must then rise to that challenge.

Occasionally, Arbitration is offered to a stressed employee spontaneously: in the form of a new and neutral line manager, one based perhaps in a different building. Or Personnel might itself contain a potential Arbiter. As with all crucial turning-points in her burgeoning or jeopardized career, the oppressed one is best accompanied by a close colleague or a McKenzie friend.° This safeguards against lingering bias, or favouritism,° to the more senior employee.　　　　RESPONSE

ARGUMENTS 6
Unfortunate indeed it is that the word Argument - like "criticism," ° "disagreement", "downturn" - has acquired an automatically *negative* meaning. Arguments can be creative as well as destructive. Some advertising agencies and school staff-rooms rely on Argument: the pros and cons of any enterprise or course of action.
Confident workers feel able to have a "good" argument with their co-workers or their managers without facing ridicule, worse condemnation. Where arguing may go wrong is resort to raised voices,° banged doors, floods of tears. And in any workplace-argument there is a power differential.° Best to   log any Arguments that come across as threatening° or destabilizing.　　　　CAUSE / MOTIVATION

ARROWS   [QUIVER FULL OF ARROWS] 6
When a co-worker° or supervisor° wishes to damage an employee, he or she keeps a few Arrows on the side : for firing as and when necessary. Your mental image: *Quiver* is significant of itself.
　　　　　　　　　　　　　　　　　　　　　MOTIVATION

[THE]   ARTFUL DODGER 4
The Artful Dodger is the co-worker who dodges all tasks, visits and phone calls so that these fall on an already-committed colleague. The Artful Dodger - who is also usually the favoured one° - has a whole set of disguises for doing nothing, whilst forever grumbling about how difficult life is! Line managers generally do not welcome reports or observations concerning known Dodgers. Instead they criticize the one or ones who *do* pick up the slack ! To exacerbate matters, the *willingly*

undertaken shortfall is itself subjected to unmerited criticism° : perhaps from the Artful Dodger herself ! *ASSOCIATION*

ARTISTIC LEANING [OR SCIENTIFIC LEANING] 6

Researchers have found that where an employee is Artistic/ Creative and her manager or head teacher or supervisor Practical/ Scientific in orientation, they will *never* be able to talk to one another successfully.... until the moment both parties recognize an almost unbridgeable gap in their respective approaches to work or tasks-in-hand. That is why so many managers feel their questions,° or their worries, go unanswered ; and why so many employees resent their work being criticized ° - or sent back for revision. See Answering Questions. *FACTOR*

ARTISTRY 3

Easily forgiven is the new recruit or later stalwart who believes Artistry to be the key to both a job and job satisfaction. Yet Artistry, pride° and perfectionism° alike risk becoming expensive luxuries. Unless Art is the final product, Artistry is seen to be an expensive overhead. The best employers spot Art and uses it to their firms' advantage : with brilliant *Powerpoint* presentations, murals in the atrium, exceptional court reports, beautifully-wrapped parcels. In other competing arenas, Artistry crushed or ridiculed° is oppression of the first order.

ASSOCIATION

ASKING ADVICE 5

One antidote to suspicion° and oppression in the workplace is where a manager seeks advice from an apprentice, a trainee or a new recruit. Provided this is not a token, or merely conciliatory, gesture, being Asked for Advice empowers the employee who would not otherwise gain voice or prestige within the organization that recruited her. To *give* Advice is to invest in an unfamiliar set-up. However, if a suggestions' box is never emptied, or is rubbished when it is opened, that sop is poor substitute for a proper and cooperative decision-making process. Round tables have a habit of providing a ministry of all the talents. *RESPONSE*

ASKING   QUESTIONS 6
If a nervous or diffident employee has been Asked Questions all through school and childhood, perhaps by a discontented parent or step-parent - later by a domineering, controlling, boyfriend or husband - she might not be able to answer *her employer's* sharp Questions with equanimity. Better by far for her manager to make simple *statements* : " I understand your home visit was a little fraught...," " I gather the Judge was very uptight...," " We seem not to have reached our target..." *Statements* give somebody under pressure far more room to reflect and respond than sharp, horribly direct, Questioning.   *FACTOR*

ASSERTIVENESS   TRAINING 7
Many employers - and overbearing husbands / boyfriends - are nervous about Assertiveness Training, because it represents a significant shift of power ; more noticeably, *an alternative* reaction to the arbitrary and injurious exercise of that power. The beauty of Assertiveness Training is that it is highly memorable and do-able. Provided always the techniques demonstrated contain an element of *surprise*. That is because bullies° are quite skilled countering the devices that might thwart them. A complement to Assertiveness Training is the provision of anger management° *for the other person.*   *RESPONSE*

[THE] AUTHORITARIAN PERSONALITY 10

When Theodor W. Adorno re-introduced the world to Erich Fromm's "Authoritarian Personality," he posited one whose state of mind or attitude is characterised by belief in absolute obedience or submission to his own authority - as well as the administration of that belief through *the oppression of his subordinates*. The label usually applies to individuals who are known, or viewed, as having an authoritative, strict, or oppressive attitude towards outsiders°- or anyone considered to be inferior. Furthermore, the Authoritarian Personality has a strict "Superego" that not only controls his weak ego (unable to cope with base impulses) but also suffers from personal insecurity : resulting in his Superego adhering, rigidly, to externally imposed conventions. Bullying° section-leaders, foremen or line managers° owe all too great a debt to Adorno : one they are uniformly unlikely to recognize or to acknowledge. *CAUSE / MOTIVATION*

AUTHORITY 7

All sorts of texts have been written about Authority : as to whether it is endowed or acquired ; inherent or earned. Another debate rages as to whether those who speak with Authority have a natural or learnt gravitas. In most workplaces, Authority is duly and freely bestowed on layer after layer of the hierarchy.° Or else the Authority attaching to a quasi-managerial position is stolen under false pretences. Here the workplace bully° pretends he has been asked to come down hard on a worker : for the sake of the entire team or floor ; to promote the achievement of targets ;° to maintain good order and discipline ;° or to attain a common goal. One thing is certain : a brand new recruit is unlikely to have any Authority - nor the means to challenge existing Authority. She then lives in fear and trembling of being disciplined° or fired before she has even made her mark. *CAUSE / MOTIVATION*

AUTONOMY 9
For many decades, Autonomy wasn't discussed. The idea that any employee, or hand, or underling,° should enjoy - let alone expect - a degree of Autonomy at work was considered so alien as to be completely crazy. Bosses and workers were *opposites*. And bosses reserved Autonomy *for themselves*. Workers existed simply to do as they were told, then queue for their meagre wages.
Only in a more liberated age did some folk ask to take charge of their own workload - without being constantly overseen, cross-questioned,° monitored° or guided. And whereas Autonomy sounds so good on paper, it represents a considerable shift of power from management to worker ; far more risk ; far more cause to wonder whether someone is in fact lead-swinging.° Contrarily, Autonomy makes for a far happier, self-fulfilled, *and productive*,° workforce. People glow when they are trusted to get on with the job. Trust° is also a sign of transition from apprenticeship, or a period of probation°, to full acceptance. *FACTOR/ RESPONSE*

AUTOCRATS   [AUTOCRACY] 7
Autocrat is a slightly kinder term for the bully° or tyrant° at work. Even so, it carries the negative connotation of *absolute* power.° A few entrepreneurs, a few nabobs, actually wear the badge of Autocracy with pride. They convincingly argue that their dictatorship° is benevolent - bringing with it the greater advancement of their organization. *CAUSE*

AWAYDAYS   [TEAM STUDY DAYS] 3
Whether doing Trust Games, Lego, Jigsaws, Group Meditation, Canoeing, or Abseiling, Team Days can only be enjoyed by those who have *already* won the right to be included. So many Awaydays provide the ideal chance to humiliate° the struggler or the rebel even further.

Who is it ? - it is worth asking - that has the unfinished business° and the luggage° ? *ASSOCIATION*

[THE] AWKWARD SQUAD 6
It is not usually a badge of honour at work to be bracketed with the Awkward Squad : people politely labelled "back bench rebels"° or "the usual suspects."° Awkward Squads prosper where there has been a history of poor labour relations,° youthful promotion,° or postponed retirement.° Where oppressed ones suddenly discover they have nothing more to lose, quite reasonably they may become even *less* subservient than usual. *FACTOR / RESULT*

BACKSTABBING 6
It is a tired Parliamentary joke that front-bench politicians are far more afraid of the enemies *on their own side* than of Her Majesty's opposition. It was ever thus : to be stabbed in the back by one's erstwhile friend or ally. And few workplaces deserve a clean bill of health on this measure. *FACTOR / MOTIVATION*

BAD LANGUAGE 8
Bad language is a complex issue at work : partly because it is almost universally heard / accepted / condoned. Yet there is a well-understood difference between hearing swearing and *being sworn at.* Oppressors are actually quite cunning. They rarely swear *at* their unfavoured one ; instead they smother her with fake kindness / condescension. Swearing at her in front of the team / senior management would look like bad form ; and activate the Manual° into the bargain.

As a rule of thumb, a climate of Bad Language ; especially derogatory or obscene Bad Language ; targeted Bad Language ; Language that isolates or marginalizes apprentices,° new recruits,° BEMs or women:

all this nurtures and sustains the tide or the scope of oppression in the workplace. Wise employers listen intently to their employees and make clear *what* Language will or will not be allowed.   *CAUSE   / FACTOR*

BAGGAGE 8
Baggage is a psychologist's summing up of all the luggage both oppressor and oppressed one carry round with them day-by-day. Baggage could be suppressed childhood memory,° an unhappy workplace in the past, domestic violence,° or simple perfectionism.° Whatever the Baggage , its weight and its impact, its weight needs to be acknowledged just as conscientiously as it would be were it an actual pile of suitcases !   *CAUSE / MOTIVATION / RESULT*

BAGGING THE CREDIT 3
What a temptation it is for the person who did not produce the report, complete the operation, finalize the sale, or mop up the mess to claim the credit. Success has many parents ; failure is an orphan. In organizations where praise° is rationed, or even non-existent, underlings get blamed whilst their managers get the plaudits. Good businesses *share* the credit - and delight in the fact that one of their workers has achieved so much.   *FACTOR*

BANTER 5
Office or conveyor belt or warehouse Banter quickly drifts from hilarity to vulgarity and sexual harassment. At its worst, Banter leads to self-loathing,° resignation,° even suicide.° The author or architect of that Banter, or practical joking, *not its intended target*, has to take responsibility for its gravity or levity. Much Banter is indeed harmless, but not in every instance.   *FACTOR / MOTIVATION*

BARK   WORSE   THAN   BITE 7
" His bark being (allegedly) worse than his bite," is one of the most fatuous excuses ever given for verbal bullying,° whether in the home or at work. It is usually totally untrue : because the bark *is* the bite.

CAUSE

BEING SHOWN UP 6
Particularly in a small team, a tiny office, an isolated outpost, the oppressed one will not want to be Shown Up as a troublemaker,° or as a vexatious, litigious, employee. Fear of Being Shown Up within a *compact* work setting maybe far exceeds fear of Being Shown Up to a new or distant employer as an incompetent, a bad signing.   *RESULT*

BLACKLISTING   [BLACKBALLING] 10
A fairly harsh type of oppression is Blacklisting. Except that Blacklisting might not be exposed till years too late. Blacklists are illicitly circulated to future employers : advice *not to touch* a troublesome° worker - quite often a previously preferred supplier or sub-contractor either - with a barge pole. And the most efficient Blacklisting happens by telephone, processed in "casual" meetings in a pub. Anything without a paper trail.   *MOTIVATION / RESULT*

BLOCKING ADVANCEMENT OR PROMOTION 9
The ruthless, heartless, or thoughtless employer or line manager actually Blocks the Advancement or Promotion of a particular employee. He might think his action is one of kindness : " She is not quite ready for Promotion," " She needs more time," " She will advance further from where she is already," "She is so happy here," " I do not think she could stand the pace," " I value her too highly to lose her."

Particularly with *internal* Promotion, Blocking is completely invisible. The relevant candidate is simply told she did not do as well in interview as the competition. It was "a strong field" after all.

With *external* Promotion, employees have the right to see a formal written reference - but do not have access to secret telephone calls, hints on the golf course, or acquired reputation.° Maybe an employer does not *create* the post a worker might go for, in the first place. At worst, he or his managers, deliberately undermines an oppressed one's confidence° until she loses *the will* to move, or to move any further up the ladder. *RESULT*

[THE] BLUE-EYED BOY [BLUE-EYED GIRL] 3

The Blue-Eyed Boy / Girl is a derisory term for the employee who is the favoured one. This employee can do no wrong. And were he or she ever to do *wrong*, those deficiencies would be filtered out° by management. Sometimes called the golden, or golden-haired, employee: with all its evocation of sibling rivalry / parental bias. Or the classroom / coaching favourite.° *ASSOCIATION / MOTIVATION*

BOMBARDMENT 7

A Bombardment at work is similar to a deluge.° The oppressed employee feels there is no end to the surge of calls, customers, complaints or commitments. It is a constant juggling act to get through the day (probably a day lightened with few *or any* breaks). But Bombardments are *not* accidental. Management can halt or redirect flow at source - or at least, not add to the Bombardment ! *CAUSE*

BONUSES | THE BONUS CULTURE | 4
Bonuses are often as superfluous as they are divisive. Especially when those so rewarded are *forbidden* from telling anyone else what Bonus they are in receipt of. Better to furnish clear increments - or a fair day's wage for a fair day's work. Besides, Bonuses quickly lead to the cutting of corners.° *ASSOCIATION*

BOSSINESS 5
It is a truism that Bosses must Boss. But some Bosses *delight* in their Bossiness. Leading to the joke : " Well, you're the Boss !" announced innocently. Not infrequently, however, Bossiness is taken far too seriously - in which case the chasm between Boss and underling° widens. Better the employee who can regard her Boss as co-worker and ally, not as enemy. The Boss still needs to lead, but to lead gently, kindly, purposefully - not wickedly or arbitrarily. *CAUSE / MOTIVATION*

BOTTOM-UP ASSESSMENT | BOTTOM-UP MANAGEMENT | 2
Bottom-Up Assessment, as opposed to the more commonly seen *Top-Down* Assessment, is so unfamiliar in the UK that it is viewed as at best a novelty, at worst a liability. Insecure managers have every reason to be absolutely petrified of Bottom-Up Assessment because the conclusions of such are disconcertingly incontestable, virtually inescapable. Immediate repercussions from *unfavourable* Bottom-Up reviews need to be instituted , unless those bad reviews are treated as mere grudges,° concerted revenge.
And if *nobody* listens to Bottom-Up Assessment, one has to doubt the motives of Personnel who approved it in the first place. Ideally, Bottom-Up commentary, in conjunction with Top-Down, should not come as a complete surprise. If it *does* come as a surprise, other internal mechanisms have already broken down. Of course, Bottom-Up

should never be used with only the oppressor seeing the comments of oppressed ones. That serves *to increase*, not decrease, suspicion and bullying. Bottom-Up Assessment is so rare because, like Peer Review, it represents a significant shift of power.°

A welcome expansion of Bottom-Up Assessment is Bottom-Up *Management* : where Head Office merely listens to, advises, and responds to, branch managers and outposted workers all of whom retain the right, and duty, to make actual decisions.   *RESPONSE*

BRIEFING [AGAINST] 8

Journalists' exposure of the behaviour of spin-doctors and Svengalis in the 1980s and 1990s brought Briefing to a wider audience. Briefing involves bending influential ears with highly unflattering opinions regarding the appearance and competence of friends and enemies alike. Needless to say, the oppressed one is almost the last one standing not to know she is being Briefed against, or incriminated.° *CAUSE / FACTOR*

BRINGING INTO LINE 8

Bringing a stray worker "Back into Line" is an oft-quoted rationalization of, and justification for, bullying° in the workplace. It has its origin in farming, rounding up the troops - or the enemy! - in battle, extended school playground playtimes, and January Sales° : all places where lining- up becomes a formality.   *MOTIVATION*

BROWNIE POINTS 3

This is a wonderfully descriptive, perceptive term, with longevity, for being rewarded, incrementally, for fine performance.° It is also a term of *derision* for a co-worker who seeks praise,° also badges, above all else. Unfortunately, it has nothing to do with Olave Baden-Powell's Brownies; rather a rude part of the human anatomy seen only when an ambitious employee is climbing the step-ladder of preferment°....usually when someone else is already perched on a higher - or the highest - rung. Of interest, American studies in the 1960s revealed how professionals often fear a colleague with *slightly* superior status, above a remoter figure with *vastly* superior status.   *ASSOCIATION*

BUGGING 5
Non conformist employees might find - or *not* find - themselves Bugged. More practical for the line manager than *actual* Bugging is close *computer- monitoring*° [maybe after an employee's day or shift ends] - or, cheaply, the strategic placing of a spy° in the office or team room. Thereby - or by intentionally overhearing telephone calls - a line manager is able to gather crucial evidence.   *CAUSE / FACTOR*

BULLET POINTS 2
In the midst of allegations, criticisms,° interrogations° and misrepresentations, it assists the oppressed one, no end, to have written discreetly on the back of a birthday or Christmas card *Bullet Points* of exactly she wishes to say in her defence,° or for clarification. She can then return to those Points if her conversation / confrontations° with management becomes subject to derailment or hostility.°   *RESPONSE*

[THE] BULLY 10
The Bully is useful shorthand, playground parlance, for the oppressor. Because we have all met playground Bullies ; because most of us have suffered at their hands or behest, it helps us to draw a parallel, at work, with *workplace* Bullies. The term is all too readily understood. We might always be able lucidly to *describe* a Bully - although under extreme pressure, many of us make a good effort ! - but we certainly recognize when that Bully is on the rampage.° The psychology of Bullying deserves a book of its own.   *CAUSE / MOTIVATION*

BULLYING 10

Bullying is another name for Oppression. It is a bit of an immature word because it is often born of immaturity. Yet the word as a description of a prevalent phenomenon has one special advantage : it is shorthand for a whole confluence of nasty traits : unrestrained power,° disempowerment,° demotion,° gratuitous nastiness, bitterness, frightfulness, physical violence,° mental cruelty,° isolation°- all contributing to Bullying - or coming under the umbrella of Bullying.

CAUSE / MOTIVATION / RESULT

[THE] BULLY'S OWN INSECURITY 8

Not affording much comfort to an oppressed junior, co-worker, teacher or seamstress : the Bully might *himself* be Insecure. In fact, he will probably have been bullied as a child by mother, father, older brother or gang. The question then arises: how much leeway should be given to the Bully himself ? After all, the Bully will quite probably be bullying his own family - and that *domestic violence*° should never be trivialized.° In this area, management must become more adept in spotting both the Bully *and* his Insecurity. Maybe a transfer to less onerous responsibilities would help, or recall to Head Office.° Somewhere, somehow, the cycle° of horrible oppression must be interrupted before a new generation is hurt. *CAUSE / MOTIVATION*

[THE] BULLY'S OWN INSENSITIVITY 9

It is no excuse, but the Bully might, over time, become immune° and insensitive° to the needless pain and distress° he is generating. Bullies are not generally the most intuitive and self-questioning of individuals. They would not have achieved dominance° without a measure of ruthlessness.° So line managers who have acted oppressively routinely express bafflement w letter arrives from Head Office. Or indeed when the oppressed one herself complains. Or when the Bully himself is called as a witness, to testify regarding his own blatantly unfair treatment of an employee or kitchen or staffroom or team.

CAUSE / MOTIVATION

BUYING OFF 6
The potentially awkward/ vocal/ brighter employee can be Bought Off with the promise of a pay rise, a handsome bonus, or future promotion.° Once Bought Off, this employee is no longer a threat to the oppressor or to management. On the other hand, the Bought-Off-one can be subject to *future* Oppression because she has ceded ground in the past. And lost her pedestal. Also *the promise* of future preferment° will not necessarily materialize.

MOTIVATION / RESPONSE

CALL CRAMMING 8
Call Cramming is the procedure whereby carers and telephonists and doctors, in particular, are expected to fit 5 assignments in the same window of time normally allocated to 2 assignments. The equivalent in heavy transport is asking a driver to make 3 deliveries in a time-span more suited to one. Pizza parlours also do Call Cramming - which puts constant - and unreasonable - pressure on the Crammer himself : a Crammer invariably on minimal pay.

CAUSE / FACTOR

CALL [RECALL] TO HEAD OFFICE 4
A request to attend Head Office - especially an *unexpected* call - comes as quite an ordeal. Is it to be disciplinary°? Or merely advisory ? Or does this recall indicate the sack? Line managers should always make clear to their co-workers why exactly an employee has to attend Head Office; also who it was who started the ball rolling!

ASSOCIATION / RESULT

CANCELLED LEAVE 7
Unhappily, in many professions or workplaces, *booked* Leave is subject to sudden, arbitrary, or unnecessary Cancellation. This causes havoc for families - to say nothing of the oppressed employee herself, her abandoned leisure, her ambitions. and her sleep ! Worse is the conclusion that proper staffing ratios° or rosters° might have *averted* Cancellation.   *CAUSE / FACTOR*

CARING REPONSIBILITIES BACK HOME 6
Most women at work have some Caring Responsibility Back Home: son, daughter, husband, partner, parent, uncle. However, where one of these dependents is gravely or terminally ill ; where one or more was born with a disability ; or had to retire from work through disability ; that Caring Responsibility is magnified. A wise or discerning employer gives flexible working and compassionate leave° to home carers. But most workplaces are ill-adapted to sudden absences, frequent crises and hospital appointments. This puts the employee with Caring Responsibility in the invidious position of perpetual begging, perpetual gratitude, for small concessions and periods away. And colleagues sniff out favouritism° immediately.   *MOTIVATION / ASSOCIATION*

CASUAL EMPLOYMENT 9
"Casual" is not just a title but also a mindset. So-called *Casual* employees carry little or no status, and absolutely no bargaining rights. As they arrived, so also they depart : unrecognized, unlamented. Defenders of Casual Employment say they desire, above all, "a flexible labour market" : the freedom to take on workers or dispense with their services at will. This supposedly aids "growth" in the economy. Problems arise when Casuals wish to complain° to an employer or

employment agency. They are quite likely to be sent away with fleas in their ears due to impertinence. Surely, Casuals should be *thankful* for being taken on ? Theirs not to reason why?   CAUSE / FACTOR

CENTRE OF THE UNIVERSE 4
Oppressed employee and oppressor alike are Centres of their respective Universes. That is part and parcel of being alive. Yet this existential perspective can help *resolve* conflict in the workplace. Coming into work is the classic collision of spheres. One orbit interacts with that of a   different planet, yet within the same constellation.   That both employer and employee have the same objective : earning power, is entirely irrelevant. These two parties have probably not *chosen* their respective paths ; less so their mutual necessity to be in one place at one time. Therefore each needs to know survival comes through a mixture of compromise and integrity.   MOTIVATION / RESPONSE

CHAIN SMOKING 5
Chain Smoking may have its origins in cumulative stress,° past adversity, parental example, teenage experimentation, bereavement, an uneasy home life, long journeys - or be the by-product of another addiction. Chain Smoking is, however, also related to work pressures: particularly those work experiences impacting on exploited and low-paid *women*; also those - usually women also - employed within the caring professions° - caring which definitely *does not* bring its own satisfaction, less so, a living wage.°
To make Chain Smoking worse, it is usually *forbidden* in most areas of a site or campus. And the working shift allows few smoking breaks. Some Chain Smokers - like long-distance coach drivers - actually have to sacrifice their duties (taking tickets, giving directions, unloading luggage) in order to have a cigarette.   ASSOCIATION / RESULT

CHALLENGING THE OPPRESSOR 4
Because the oppressed one might be too newly-recruited, too subordinate,° too demoralized° to Challenge the Oppressor, it is incumbent on her co-workers, senior managers, or Personnel to do that Challenging on her behalf. Conversely, the *unchallenged* bully° lives to see another day, thus entrenching his power.   *FACTOR / RESPONSE*

CHILD-FREE EMPLOYEES [CHILD-FREE ALLOWANCE] 3
Offices, staff-rooms and factory floors are like wombs. Anybody coming to work and announcing she's "been caught," or is expecting - or is to become a granny - is instantly celebrated and justified. Soon, collections, gifts, midwifery and maternity leave come into play. Which all leaves single, and bereaved, and Child-Free, employees - or those still too busy caring for elderly parents, uncles and aunts - out in the cold. *They* cannot join the rejoicing. Moreover, Child-Free workers will be put upon : expected to fill in for those whose infants are ill, collecting their badges, or in the Nativity. Not uncommonly, Child-Free recruits resent not being on the same flexible hours° as their child-laden co-workers. And we are light years away from understanding such Child-Free men and women, or conversing about subjects *not* involving other people's children and grandchildren.   *FACTOR*

CHILDHOOD MEMORIES 4
Bullying° or punishment° of any sort reminds us of Childhood - as does criticism,° the unrealistic setting of goals,° rivalry° and scapegoating.° We can only take into adulthood our childhoods, good or bad. We have no other reference point - with the possible exception of loving friends and partners or spouses. Workplace oppression literally becomes a nightmare when old doubts and fears and humiliations° re-surface.

ASSOCIATION / MOTIVATION

CLASS [SOCIAL CLASS] [CLASS CONSCIOUSNESS] 6
Class rears its head everywhere in the field of oppression in the workplace. At its crudest, a new or established employee can be criticized, or vilified, for being "too posh," "a country bumpkin," "hoity-toity," or "the dregs."
Sometimes an organization such as a club, the Army,° a cricket team, prison° or private school has, or had, separate entry ranks, separate grades for gentlemen or conscripts. Additionally, in most smaller businesses, wealth is inherited, not earned : so the son of the owner, his nephew, or chosen representative, might *de facto* be beyond question or correction.
Class Consciousness can, of course, be *un*conscious - if that's not a contradiction of terms. Additionally, defenders of the *status quo* frequently allege that class barriers are *surmounted* by distinction in what you do, promotion, ° marriage, or exceeding effort. One thing is certain: Class will not appear in any Manual°!   *CAUSE / FACTOR*

CLEARING YOUR   DESK 9
Should an employee work from a desk - and relatively few employees do work from a desk - the action of Clearing that Desk is immensely symbolic. Maybe the oppressed one finds her desk cleared *already* when she returns from lengthy absence from work or from sickness. Maybe her line manager° Clears her Desk because she is drawing too heavily on the sympathy / support of an adjacent co-worker. Or else she is marched off to Personnel, marched back, then given 15 minutes precisely to clear her desk, her locker, and Security.   *RESULT*

CLOCKING   IN   [CLOCKING OFF] 7
Both the act of Clocking In and the act of Clocking Off can be oppressive. If time and privileges and money are deducted for occasional lateness, the employer must be sure his workers were not

held up by caring responsibilities,° by bad weather, by bus or Tube strike - or by having to queue behind fellow Clockers In !

Clocking *Off* is sometimes the first resort of the employer who only wants zero-hours' contracts.° Getting someone to Clock Off every time a customer leaves the shop; or every time a carer leaves an old lady's house; or every time a conveyor belt halts, is plain wrong. The test should always be : either a worker *wants* to go home and / or that a worker has sufficient minutes or hours to benefit from before the next shift or assignment. *ASSOCIATION / CAUSE*

COFFEE BREAKS 3
The Coffee Break is yet another fertile breeding-ground for complaint,° gossip° and banter:° all faithfully relayed back to the oppressor as "proof" of the oppressed one's silliness / laziness / wickedness. Meanwhile, the Victim has, naively, actually *looked forward to* her Coffee and her lunch! *ASSOCIATION / RESPONSE*

COGNITIVE DISSONANCE 7
Cognitive Dissonance is not too difficult a concept to take on board : the *gap* between one behaviour and another ; one perception and another ; and the unwelcome challenge to *all* preconceptions when confronted with reality. Everybody needs to bridge the gap between what they would like to see and what they *actually* see - so they will make adjustments to either in memory or persuasion. The unscrupulous employer, on a good day, perceives an employee he does not like; yet at the same time he is being asked or forced or tempted to acknowledge she is performing well. Therefore he dismisses these or any other achievements. On the other side, an oppressed employee sees a horrible manager, yet is asked or forced or tempted to acknowledge that person has a very successful track record. Teams are sometimes told a newcomer will be God-sent - then face disappointment.

Cognitive Dissonance is never more present than in filtering:° where all good feedback° is toned down or obliterated if a worker is perceived as a failure/ nuisance / liability. At the same time, all *negative* feedback is diluted, even completely discounted, where a valued employee is compliant, has blue eyes°, is the boss' favourite,° or is a relative, part of the establishment or too good to let go. Filtering° is probably the magic ingredient of - and archway to - *all* workplace oppression : a process - also answer to Cognitive Dissonance - nobody should ignore.   *ASSOCIATION / MOTIVATION / RESULT*

COLLABORATION 5
Collaboration [cooperation] is the direct opposite of hierarchy.° When all employees enter a partnership for the greater benefit of the organization, there is an immediate uplift in staff morale.° Because Collaborative employees are talking to each other, and helping each other out, rather than cutting their co-workers' throats, or striving to please an implacable superior, Collaboration is a useful alternative to competition.° Amazingly, Collaboration has frequently not been tried and found wanting but has been *wanted and not tried.*   *RESPONSE*

COLLEAGUE SOLIDARITY 7
It is absolutely essential that Colleagues stand together in the face of a tyrannical ° line manager, team leader, section head, or office bully.° Such Solidarity greatly reduces the isolation° of the oppressed one. Solidarity can take the form of unadvertised Colleague get-togethers, coffee and a chat, or discreetly-arranged home visits : the latter unlikely to be spied upon.° Remember : certain Colleagues might be going through the mill, to Hell and back: beset by troubles, doubts and anxieties, *entirely* unbeknown to anyone else around them. *RESPONSE*

COLLEAGUE BULLYING [CO-WORKER BULLYING] 9
Bullying at work° is automatically associated with hierarchy° : the bucket of manure swilled downward till it reaches the humblest underling.° Linked, however, to top-down Bullying is spite shown by new, or established, or formerly trusted, Colleagues. A Colleague's motivation° to add to the culture of oppression° might include envy,° grievance,° innate hostility,° or - at its most charitable - the Colleague's wish to stay safe.° Most to be pitied is the oppressed one who *believes* her Co-workers are sympathetic, and rooting for her, when they aren't !
CAUSE / MOTIVATION

COLLEGIATE MANAGEMENT STYLE 6
Collegiate Management is usually the opposite of confrontational° or adversarial Styles of Management. Another word for the Collegiate Management Style is the emollient style. To be emollient is not to be weak or feeble. Indeed, the Collegiate Manager might expect - and get- more out of his workers than the bully.° Kindness° : from top to bottom in a work setting, always carries its own reward. In a kindly atmosphere, employees are gladder to get into work, more committed, less nervous. And when the going gets tough, solutions are sought more quickly where co-workers and line manager° can share a joke, and enjoy working together towards a common goal. More than one oppressed employee - perhaps oppressed at home as well as at work - is dumbfounded by the Collegiate Management Style exercised by a next or subsequent employer. There is nothing bland, or slack, about expansiveness at work, rapidly *reciprocated* with generosity - and forgiveness ° upwards.
RESPONSE

COLLUSION 7

If an employer or his Personnel Department cannot demote or get rid of a bully, the temptation is Collusion. No fuss. Better to sacrifice a few minnows than a big fish. Also, as with domestic violence, it is possible for the oppressed one *also* to collude with the oppressor, in the forlorn hope he might be better to-morrow [which usually he isn't!]. Nobody should condemn this complex interaction : simply because it might be *the only* survival strategy° available to the tormented one. *CAUSE / MOTIVATION*

COMMISSION-ONLY   EMPLOYMENT 8

Being paid Commission Only can be just if every single employee or associate or agent has equal chance to make a decent living - and that there will be an appropriate reward at the end of any and every contractual period. Commission-Only comes unstuck: first where targets° are impossible; second where achieved targets° are grossly underpaid;° third where targets° are dangerous;° fourth where the whole transaction is dodgy and off-the-books ; fifth where a worker struggles *or starves* in the process, or on the production line. For instance, door-to-door sales are frequently Commission- Only : dreadful products; hundred mile journeys unpaid; lamentable, also unpaid, training; high-pressure sales' techniques : the whole operation a subversion or circumvention of Minimum Wage° legislation. To say nothing of the terrible, indeed disgraceful, also unpunished, exploitation of immigrants, trafficked women, servants, those with learning difficulties, casual labourers and "Neets." *CAUSE / FACTOR*

COMPASSION 7
Very few Organizations set out to be Compassionate : their aim being the completion of jobs and orders with minimum fuss, maximum reward. This is even the case in Hospitals° and Care Homes°- where Compassion might initially be *a given*. This leaves a lone, *Compassionate* employee torn: should she do management's bidding *or* listen to her patients, her service users and her struggling co-workers? Particularly in times of freeze and squeeze, Compassion is sacrificed first. Its absence then becomes part of workplace culture °, an incubator for low staff morale.°   *ASSOCIATION   /   RESPONSE*

COMPLAINTS 9
Oppressors in the Workplace *love* Complaints. That sounds counter-intuitive. Surely, Complaints reflect badly on the Organization and its prospects. Far from it. Complaints - whether from co-workers ,° other line managers,° customers, visitors or allied agencies - are grist to the mill. Furthermore, if the oppressor runs out of Complaints, he can always manufacture - or solicit - one or two *himself.* The impact of Complaint on the oppressed one is gratifying for her adversary. She becomes ever more paranoiac, ever less resourceful. She then looks to higher management for support - whereupon they all reply: " but look at this pile of complaints !" The best complaints to whack someone with are *written*. Even though such carefully researched, and orchestrated, written complaints *look* spontaneous - they turn out to be vexatious, also unanswerable from below. *CAUSE   /   FACTOR   /   MOTIVATION*

COMPROMISE 7
Compromise is a minefield. Just where you would expect to find peace and quiet, a true meeting of minds, along comes suppressed tumult. For Compromise to work, it must be *desired*. And neither the oppressor nor

his victim is likely to be in a position to Compromise. The victim's reluctance often rests heavily on power° differential. Her line manager° will always be superior: therefore in a stronger position. Yet there is hope : through skilled supervision - preferably by an outsider - and the intervention of a mediator° / McKenzie Friend.° *RESPONSE*

CONFIDENTIALITY 6

Oppressed one are not usually allowed to know what the oppressor has said to *his* Supervisor / Manager / Union Rep . [*Confidential*] Taking up a grievance procedure°? : do not tell your co-workers. [*Confidential*] Receiving a bonus / increment? : do not tell competitors. [*Confidential*] On the other hand, you, the oppressed one, are allegedly guilty because you *broke* Confidentiality!   You told one client about another client. You told a service user something contained in a private memo° / manual° in the office.   You spoke to someone in another Agency without permission.   You informed a parent of something a teenager said in the course of youth work. You are therefore deemed "unreliable" - because you act like a sieve. *FACTOR*

CONFLICT   [CONFLICT RESOLUTION | 8

Conflict Resolution   improves work life and dispenses with the need for sit-ins or walk-outs. The mechanics of Conflict Resolution include arbitration,° mediation,° grievance,° the annual appraisal° - or a McKenzie Friend.° There is nothing to stop either the oppressor *or the oppressed one* approaching the other - *or a valued another* - to ask : " Is there anything we can do to better this situation ?" *RESPONSE*

CONFORMITY   [CONFORMISM | 6

The primacy of Conformism needs no testimonial beyond the religious phenomenon known as *Non-Conformism*. Non-Conformists in every age are distrusted and marginalized.° Ironically, many dissident recruits were *first and foremost* Conformists before the issue(s) arose that altered their persuasion, in turn making them immune to persuasion. Perhaps everyone has rebellious instincts lying dormant. Most workplaces are like ships - where an "even keel" is the essential *balancing* mechanism.   CAUSE / MOTIVATION / RESPONSE

CONFRONTATION [CONFRONTATIONAL MANAGEMENT] 10
Confrontation is as ugly in the workplace as its passage and reward anywhere else: home, road, committee, restaurant: the eyeball-to-eyeball wearing down of a worker's resistance - also her coping mechanisms - by constant criticism° and fault-finding.° Unhappily, Confrontation is both a learnt° and retrieved behaviour. Certain organizations preach Confrontation: ironically to increase productivity°! Agencies might say they are more "dynamic" through exposed aggression.° In contrast, the management style of *Non-Confrontation* - oft-times, emollient or collegiate° - *builds workers up* rather than knocking them down. As such, this oasis brings the oppressed one *on-side*, without leaving her outside. Crucially, Confrontation is both a repeat and oft-imitated reaction to *displeasure* : an instrument also fervently, unrelentingly, practised, and honed, *in the confines of a troubled home.*   CAUSE / MOTIVATION

CONSENSUS   [THE CONSENSUAL STYLE OF MANAGEMENT] 8
Consensus is not just for Christmas. Consensus : the acknowledged will of the great majority, is actually everso easy to achieve. Simply sit round until there is rudimentary agreement. Inevitably that means some compromise°- but not necessarily so. Most people prefer Consensus to conflict.° And a Consensual Style of Management, when observed or experienced, is very real - and very satisfying. Worth trying. If only for the resulting Presenteeism.°   *RESPONSE*

CONSTRUCTIVE DISMISSAL [CONSTRUCTIVE DISCHARGE]....8

If ever there was a contradictory and nonsensical legal term, Constructive Dismissal - forced, or engineered, resignation°- would be up there with the greats. There is nothing "constructive" about being marginalized° and edged out of a paid position by a mixture of bullying,° harassment,° underwork,° overwork,° inflexibility°- and altered goalposts.° *MOTIVATION / RESULT*

[THE] CONTROLLING PERSONALITY 10

The Controlling Personality - sometimes called the Authoritarian Personality° - exists only to dominate or intimidate° other people, whether at home, in the bank, at the golf club, or on the factory floor. The bully° has less need to be respected than *to Control*. The Controlling Personality has power°; and no wish whatsoever to concede ground, share solutions, or accept compromise.° *Control* is the Authoritarian's byword : his reason to take up the reins; in the process suffocating, and marginalizing, all those in his orbit.

There have been attempts to codify, therefore understand, the Controlling Personality: low birth order, childhood submission, unhappy schooling, narrow interests, bigotry, racism,° sexism,° intolerance° of difference, inability to listen or to relent, misogyny,° insensitivity,° whatever. Control freaks are given 20 statements to agree or disagree with. Test-in-hand, the less cunning of their breed are enticed out of the woodwork.

The Controlling Personality picks out his victims a mile off. Having got his fish on the hook, he quite probably enjoys watching it wriggle. That is another sign of that wish to Control the world: the *objectivising* of others. Heaven help the employee, new or established, who stumbles across the Controller, or the Controller's willing acolytes, in the shop or on the shop floor. *CAUSE / MOTIVATION*

COPING MECHANISMS 9
The "Coping Mechanism" is a general term for any survival stratagem: escape,° coffee,° self-pampering, reward,° jettisoning of work - or the simple saying of the word : NO!° There are many *other* ways to keep your ship afloat when under pressure, or whilst facing a barrage of criticism: devices that shelter under the umbrella of assertiveness training.° If an employee does *not* Cope, however, she then appears as if failing to achieve that precious balance between productivity° and survival. ° She then stands the risk of going under and not resurfacing.

RESPONSE

CORPORATE EMBARRASSMENT 6
Much debate could fruitfully be held as to whether a Corporation can possibly feel guilt° or shame° or loss or sadness. In many ways, Corporations can feel *nothing*. Their owners are immune to any setback except a threat to their share price *or to their own survival*. An outsider might fondly imagine a firm riddled with guilt°, when outed as oppressive. Conversely, oppression might be a firm's badge of honour: a sign of robust° leadership,°a purposeful management style. One minnow can be let go. However, if the whole organization becomes riddled with discontent° and dissent, it will not, indeed cannot, prosper in the long run.

ASSOCIATION / RESULT

CORPORATE IMAGE 6
Many organizations need to appear to the wider public as cuddly-feely : breakfast cereals, children's television, toy manufacturers, social services, adult care agencies, housing associations, charities, to name just a few. Ironically because the Church° - and allied bodies - are *so innocent of* guile, and so "benevolent," that conspires to act as a cloak for severe workplace misery° and oppression. The assumption is that bullying° therein is so unthinkable as to be discounted - and left

unaddressed. The modern name for a firm's dented Image is "reputational damage." *ASSOCIATION*

CORRECTION 8
There used to be Schools of Correction in Britain ! It is not a very pleasant experience being Corrected. On the other hand, it is marvellous if your reference calls you "Correct in approach." One branch of bullying° at work is Correcting absolutely everything, almost for the sake of it. This practice is both destabilizing° and dispiriting.°
CAUSE / MOTIVATION

CORRUPTION [CORRUPT PRACTICE] 7
Corruption spreads its wicked tentacles to the very heart of schools,° the Police,° factories and the armed forces.° Sadly a lot of junior staff and new recruits also get drawn into Corruption - unexpected participants in unexpected settings. And Corruption can usually be neither detected nor eliminated. Otherwise it would not flourish : so meandering its way in and out of every crevice of a slack organization.

And the difficulty of being *an honest* employee within a corrupt outfit is that you are the first to be blamed,° the first to carry the can.° Ideally, few people would want to join in Corruption ; yet the temptation to join Corrupted co-workers°- with all the attendant cash in pocket - are immense. *FACTOR / MOTIVATION*

[THE] COST OF BULLYING 7
By its very nature, the Cost of Bullying is unquantifiable : all that underperformance, stress,° sick leave,° missed targets,° conveyor belt breakdown, walkouts, whatever. One estimate for the Cost of Bullying at work is £ 2 billion per year, 10% of gross profits: far too conservative a figure in many managers' experience. No owner, no Head Office, should ignore the Cost of Bullying. A happy workplace is generally an enriched *and enriching* workplace. *ASSOCIATION / RESULT*

COUNTER - CLAIM [COUNTER ATTACK] 4
One of the biggest deterrents to whistleblowing,° obduracy, or a complaint to management° is the risk of Counter-Claim. Bullying° managers and co-workers° know no scruples - nor any restraint in preserving their "good" names. Thus the Counter-Attack is launched, whereby Senior Management is assured the complainant has already been branded a troublemaker,° underperforming,° and with "poor interpersonal skills." Risk averted.   *FACTOR / MOTIVATION*

COVENTRY [BEING SENT TO] 4
In Coventry, nobody talks to the oppressed one. Not always as extreme as *no communication whatsoever*. More likely to be a *shunning* of the oppressed one : leaving her out of the frame ; out of the magic circle. An unpleasant place to be : Coventry.   *FACTOR*

COWARDICE 8
There are two ways of interpreting Cowardice in the workplace : either the oppressed one is afraid to answer back ; to release herself from the servitude of bullying ; or - far more likely - the bullying° or scheming middle manager / co-worker° shrinks at facing down a more powerful person or faction - so picks out, and picks on, a target perceived much weaker, in order to escape their own shortcomings by exercising arbitrary authority and baseless superiority. *CAUSE   / MOTIVATION*

CREDIT GIVEN [CREDIT, WITHHELD] 8
Credit, like praise,° is all too often *withheld* in the workplace, rather than granted. Giving Credit is actually quite a downer *for the oppressor*. Credit might give the oppressed one some encouragement° and satisfaction, empowering her in a workplace setting that normally sees - wants - her powerless.° Sometimes, Credit is sought by a manager *at*

the expense of his underlings.° Unions used to chant : " It's the rich what get the glory and the poor what gets the blame." Success has many parents. Failure is an orphan. And perceived failure° is everywhere just down the corridor : bestowed on whomever is prepared to accept it.

FACTOR   /   MOTIVATION

CRITICISM 10
Criticism is a necessary - though not intrinsically desirable - component of work life, facilitating as it does the achievement of management goals.° Unfortunately, not all employees are equally well-placed to listen to Criticism and act upon it. Improbably, some employees *welcome* Criticism ! Happily, established and secure workers have no fear° of reasonable Criticism. But the wise manager will go out of his way to praise° those who, through no fault of their own, cannot live with Criticism, let alone complaints.° The alert manager couches his Criticism in kindly language, and indicates how he himself would respond were he Criticized, as he undoubtedly has been in the past. Much depends on filtering.° The favoured one° will be protected from most Criticism because her managers treat negative feedback as a fluke. Conversely, the bully° actively *garners* Criticism for future ammunition, where his sole desire is the humbling of anybody brighter, or more knowing, than himself.   *CAUSE / MOTIVATION / RESULT*

CULTURE OF BLAME 10
Not a few arrivals in a new workplace comment on the welcome *absence* of Blame. They cannot understand a climate of praise,° trust,° and partnership. On the other side of the divide - where only Blame is dished out - workers will forever be dissatisfied, and on the defensive.

FACTOR   /   RESULT

CULTURE OF BULLYING 10
All too many workplaces tolerate bullies° because management - like most of their appointees - dare not stand up to the bully.° Better the bully you know ? Robust° leadership is called for. Someone is "too good to lose." That constitutes supine collusion° with the oppressor : much easier than dismissing° him. And so an *Ostrich Culture* thrives more years into the future.   *CAUSE   / RESULT*

CULTURE OF FEAR 10
Cultures of Fear infiltrate classroom, board-room, sewing room, back room : wherever there   is going to be a big shake-up° ; mass redundancies° ; a clear-out ; removal of one tier of management ; a Stitch-Up. Cultures of Fear are endemic in certain Hire-and-Fire° industries ;   also in local and central Government, and in quangos°: anywhere you least expect poor labour relations. *FACTOR / RESULT*

CUTTING CORNERS 8
Invariably, the Cutting of Corners is counter-productive, and leads to a blame culture.° Much better to go the long way round. Reputable and upstanding employers actually *prefer* their employees to take their time and so keep to the plan. Also, the initially more difficult and expensive way forward often turns out the cheapest in the long run. Even so, it is not in the interests of shadier shopkeepers and factory owners that their workers display too much pride° in their work. Pride gets in the way of output ; also impeding the burial / denial of unsafe or shoddy or dishonest practices.   *FACTOR   /   RESPONSE*

CYBER-BULLYING 7
This is a relatively new term for the phenomenon of using E-mail/ Facebook / Twitter / smart phone / photograph retention, to put extra

pressure on a fellow-user of that medium. Cyber-Bullying does happen at work too - and is equally unlikely to be detected / reported. Can lead to resignation,° even suicide.°   *CAUSE / MOTIVATION*

CYCLES OF OPPRESSION 8
The Cycle of Oppression works in one very many ways :
1) Oppression >> "Success" >> More Oppression ; 2) Oppression>> Resignation°>> More Oppression ; 3) Oppression >> Obedience°>> Appeasement° >> More Oppression ; 4) Oppression >> Resignation >> New Employee >> More Oppression ; 5) Oppression at home >> Oppression at Work ; 6) Manager enjoys Bullying° >> therefore Bullies more >> Resignation° of Oppressed One >> New Recruit°>> Manager moved >> More Oppression in new role...etc. On the other hand, the notion of Cycles is itself contentious. It could be argued that Cycles presume, also promote, *unavoidability* - therefore undermining people's ability to override mood° and misery.°   *CAUSE / RESULT*

DECISIONS OVERTURNED 6
Nobody minds *insignificant* decisions being overturned at Board level - or anywhere else high up in an organization. Upsetting indeed is when an immediate line manager's decision is overturned, unless it was unfair in the first place ; worse when the oppressed one's own decision-making is overturned, countermanded, forbidden. The oppressed one is frequently so low down the pecking-order that she can only decide a bit before company policy comes into play.

Even so, there are certain offices and service industries where independent decision-making has been a traditional part of the job. Here, to have your best and most sensible decisions overturned is devastating.

Maybe a co-worker or line manager waits till holiday time or unplanned sick leave to change everything previously agreed or rubberstamped.

And that overturning does, in its turn, become irrevocable. If the oppressed one wants to regain ground and win back favour, she cannot - because her bridges have already been burnt. *FACTOR / RESULT*

DECLINING PRODUCTIVITY 6
As with declining profitability and increased staff turnover, Declining Productivity on one belt, in one division, one small sector, might be indicative of bullying and widespread dissatisfaction. Cure the shortfall in leadership and other shortfalls quickly cure themselves. *CAUSE / RESULT*

DEFENSIVENESS 6
Defensiveness is a negative and unsatisfactory response to aggression.° The more the aggressor triumphs [an essentially military concept], the more Defensive the oppressed one becomes. It is almost as if she is on trial and *has to* mount a Defence. In turn, that Defensiveness becomes a learnt behaviour. *An employee always feels she is on the back foot*, or about to be wrong-footed ; on the rear-guard, in an unguarded place. And then the Defender, in her Defensiveness, comes to expect attack. That becomes her default position at work : a state of siege. *FACTOR / RESPONSE*

DEFERRED APPRECIATION 7
So desperate are insecure, oppressed, employees for Appreciation that when it is delayed, postponed, denied or suppressed, those same employees struggle to survive. It is no use only appreciating a worker when she has resigned°/ retired. *FACTOR / MOTIVATION*

DELETION OR SUPPRESSION OF RECORDS 6
Many reasons exist why an employer - or an individual within an organization - would wish to destroy Records. And that Deletion or destruction is relatively easy in an age of computerized record-keeping. Then no awkward questions can be raised at a later stage. On the contrary, the oppressor or oppressive outfit can say, "honestly," that no evidence of discrimination or harassment exists or has existed.

An employee's letter of grievance° can be suppressed or the record of her first grievance° interview [which might have gone in her favour] can be lost. Or related complaints° can be obliterated. Alternatively, that one Memo° that could exonerate an accused employee could be torn up. In fact, praise° of that worker - maybe a letter from a member of the public or a parallel agency expressing Praise - could also "go missing" through the process of filtering.° Employee files - though technically accessible to the person being written about - are compiled in a mysterious way.   *RESULT / MOTIVATION*

DELUGE 7
A Deluge at work is similar to a siege,° an avalanche or a bombardment.° Too much work to do, too hurriedly, in too short a space of time. Yet schedules° are not at all *accidental*. Management could recruit more people to respond to the Deluge ; or indeed, restrict the flow of demand° far earlier in its build-up. For instance, management might already know the first day of a Sale will be hectic, or the first day of after a pub's renovation . They could get in more assistants for that day - or arrange a couple of preview days. And there are firms and offices where *every* day is a Deluge !   *CAUSE*

DEMANDS [HIGH EMPLOYER EXPECTATIONS] 10
The word Demands is so universal that it is difficult, here, to tie it down to the Workplace. But tie it down we must. Where Workplace Demands come to impinge or impose on workplace oppression is the actual *breaking point*. The demands of commuting, filing, paperwork, production, sales, reaching targets, pleasing co-workers, whatever, all accumulate to the point where an employee feels she cannot survive as things are. And it is quite possible *all* the Demands are humble ones- yet not too humble to ruin work performance as well.
Other Demands are the Demands employees or their Unions make of a reluctant management. Even these Demands are often dismissed as totally unreasonable before they are actually assessed and quantified. That, in turn, leads to hostility and distrust. *CAUSE / ASSOCIATION*

DEMONIZATION 8
Demonization   is sometimes regarded as a more extreme form of scapegoating.° In such adverse conditions, the unfavoured employee literally becomes the Devil : that worker on whom all loss of output or change in corporate fortunes can be blamed.° And it is a paradox of oppression in the workplace that that "Devil" was once - or is now - a new recruit.   *CAUSE / MOTIVATION /   RESULT*

DEMORALIZATION 10
Demoralization is puzzling, as it is both impetus for, and result of oppression in the workplace. No one doubts that a persistently blamed,° marginalized,° or criticized° employee can be Demoralized both at work and at home - and carry low self-image ° into work. But some workplaces are so chaotically or irresponsibly organized that Demoralization within those settings is inevitable, whatever happens outside.   *FACTOR /   RESULT*

DEMOTION 7
Demotion is a heavy, but accepted, tool for alerting someone who has lost the trust° of her employer through misconduct° or inability to fulfil her prescribed role. Less welcome is the use of Demotion as a tool to bully / threaten someone. Demotion can more speedily be achieved through a timely reorganization.° *MOTIVATION / RESULT*

DEPENDENCY 7
Dependency is a counselling term for an afflicted or confused or downtrodden person who develops an unhealthy Dependence on the more dominant person in her proximity - whether friend or foe ; *or* on the perpetuation of a damaging sequence of events. Oppressed employees *do* actually Depend on their bosses for a wage-packet and a good reference. *Psychological* Dependency is altogether more contentious; potentially more hazardous - as when a worker comes *to expect* gradgrind both at home and at work. *CAUSE / RESULT*

DEPRESSION 10
Another vast subject. Nobody can escape the deepening and hastening of Depression when the oppressed one is going under ; when she cannot even face going to work - even where work is neutral ; or, at worst, where her workplace is Hell. It is, of course, possible to be Depressed before work, in the home, or independent of the workplace. But it behoves everyone to make work as happy and fulfilling as is humanly possible. Also for managers at every level to inspire so much confidence in their workers that anyone with pre-existing Depression can talk about it, especially on bad days. Good managers recognize how a Depressed employee can be very good and very reliable - if only because Depression can promote greater awareness; and greater determination to safeguard others from distress.° *FACTOR / RESULT*

DE-SKILLING 7
If one huge combine takes over a smaller workplace ; or if new legislation makes previously qualified workers unqualified ; or if a manager wants to do absolutely everything himself ; or if previously gained skills are not updated through top-quality in-service training: then people will become De-skilled. They will then become less confident, *not more confident*, in the smaller field of endeavour they are left with - which, ironically, might not be their employer's most savvy deployment of his available resources.   *CAUSE   / RESULT*

DESKS   [HOT-DESKING,   DESK SHIFTING] 4
On a turbulent and pressurized working day, finding your Desk occupied - worse, cleared - by somebody else, is the straw that breaks the camel's back. Due to flexi-working, not everybody in an office is now promised a Desk of her own. She might have to share it, shift it - or go to any desk / or take any depersonalized work-station that is available. That might well be unsettling. Not infrequently, disciplinary procedures include a raid on Desks or having to clear them in 15 minutes. Alternatively, a line manager might exert greater control° over an underling° by making sure something menacing / unsettling / unpleasant is already on her desk when she arrives at work.   *FACTOR*

DETERMINATION 8
Certain employees are so full of Determination, they are able to survive jealousy, brickbats, setbacks and snares. But Personnel should never, ever, *rely* on an individual worker's Determination to withstand oppression.   *MOTIVATION   /   RESPONSE*

DIARY IN HAND / TO HAND 4
When the atmosphere is tense and full of mistrust, in an office or on the shop floor, access to a Diary is essential. The Diary is something to hold. Maybe it already contains the answer to a question. And if a boss is in the middle of a tirade, he will be thrown aback by his intended victim scribbling in her Diary. For he has no way of knowing what she is writing - or when it will be held against him ! *RESPONSE*

DICTATORSHIP [THE DICTATORIAL APPROACH] 8
Dictatorial management techniques and devices speak for themselves as irredeemably oppressive. It cannot be much fun to go to work for a Dictator : the office mogul, or the supreme mandarin. Calling your boss "Napoleon" is a very tired joke. *CAUSE / MOTIVATION*

DIFFUSE - OR DISPERSED - RESPONSIBILITY 4
The more employees / junior managers share Responsibility : in a shop or factory or outlet, the better. Responsible workers rise to the occasion gratified to be receiving such trust - and a commission ! *RESPONSE*

DIGNITY 9
Dignity is an all-embracing term for arriving at work each day; more important leaving at the end of each day, with a clear conscience, happy to face oneself , one's family, and the outside world. So it is a calumny that so many jobs and workplace dilemmas leave workers - especially vulnerable workers - stripped of dignity and self-respect.° Dignity is also a possible *response* to bullying in the workplace : head held up high, refusing to be bowed, determined not to repay in kind.

ASSOCIATION

DIRTY TRICKS 7
Dirty Tricks at work - and the climate that promotes or condones them - need no further amplification or condemnation. That they are still possible, and undetected, is beyond belief. *FACTOR   / MOTIVATION*

DISAPPROVAL 5
An employee subject to Disapproval certainly knows it ! Thankfully, the Disapproval registered at work is usually temporary. In other words, the worker in the dog house one day is readmitted to the magic circle the next. Something reintegrates, or re-ingratiates, her, in the same way as a naughty schoolboy rehabilitated by his class or his mother. And Disapproval operates in reverse: where a group of workers Disapprove of new working methods, conditions or remuneration. *Perpetually* to be Disapproved of, or unheeded, or labelled° Unperson, constitutes very miserable, and unanswerable, oppression.   *CAUSE*

DISCIPLINARY   PROCEDURES 7
Disciplinary Procedures - often simply called "Disciplinary" - are as many and varied as Manuals.° Universally, the Disciplinary is *a Threat.*° It is impossible for a new employee not to know she could fall foul of Disciplinary. With violence, drunkenness, lateness, fraud, embezzlement, dangerous driving, some Disciplinary is automatic. But *Underperformance*° is far more of a grey area. Here the line manager's support° / withdrawal of support is crucial. There is nothing intrinsically *fair* about Disciplinary, whatever safeguards are built into the system. As with racism° and sexism,° best practice often exists only on parchment: perversely that parchment *replacing* best practice. Other grey areas are sickness° ; work-to-rule ;° disobedience ; or refusing guidance.° And, throughout Disciplinary , if Human Resources or senior

management or line manager° mark, or call up, your ticket, nothing changes their corporate minds. Therefore, call on a Patron,° and certainly a McKenzie friend.°   *FACTOR / RESULT*

DISMISSAL [S] 9
Not everybody dismissed is justifiably sacked ; and Employment Tribunals are all too acquainted with the concepts of Constructive° or Unfair Dismissal. Being given your P45 is not an entirely logical, less a principled, outcome. And the threat of Dismissal hangs over many more employees than actually get dismissed.   *FACTOR / RESULT*

DISPUTE [S] 8
A Dispute in the workplace need not necessarily be an Industrial Dispute.° Instead it can be any difference of recall or interpretation of developments that have happened. Human memory is notoriously selective and unreliable. Thus an overbearing line manager° is quite likely to see a shortfall,° an act of omission, or a confrontation° [maybe the confrontation in which he is currently engaged] in an entirely different light from the one that illumines the oppressed one. The territory is then set for bitter recriminations:° all the more reason to bring in a mediator,° an arbiter° - or to keep a diary° of oppression.
FACTOR / MOTIVATION / RESULT

DISSENT [AN ATMOSPHERE OF DISSENT] 6
A degree of Dissent in any work setting is actually very helpful. It deters steamrollers and steamrollering.° Dissent blossoms either where disagreement is encouraged - eg. in creative professions like journalism and advertising ; or where it is forbidden. Dissent may go underground, and certainly will go underground if there is a culture of fear.° And should. its disguise *not* be successful, Dissenters will be easily picked

off, sidelined, marginalized,° indeed, ostracized ° by management. And, naturally, Dissent breeds Dissent.   *FACTOR / RESPONSE*

DISTRESS 8
Distress at work is very difficult to disentangle from Distress at home, Distress at Church or in a hobby, Distress due to the car breaking down- or Distress concerning elderly parents who might live a long way away from home and from work. Nonetheless, some Distress can be identified as actually *originating in* the workplace or office or outpost where the nature of workload° or supervision° exacerbates stress.° Kind management is alert to Distress *wherever it comes from.*   *RESULT*

DISTRUST 10
Distrust is the opposite of trust : and tends to be endemic in insecure or non-unionized organizations. Oppression is sometimes called a Breakdown of Trust: requiring, or resulting in, demotions,° suspensions,° resignations° or dismissals.°   *CAUSE / RESULT*

DISTURBED SLEEP PATTERNS 7
Disturbed Sleep is one of the earliest indications of oppression experienced - or expected - in the workplace. It is important that the two are seen as reaction one to the other.   *RESULT*

DIVIDING THE FLOCK [DIVIDE AND RULE] 7
Oppressors at work become expert at dividing a group of colleagues just as a shepherd might divide his flock. A Team thus becomes half pro-boss, half anti-boss : favoured ones, out of favour. And there is far less chance of open dissent° / questioning of the line manager, if dissenters cannot or will not present a united front. *MOTIVATION / RESULT*

DOCKED WAGES 9
Wages docked for lateness, missed targets,° the malfunction of machinery, breakages, an unbalanced till or float, industrial action,° or for any other reason, are immediately unjust. If there *has* been some malpractice, or underperformance,° these are better dealt with through advice °or an organization's disciplinary procedures.°   *CAUSE*

DOMESTIC VIOLENCE 10
Throughout this Dictionary, oppression in the workplace has its parallels in Domestic Violence. The two phenomena depend on similar urges expressed in different arenas. Crucially, the (shielded) domestic tyrant carries that behaviour into the workplace. Similarly, the subject (object) of Domestic Violence arrives at work with the same responses - usually the same learned helplessness - she has had to be content with at home. So there is potential for an overlap of victimhood.° Weakening of morale° at work will be instantly noticed by new tyrants at home. And it goes without saying that the employee who arrives at work bruised by her "lover" will then be more susceptible to criticism° in that workplace *even where* the appointed manager there, perhaps also a male, is benevolent ! And all managers and co-workers° need to be on the watch out for signs of Domestic Violence, usually *unreported* Violence, Violence not the preserve of any one social class.° Larger firms actually have protocols° for combating Domestic Violence, comforting survivors, *blocking* telephone calls / visits by the offender, in work time / space. *ASSOCIATION / MOTIVATION / RESULT*

DOMINANCE AND DOMINEERING 10
Hierarchies° would be lost without Dominance. Dominance is instrumental to GOAD : Good Order and Discipline. But *complete*

Dominance is overpowering, disempowering,° frightening and frightful. It is also terribly reminiscent of the domestic violence° that employees have often suffered prior to arriving for their shift. Most good team leaders have to be a tiny bit domineering in order to get anything done. But a bully's° dominance - his unquestioned status - is what most organizations can do best without. That means a sensitive management structure weeding out Sergeant Majors ; being aware of harsh, exploitative, practices in the workplace ; forbidding - or at least curtailing - tyranny. °   *CAUSE / MOTIVATION*

DOMINATION 9
Domination is the actual act of seizing power over a worker before, during or after work. That can be a single or a group stratagy. In some workplaces, men are always superior to women : pilots to stewardesses, shop managers to shop assistants, section heads to typists.   Or Domination could be a by-product of religion° or race. Sometimes the sisterhood exercises Domination, freemasonry,° the golf club, the executive dining room, or the car pool. We all have it in us to Dominate, and to   retain that superiority through thick and thin. Domination is raw power.°   *CAUSE / MOTIVATION*

[THE] DOORMAT 7
"Doormat" is the rather tactless, graceless, description handed out to a man or woman - more usually a woman - who appears to consent to their own subordination or persecution. The term Doormat is somewhat redeemed by its rich sado-masochistic° associations. It is also an unusually *long-lasting* word picture : filling as it does a gap in the language.   *FACTOR / RESULT*

DOWNTRODDEN WORKERS 9
From time immemorial, the majority of employees have been Downtrodden : at worst, ground into the dust. In some professions, it is taken for granted low-paid, unmotivated, workers will also be Downtrodden. As long as there is plentiful supply of labour, labourers will not generally be appreciated, nor rewarded more than the minimum any employer can get away with. That certain employers are *proud* that their workers enjoy few rights, few days off, few pounds in their wage-packets, is a matter of deep regret. Better employers have happier workers, greater productivity, and increased footfall in their retail outlets.   *MOTIVATION / RESULT*

DRAGGING OTHERS DOWN 7
Should an employee fail to keep up the work-rate, to finish the assignment, or to sell enough, she is told she is : "Dragging the Others Down." Her co-workers are going without commission or reward or time off *because* she came along. In fact, it is stated : nobody can be happy again at work until she resigns° or is allocated to other duties / or dismissed.°   *MOTIVATION / RESULT*

DRAMATISTS [DRAMA QUEENS] 5
Dramatists are needed in the workplace to keep everyone cheerful and motivated. The only trouble is : so-called Drama Queens can act as bullies° *and hide their true intent behind melodrama.*   *MOTIVATION*

DREAD 10
The oppressed one's Dread is a little broader than her fear.° Dread is a seizing up of any residual coping mechanisms.°   Dread even encompasses seeing the Oppressor's *car* and crying ; or hearing of the

oppressor's illness - and rejoicing. And Dread does not differentiate between worker and workplace, between lower and higher management, between coming to work and leaving for a home even crueller.   FACTOR / RESULT

DRESS 7
You might well conform to office or factory Dress Code, yet *still* fall foul of a co-worker° or supervisor. Dress too casual, too formal, too revealing, too flirtatious. Dress inappropriate for the task at hand. Wrong colour. Wrong size. Wrong match. "Look at that idiot who took Dress-Down Friday at its face value!" Other words are purportedly words of " advice" : " I hope you don't mind my mentioning..."
Comments regarding Dress are sometimes most bitchy from co-workers° : more likely to be overheard than comments addressed to the oppressed one *directly*. Dress is a touchy issue, indeed.   FACTOR

DRESSINGS DOWN 10
A Dressing Down at work is much to be feared : particularly behind closed doors, without representation, without justification, or when the said Dressing Down happens at the very start or end of a day, start or end of a week, start or end of a term. Dressings Down are intended to be both intimidating and peremptory. They are also timed exactly to coincide with an employee's high spirits, her dread return to work - or her best assignment / greatest triumph.
The reason Dressings Down are used so often is that they exact most harm, with least notice, or right of reply, or *ability* to reply.
Dressings Down are very *sudden* . The aggrieved or resentful manager has bags of time to plan his Dressing Down : indeed to root round until he finds something requiring a Dressing Down. The manager then starts his Dressing Down with a mock-friendly disposition, even to the

extent of smiling and offering his victim a cup of coffee. And it is to his greatest advantage that he knows what his agenda° is, whereas his victim has no clue. Because a Dressing Down is automatically a negative experience, she is unable to reflect positively on the eruption at a later time or date. In fact, the Dressing Down destabilizes , even incapacitates, her. Worse, *another* Dressing Down is only just round the corner, due to her oppressor's filtering-out of positive feedback ; and his lavish welcome of negative feedback.° *MOTIVATION / RESULT*

DRIVEN TO DRINK 7

It is accepted as a colloquialism that some people are dominant,° also ruthless, enough to Drive you to Drink. That is not be a compliment. Instead, the actual or potential manager from Hell ought to be challenged or weeded out *before* he Drives someone to Drink!

RESULT

EARLY WARNING 7

Early Warnings come in two forms. At its best an Early Warning from existing or future co-workers can protect a new recruit from workplace bullying° or from more general oppression. Better to know straightway which managers to avoid, or to deal with in a specific manner.
Then there is the negative Early Warning : where a new recruit suspects something is seriously amiss *without* anyone shock-proofing. Not unusually, clashes of perception / expectation / satisfaction in the first few weeks or months of employment, or following a change of manager, constitute in all but name Warnings ; blots on one's record of employment and employability. *MOTIVATION / RESULT*

ECCENTRICS [ECCENTRICITIES] 6
Eccentrics, like outsiders, can make a wonderful - and distinctive - contribution to any office, shop or factory. A wise employer will note Eccentricities and play into them. Eccentrics sadly take quite a bit of bedding in after recruitment - because they do not commonly "fit the bill."   *CAUSE / ASSOCIATION*

EMBARRASSMENT 9
A vulnerable employee joining a new organization will either be Embarrassed already by weight, self-presentation, accent, dress,° divorce, inexperience, whatever - or Embarrassment *follows* bullying,° belittlement, and irresponsibly negative feedback.° It is all too easy to feel isolated : by being "the only" target on the range, "the only" victim, "the only" underachiever. Embarrassment matters because it is inseparable from preparedness for the working day / working week ahead.   *FACTOR / RESULT*

EMOLUMENTS DENIED [EMOLUMENTS REFUSED] 8
Many industries and professions can only operate with Emoluments. Such employee benefits - rarely mere "perks" - include food, drink, subsidized travel, lodgings, tied cottages, bed-and-breakfast, hotel accommodation, haircuts, costume, and entertainment - or an entertainment allowance. Emoluments are more than normally present in freight transit, hospitals,° hospitality, care homes,° farming, policing,° surveillance, sales. Also commercial travelling.
Given freely and equably, Emoluments are not of themselves oppressive. Yes, they restrict employees' normal leisure and family commitments.° But that drawback is offset by extra comfort, challenge, novelty. Emoluments *Denied* constitute the bigger problem. Not uncommonly, especially in times of freeze-and-squeeze, Emoluments are actually *refused* . Where that happens, the employee himself or

herself becomes responsible for overnights and extras, out of residual income. That deficit results in not only financial hardship, but *actual* hardship. People report seeing builders, couriers, decorators, electricians, contractors, or agents, sleeping on park benches or behind their steering wheels. Other employees Denied Emoluments go hungry or unkempt. Such distress is compounded by the need to keep up appearances, and not to complain.° *Nor to lose the job* for the sake of pennies and pride.° So it is that tight employers are unfairly - and unjustifiably - subsidized by their own employees ! *CAUSE / FACTOR*

EMPLOYEE ASSISTANCE PROGRAMMES 7

No organization employing more than ten or so people should neglect its Employee Assistance Programme, if it has bothered to set up one in the first place. The best Employee Assistance Programme is independent of line management ; also confidential for as long as the employee asks for it to be. It might seem a waste of time and money to set up possible competition to Personnel. After all, management wants to get vibes that every employee is already the member of one big happy family. And management itself might have been deceived or misled by a trusted foreman or a line managers anxious to prop up his reputation for bullish, and robust,° staff relations.   *RESPONSE*

EMPOWERMENT 10

Empowerment is the opposite of *Disempowerment*.
And Empowerment is very rare : simply because it is the product of transferring power° from manager / management to managed one / worker / underling. °   And such a transfer is very risky.
All Workplaces will *profess* the promotion of worker Empowerment (how could they say anything else ?) - but the reality is everso different. Some Empowerment is in the mind only, but none the less

gratifying for that reason. Some assertive courses° enable attendees to feel more Empowered, potentially more resistant to oppression.
The Empowered one is soon, and visibly, more confident,° more vociferous, less compliant, less marginalized.
Nonetheless, Empowerment need not represent a threat to the system. In advertising, the law and PR, in particular, empowered employees value their autonomy.° Those trusted with responsibility volunteer to work late, unpaid, so helping management succeed. In these instances, the whole workplace is infused with goodwill. Empowerment is not such a loser after all. *FACTOR / RESPONSE*

EMPLOYMENT TRIBUNALS 7
The rules and procedures governing Employment Tribunals are always evolving - partly because these Tribunals can do *too good* a job: tilting the balance from employer in favour of employee (not on any Government's wish-list in a low-status, low-wage° economy). The oppressed one gambles the Tribunal will provide her first platform ; her first *sympathetic ears* to hear what she had to go through before electing- *and paying* - for formal Tribunal. The third of Employment Tribunals still happening are perhaps best postponed until a last resort after internal grievance procedures° have run their course. *RESPONSE*

ENVY 8
Not uncommonly, the oppressor in the workplace is Envious of a newcomer, or of someone brought in from another branch of the same business. Envy reveals itself in the creation of failure, deliberate fault-finding. Secretly, the oppressor is himself insecure - and imagines his target will do far better, attract more praise, even supplant himself.
More cause for Envy is where a co-worker of equal status in the organization resents a newcomer's looks, glamour, ability or output.
FACTOR / MOTIVATION

ESCAPE 10
During or after oppression, the tortured one prays for Escape. Escape comes in three ways. At its most extreme, Escape entails resignation,° retirement° or being sacked.° More subtle Escape comes with mental absenteeism° : being there but not there. Retreat to a secret garden. Quiet reflection. Coffee and cake rendezvous with a trusted colleague, or partner, at lunch time or after work. In between these extremes : legitimate, permitted, undetected, Escapes are the back office, the filing room, the water-cooler, the photocopier, the works' vehicle - or the toilet ! Of course, it is not unknown for stressed employees to run screaming out of the building: some sight ! That this does not happen more frequently is tribute to the endurance - and fear of change° - of both survivors° and oppressors alike.   *RESPONSE*

ETHOS 10
As apparent throughout this Dictionary, the work and workplace Ethos is all-important in determining whether individual employees dread° the prospect and reality of a day's work - or skip down the road to make an early start.   *CAUSE* / alternatively *FACTOR*

EXCUSES 6
Just as Excuses are discounted by the bully,° so should the bully himself not be Excused. "I had a bad morning!" "My wife's leaving me!" "We've got a very tight schedule," "You haven't been an asset to this team," " I myself am being leant on by management...." Whatever the Excuse, it will assuredly be followed by another one.   *MOTIVATION*

EXIT INTERVIEWS 7
Exit Interviews have been around for some time now - but are approached with a degree of nervousness on the part of employer and employee alike. The best Exit Interviews are frank, purposeful and

conducted in a relaxed atmosphere. There is absolutely no point in the perceived aggressor interviewing his own putative victim. Some leapfrogging is essential. Maybe a short written questionnaire could be filled in first, which includes the ultimate employer saying why he thinks someone's work experience has led to resignation°/ retirement.°

RESPONSE

EXPENDABILITY 7

One reason for intractable worker/manager conflict, and reason for stalemate, is the junior - even senior - sufferer's Expendability. Employers are quite seasoned in their calculation as to whom should be first to go. To the outsider, Expendability might seem harsh - certainly unjust. Not a few people in Personnel pray for the day the dilemma will sort itself out by the oppressed one, even the oppressor, resigning° - or taking long-term sick leave.° *FACTOR / MOTIVATION*

EXPLANATION REJECTED 8

During filtering,° whatever explanation [mitigation] the oppressed one comes up with will automatically be rejected as specious. " She would say that, wouldn't she ?" "Covering her back !" And why is any Explanation demanded ? The original sin is just one of many held in the manager's arsenal, quiver,° of guided missiles. *CAUSE / RESULT*

EXPLOITATION 10

Exploitation is a general term for squeezing as much out of a secretary, doctor, machinist or functionary as is humanly possible - and at the lowest price or wage. Exploitation also applies to the much-heralded "flexible workforce,°" any recent manifestation of goodwill, past excellence, former willingness. Many times : the lonely, non-unionized, employee feels utterly powerless° - without voice or means or ability or alliances° to protest effectively in the wake of Exploitation.

In recent years successive Governments have made strident efforts to combat Exploitation : child labour, home-working,° part-time employment,° agency working,° unequal pay,° circumventing the minimum wage,° gangmasters,° slave owners, human trafficking, whatever. As soon as one type of Exploitation is disguised and undetected, a new instance of Exploitation surfaces. Some commentators eloquently maintain that *all* wage labour is Exploitation.

MOTIVATION / RESULT

EXPOSURE 8

Oppression in the workplace is very *unlikely* to be Exposed - because *all* oppression, especially domestic oppression behind a firmly closed front door, builds into itself the means of its perpetuation : fear,° threat,° self-justification,° logic, inevitability, irreversibility.....learned hopelessness° intended, and not offset by, a bully's seemingly harmless demeanour.

ASSOCIATION / RESULT

EXTRA RESPONSIBILITY 5

Providing she welcomes it and has time for it and is encouraged whilst exercising it, Extra Responsibility is a boon and boost for otherwise oppressed employees. It may be only through the allocation to her of those Extra Responsibilities that she can prove her worth. On the other hand, she should not *need* to prove her worth. *Every* workday should be an exciting opportunity for the expression of praise° and satisfaction° - not the opposite.

ASSOCIATION

EYE   CONTACT 8
Shy individuals, or children brought up in harsh, confrontational,° households, may find Eye Contact difficult, even impossible, for the rest of their lives. Or they might only ever be able to resume Eye Contact with their partners and spouses. Eye Contact is a far more sophisticated interaction than most people realise. For instance, some Eye Contact might only be spasmodic, or restricted to listening as opposed to speaking [this a puzzling response in the Western World]. Where Eye Contact impacts upon workplace oppression is the recurring, instinctive, blockage many oppressed ones experience when face-to-face with the co-worker ° or line manager° who is on their case. To exacerbate their fearsome sideways glance, or direct gaze, several oppressors do actually have quite sharp, and bright, and demonic eyes.   *FACTOR   /   RESULT*

FACE THAT FITS 5
A Face That Fits is another name for blue eyes,° favouritism,° or preferment.° Yet if you are out of the loop,° none of this applies.
FACTOR   /   MOTIVATION
FAILURE 10
Failure is a complex attendee on target° or appraisal° day. On the face of it, Failure should merit possible demotion° or dismissal.° However, a wise employer builds Failure into his equation, makes room for it on his balance sheet. After all, judicious Failure points to later success. Failure is a stage of learning. Some failure is a jog to the memory. Failure in the workplace, as in the worlds of sport, leisure, domesticity and charity, is actually a fact of life, a given : unwelcome on most occasions, but inescapable. Failure compounds oppression when a foreman or line manager° panics, thus endorsing a culture of blame.° And who better to blame than the newcomer,° the troublemaker,° the shrinking violet - or the scapegoat ?°   *CAUSE / FACTOR / RESULT*

FAIRNESS 10

Workplace oppression is all about *unfairness* - so any transformation in that situation, any indication of *Fairness*, is a useful corrective. Little children say " It isn't fair !" - and quite possibly they have stumbled on a truth. But there is a difference between fairness and justice. Employment Procedures are not written with Fairness in mind. More overarching considerations are profitability,° the allocation of responsibility,° job description,° assessment° or appraisal° criteria, management expectations, safety° and conflict resolution.° In turn, conflict resolution° demands justice, not Fairness !   *FACTOR*

FALSE ALLEGATION 8

Like the rumour, the False Allegation against the oppressed one, not usually the favoured° one, never fails to succeed. Biblically. Not only is there no conceivable chance of ° it ; if a False Allegation *is* ever quashed or rebutted, mud sticks. The Allegation thus becomes one more arrow in an oppressor's quiver.° And , like the complaint,° the ruthless line manager° actually *welcomes*, orchestrates, its appearance. Tellingly, the denial of a False Allegation legitimates it ! " She would say that, wouldn't she? "   *MOTIVATION / RESULT*

FAMILY COMMITMENTS 7

Wise and generous employers make time and room for workers with heavily Family Commitments. Because in the end, both productivity and employee-satisfaction levels will *soar* if the wider Family is settled, in the right place, and adequately catered for. One good turn deserves another. Not a few people given compassionate leave° later excel at the workbench or word-processor.   *ASSOCIATION*

FAULT [FAULT-FINDING] 10
Due to the effectiveness of filtering° : that is, filtering out good news, also positive feedback,° Fault Finding at work is as universal as it is counterproductive. Naturally, everyone is at Fault some of the time. But to go out *looking for* Fault - *wanting it* to be discovered - is as distressing as it is ridiculous. Yet it happens : to the detriment of thousands of conscientious employees. Fault Finding is nothing if it is not dreadfully oppressive. And knowing it's happening creates frozen awareness,° incapacitation, and worse - not better - performance !°
CAUSE / MOTIVATION

FAVOURITISM 5
Favouritism is a sign or consequence of having a face that fits,° or blue eyes.° Favouritism is also the result of filtering°- where all negative feedback° has been discounted. The trouble with Favouritism is that it might have *already been bestowed upon* the oppressor now showing it. How patronage° counts : everywhere !
CAUSE / FACTOR

FEAR [CULTURE OF FEAR] 10
Fear is an all-encompassing term for workers' trepidation as to what will next go wrong in their work settings ; who will next rise up against them, who is up for the high jump. Fear not only induces paralysis ;° it reinforces learned helplessness.° Yet many ruthless or macho° managers exist to *promote* governance through Fear. It was especially popular before the turn of the Century to attribute increased productivity° to a very useful Culture of Fear, with an accompanying reduction of employee rights.
MOTIVATION / RESULT

FEEDBACK LOOP 9

The Feedback Loop is a continuous - and virtuous - circle where Management is receptive to, and welcoming of Feedback (even critical Feedback) - and where all employees receive constructive Feedback from management, co-workers,° other agencies ... and customers.
Feedback never ends, because one response elicits another, then another! Needless to say, *negative* Feedback needs to be dispensed in a kindly manner ; and needs always to be balanced, and diluted, with heaps of *good* news. Again, the manual° usually says that workplace Feedback is commonplace. (On parchment only ?)   *ASSOCIATION*

FINAL WARNING [S] 8

Final Warnings : a reluctant or regrettable tool° in the management tool-box need handling with care. At best, the Final Warning is a useful alternative to outright dismissal.°   At worst, the Final Warning hangs round somebody's neck for months, so disabling her from useful toil. All Warnings need proper grounds and process ; also adequate employee representation.   *CAUSE / MOTIVATION*

FLEXIBLE WORKING 7

To the outsider, also to many insiders, Flexible Working, in its truest sense, is an undiluted good, a virtuous circle. Why not come in at 7 in the morning and leave at 2pm for the caravan ? Unfortunately, some managers are distinctly suspicious of their dawn workers. How can they know what is being produced when they themselves are still in bed ? So, Flexible Workers, and workers from home, are wrongly thought to slacking.   Crucially, the granting of Flexible Working - as with compassionate leave° - is *optional* in many work settings. It is a favour to be granted or withheld. Not a few employees are convinced they have

been deprived of the benefit of Flexible Working or home working unfairly,° or arbitrarily. Or else Flexible Hours are available to the parents of children under 11 only - thus placing a greater burden on employees who are child-free° or who have the responsibility of ageing parents to look after.° Surely an opportune time to involve Personnel!
The other, more recent, Government use of the term Flexible Working is far, far more insidious. As a sop to outsourcers,° back-street shysters, everything-for-a-pound shops, and burger bars, many a Minister proclaims the infinite value of zero hours,° re-training, futile job-centre° attendance, the refusal of access to employment tribunal,° split shifts,° whatever, as a boost to the national economy. But one man's Flexibility is another man's incarceration. *CAUSE / RESPONSE*

FLIPPING JOBS 5
Times have changed since the 1960s and early 70s when workers were able to leave one job to be hired straightway by the shop or the builder or dockyard just down the road. But the Flipping of jobs, churning, still happens - especially in fields where there is an acute skills' shortage. Exit interviews° are a means by which one public house, for instance, can find out why its bar-man is now serving in *a different* public house; or for a hospital to discover how it lost so many nurses to " Care Homes". The answer can be quite uncomfortable. *RESULT / RESPONSE*

FORCED LABOUR 9
Forced Labour has much in common with trafficking and slavery° - but not exclusively. Some labourers are *forced* to work by prison officers,° by the courts, by job centres,° by dominant spouses - or by parents. Forced Labour is less common in Western countries than it used to be; and is, by its very nature, poorly remunerated. *CAUSE / MOTIVATION*

FORCED   RETIREMENT 6
Recent legislation has slightly halted - or postponed - Forced Retirement. But thousands of employees resign° each year because they perceive themselves - or are perceived - to be too old, maybe too outdated, too unqualified, for the job. Forced Retirement takes many forms : redundancy,° suspension,° reorganization,° outsourcing,° or inflexible rotas, ° as well as straightforward marginalization,° being edged out.   *RESULT / RESPONSE*

FORMAL   GUIDANCE 6
This "Guidance" is best treated with caution, lest it be a veiled threat° of disciplinary.° The form it most often takes is an interview under duress - *often without others present* : announcing that the employee, frequently the oppressed one, must do far better.°   *MOTIVATION*

FREE MEETINGS 4
Free Meetings, or agenda-free° meetings, are ideal for unburdening staff when otherwise they might perform in a strained or unproductive manner. Free Meetings should however be barred to infiltrators. The best Free Meetings have some managers attending who are *not* part of line management.° Free spirits !   *RESPONSE*

FREEMASONRY 8
As with Freemasonry, so with all cabals and secret societies: preferment° - sometimes total exoneration from wrongdoing - is bestowed on the insider,° whilst the outsider° is granted no such privilege. Particularly in organizations that are strictly hierarchical,° a complaint° against one ruthless officer / supervisor° goes entirely unaddressed because he is a Freemason. Conversely, *the non-Mason* is easier to marginalize° in any dispute,° or difference of perception / interpretation.   *ASSOCIATION / MOTIVATION*

FROGMARCHING 7
Frogmarching is inherently humiliating.° Frogmarching does not just happen in the armed forces. A retiree, or victim of shake-out, might be frogmarched away by Security. In such circumstances, it is imperative nothing is done to kick someone while she is already on her benders. Other acts of humiliation in the workplace are having car keys confiscated, having one's desk cleared,° having one's locker emptied, being ordered to leave an important meeting, or being suspended° without due process. *RESULT*

FROZEN AWARENESS 8
The concept of Frozen Awareness was established by Child Psychologists in order to define - and draw attention to - frightened children fearful of the next smack or shout or put-down, or their father's next outburst: one that inevitably ends with *mother* being attacked. Social Workers would do well more assiduously to look out for Frozen Awareness : the response of a rabbit in front of car headlamps.
Now the reality of Frozen Awareness has been extended to *all* women subject to domestic violence; ° to asylum-seekers under the thumb of gangmasters ; ° also to the elderly residents of poorly-run care homes. ° Frozen Awareness certainly informs any image we have of bullied° workers : and of all employees who are unable to relax.   *RESULT*

GAGGING ORDERS 5
Gagging Orders are never fair. It often becomes a condition of suspension,° resignation,° redeployment, pay-off, or redundancy° that the aggrieved employee / manager / doctor / whistleblower° makes no statement at all to fellow workers or journalists or tribunals. ° Yet Gagging Orders, however absurd and undemocratic, are *completely legal* ; usually adhered to, to the letter ! *ASSOCIATION   / RESULT*

GANGING UP 6

It is an extremely unpleasant experience to be Ganged Up against. Perhaps the whole team or conveyor belt or department Gangs Up against the oppressed one. Result : further misery,° scapegoating ° and marginalization.°
CAUSE / RESULT

GANGMASTERS 8

Gangmasters are employers - more likely *casual* agents or overseers - charged with the instant employment and dismissal° of immigrants or unsettled workers, not a few of whom are unregistered with their local job centre° - and without fixed abode. Gangmasters are strongest, though not exclusively active, in agriculture, horticulture or the harvesting of shellfish.

For about a decade, there has been a Gangmasters Licensing Authority: in response to public disquiet, and fear° surrounding migration and tax evasion; also deaths in the fields, on country roads, or on the sands.

Nevertheless, many anonymous young men are still picked up at anonymous lay-bys, early in the morning, and transported in equally anonymous white vans to suitably anonymous sheds, or lock-up units on anonymous industrial-estates : wherever they can be anonymously exploited° most and paid *least*. Gangmasters would not flourish *unless* they could stay covert, relying entirely on their victims' compliance, moreover silence.
CAUSE / MOTIVATION

GANGS OF FOUR 3

A " Gang of Four" is useful shorthand for the four people at the top of any organization. In the case of three, it is technically a Trinity or Triumvirate ; in the case of two : a Duopoly. Some workers admire and revere their Gangs of Four, in equal measure. More *distrust* °them - or at least, joke about them.

The idea of a Gang of Four is that each of its number shares joint responsibility for the prosperity and progress of the whole operation: joint credit, joint blameworthiness, joint remuneration. Where Gangs of Four impact on workplace oppression is the clear notion shared by a number of their underlings° that if you speak to one of the privileged owners, nothing will happen without the connivance or say-so of the other three, two, one, personages. Iron masters act in concert - effectively beyond challenge or redress.   *ASSOCIATION*

GATEKEEPER [S] 3
Not merely anecdotal is the institution and presence in any organization of Gatekeepers : individuals charged with financing - keeping secret? - the deliberations and senior management. Sometimes the Gatekeeper is parodied as the Tiger, the Dragon, "She Who Must Be Obeyed," or simply: the Road Block. Quite possibly, the Gatekeeper will act oppressively, condoning oppression in the workplace - indeed *perpetuating it* ; OR become the facilitator of a less harsh, more accountable, even a more generous, administration.   *FACTOR*

GOALS 6
Goals are set for each team, each conveyor-belt, each floor, sometimes for each employee. But Goals tend not to be merely an innocent tool for measuring performance.° Goals can actually be quite intimidating - especially if not reached. See Targets°)   *FACTOR*

GOALPOSTS [SHIFTING OF GOALPOSTS] 7
Here the employee is told the exact requirements of her day/ week/ assignment/ task; or else she is told how her personality and performance needs to change,° to fit more nearly the terms of her continued employment. And when she has done all that, the oppressor

comes up with new and wider Goalposts - because it is not in his interests either to offer praise° or to express satisfaction. *MOTIVATION*

GOOD ORDER AND DISCIPLINE [DISCIPLINE] 6
GOAD is (Police °) shorthand for a compliant and obedient° workforce. Conversely, *its absence* is a charge to be held against "rebels," "misfits," & other troublemakers.°   *MOTIVATION*

GOODWILL 8
Goodwill is so intangible, it is difficult to describe. But you know it when you see it. Goodwill comes with a lot of smiling faces, autonomy, and workers duly empowered :° workers happy to talk; happy with their wages; workers anxious to *get to* work rather than get out, at 5pm. on the dot. Goodwill is commonest in cooperatives° or small businesses where everyone knows everyone else. Where each employee, however senior, depends on every other employee. Where nothing seems too much trouble. Wherever praise° abounds. Goodwill also has religious connotations.   *RESPONSE*

GOSSIP 4
The workplace - any workplace - is a hotbed of Gossip. Some of this Gossip is absolutely harmless. But even harmless Gossip can exclude or marginalize ° the oppressed one. " Didn't she know ?" " Hasn't she heard ? " " Not seen it on TV ?" " Clearly out of the loop." °
Harmful Gossip often starts with derision of the management / the system. But even this is a quagmire. You are encouraged to join in the chorus of disapproval of what's happening ; then you are shopped to that same management! You are clueless fodder for the planted *agent-provocateur.*

Even more harmful Gossip is about *the person herself* : "Out of her depth," "too distracted by what's going on at home," " blue eyes,"° "came to us on false pretences," " clearly not up to the job," "*reprimanded* : did you not know ?" And whatever the manual° says, work Gossip is both permitted and perpetual.   CAUSE   /   FACTOR

GRADES   [GRADING   ] 4
Grades are part of both the power structures and the salary/. bonus allocations of trusted businesses or organizations. You are allocated a Grade upon entry, promotion° or demotion.°   That leads to acute Grade-consciousness, sexual discrimination, a lot of envy,° - also the fierce protection of differentials.   Grades are inextricably entangled with the establishment : whether you are a casual,° or "on the books."
ASSOCIATION

GRIEVANCE   PROCEDURES 6
The danger of Grievance Procedures written on parchment, laminated, and bound in grand ring-folders, is that - like "tackling racism," "confronting sexism," and "terms and conditions" - they are codified, then *ignored*. The very existence of a formal Procedure should not be taken as reason for not confronting flagrant breaches of their guidelines. Nor must employees be despised, dismissed° or demoted° *because* they have resorted to Grievance. One grievous Grievance needs to be brought into the foreground *explicitly* : bullying.° Amazingly, some established Grievance Procedures pussyfoot, or skirt round, the issue of outright bullying°: a bad instance of corporate embarrassment....if organizations *can* ever be embarrassed.   RESPONSE

GRIT 3
Grit in the workplace is as unpleasant as it sounds. Either the unscrupulous management figure is "showing Grit" by bullying ;° or the oppressed worker is "lacking Grit" by being unable to take the aggro.
MOTIVATION

GROPING [GROPERS] 7
Groping is possibly a much greater issue in the workplace than it is given credit for. Many men, though not necessarily women, going about their lawful occasions, *thought* Groping had died a natural -or unnatural- death in the more liberated 1970s and 1980s. Which makes this continued fixation on women's extremities even *more* perplexing.
Most Personnel departments explicitly forbid Groping, as they do all forms of sexual harassment ; and request that Groping be brought to management's attention. Transgressors are usually warned° or dismissed ;° yet *touching* an employee - male or female - whilst addressing them, is generally tolerated. Also, not a few Gropers are in a higher, more powerful, positions than the one being Groped. *CAUSE*

GROUP COHESION 7
Group Cohesion is shorthand for sticking together, true comradeship. Society is generally suspicious of both comrades and trades unions.° Yet no part of society : from football terrace to boardroom, can progress *without* Group Cohesion. A Group forms effortlessly wherever its members share a common purpose. Then a Group gains some permanence. In these circumstances, everybody is either an insider° or an outsider : ° "one of us," or "one of them." So it is that established Groups do not always welcome newcomers - not even for their novelty value.
ASSOCIATION / RESPONSE

GROUP   DYNAMICS 8
Group Dynamics is far too immense a subject to be properly tackled here. Sufficient to say it is that branch of Sociology that attempts to understand how Groups work. That includes recruitment, initiation,° retention,° departure,° dissolution, trust,° cohesion,° survival.° Group Dynamics labels different joiners according to their attributes : as fixers, leaders,° negotiators,° facilitators, clarifiers, maintainers, whatever. In the workplace, it follows that every employee damned, or deemed, beyond redemption, has a role to play in task fulfilment.°
Team Study Days° should include a study of <<How Groups Work.>> That scrutiny is made less likely due to *the delicacy* of the topic and its huge   ramifications.   It has *already* to be a wonderful Group to feel freed enough to discuss Group Dynamics ! Yet it is time well-spent. Little do many Personnel Departments know that here they have the key to nearly every door. Why leave it on the key-rack ?
ASSOCIATION

GROUP   THINK 5
Thinking outside the box, outside the Silo,° is lauded in mission statements - but not always *in reality*. Group Think is compelling : the ability to throw up ideas and know they will be warmly embraced by one's peers. Group Think is cosy.   Then comes the time the whole edifice comes crashing down - not least where a quango,° or the Civil Service, has had some input ! Wise estate agents, PR agencies, schools, hospitals, wherever, welcome *Un-Group* Think with enthusiasm.
See Silo. Also see Wilful Blindness. *ASSOCIATION*

GRUDGES   [HOLDING A GRUDGE] 7

Grudges are sadly not easily forgotten, less so resolved. Many are the office bullies° who harbour fierce Grudges against underlings ° in their teams or shifts - or, contrarily, Grudges concerning *their own superiors*. Lingering Grudges intrude on every work space, every working day - and so act to perpetuate oppression; thereby cultivating distrust and misunderstanding into the bargain.   *CAUSE   /   MOTIVATION*

HANDICAPPISM 6

Although the word Handicap is understandably out of vogue, Handicappism is alive and well. This -ism incorporates making little or no provision for a disabled employee, dwelling too little - or too long - on her disability, not adjusting work allocation to take account of disability, and not correcting / reprimanding co-workers° who make light or make fun of a colleague's disability. And Handicappism impacts upon oppression in that a disabled or differently-abled employee might suffer first when travelling to work; second on arrival at work; third while doing the work; fourth when managing expectations that she can / cannot do work as completely as the able-bodied person can; fifth a persistent feeling of not being part of a team; indeed acting as a possible *drag* on that team.   *MOTIVATION   /   ASSOCIATION*

HAND-WASHING 6

Ritual Hand-Washing is seen all too often in the workplace: sometimes with clinical dereliction of duty. All those who *could* speak out against sharp practice, mis-selling, false accounting, fraud,° misdemeanours, unprovoked anger,° victimization,° the rigging of contracts, whatever, often choose not to. They would prefer to Wash their Hands, Pontius-Pilate like. That makes the lone objector, the snout, the whistleblower,°

the alleged troublemaker,° a voice crying in the wilderness. After each shocking scandal, people always ask : " Why did this not come to the surface before now ?" The answer is : there wasn't a channel or device or incentive or reward for coming forward. Conversely, speaking out of turn in many staff rooms, offices or agencies is deserving of the heaviest of the heavy squad : the Mafia.   *FACTOR / RESULT*

HARASSMENT 9
Harassment is an all-embracing word for workplace oppression. It has the nice, or nasty, connotation of stalking. Harassment is also eerily reminiscent of the domestic violence ° facing far too many employees when they go home after a stressful ° day at work , with stressful° journeys to accommodate as well. Harassment takes very many forms, filling the whole of this Dictionary.   *CAUSE / MOTIVATION*

HARMONY 8
Harmony is difficult to describe but you know it when you see it. Immediately the visitor enters a school or hospital or shop or restaurant, he or she will be attuned to signs of harmony or disharmony. Unreasonable levels of rush, stress, noise, panic or conflict are immediately evident. Yet a *Harmonious* workplace is relatively cheap and effortless to achieve.

Harmony does not mean everybody is a close buddy, even less a paragon of virtue. But there is a common purpose, a commitment to achieve the best outcome. Conversely, nobody can be bothered to invest in a disharmonious workplace. A place where managers have simply given up. Astonishingly, some hotels, warehouses, manufacturers and elderly persons' homes fondly believe nothing is wrong; nothing has ever been wrong ; so nobody is needed to hand to pick up on shortcomings that do not exist. *ASSOCIATION/ RESPONSE*

HEADACHES 6
Headaches can again be literal or metaphorical. Real Headaches and migraine are still a bone of contention in the world of medicine. Everybody know Headaches exist - but how ? Some result from caffeine-withdrawal : the excess caffeine, ironically, being consumed at work or on the way to work. Should any sufferer suspect oppression at work is the cause of continuing Headaches, then that stressor should be addressed first, in preference to mere medication. *RESULT*

HEIGHT 3
An employee's Height matters enormously. Nobody argues with a 6 foot-8inch man ; whereas a 5 foot-1 inch woman presents a different target. But whatever a worker's Height, or the high heels with which she vainly attempts to boost that Height, she should refuse to sit on lower chair than her interviewer / accuser or talk to her line manager's° abdomen. *ASSOCIATION*

HIERARCHY 7
Organizations and businesses *can* be run on non-hierarchical lines. John Lewis has famously opted for the Partnership model, as have hundreds of tiny shops, doctors' surgeries, and two-man outfits. Also, many advertisers and PROs, or those in sunrise I.T. who sit round in a circle, spurn Hierarchy in favour of broadening out the decision-making process. Workplace oppression is far commoner in big, long and strong Hierarchies where everyone covers their back apart from the oppressed one who is most exposed to disapproval. *FACTOR*

HIRE-AND- FIRE 6
The practice of ruthless Hire-and-Fire is allied to a culture of fear.° "If you don't like us, we maybe let you go..." Hire-and-Fire operates best in low-pay, low-morale, low-job-security, workplaces- or where zero

hours° only are on offer. Also jobs involving door-to-door visits, fast food production and distribution.... and ironically : security !   *CAUSE*

HIT-LISTS....7
Unscrupulous employers keep a Hit-List of workers due for demotion° or dismissal, ° and transfer to the front line. Sometimes the Hit-List contains the names of employees who have been on strike,° who have blown the whistle,° who have been "insubordinate," °who have sold less than they should have sold, or who have slept with a love rival. The top tier of the Hit-List are usually the first for redundancy,° first for demotion,° first for the glasshouse, first for fatigues. Hit-Lists are generally kept secret. Their very *existence* is denied.   *RESULT*

HOME WORKING 5
Home Working - like flexible working,° part-time working,° four-day working, job-sharing, and compassionate leave° - is granted as a favour in many work settings. There is lingering suspicion that the outposted organization's input or output is losing out to Scrabble, crosswords, husbands, baking, screaming kids, dusting, whatever, where workers work from home. A doubting manager might actually permit Home Working during heavy snowfall; or when an employee's family is ill; when their teachers go on strike. But, even then, several Home Workers *feel* they are living on charity. Moreover, equal-status colleagues *tied* to the workplace resent the (lazy?) Home Worker. Conversely, the floodgates are opened to every Tom, Dick and Harry actually at base to ring or e-mail the oppressed one at home 24/7, 365 days a year ! After all, it was she herself who opted to work from home !   *ASSOCIATION*

HOMOPHOBIA 7
Homophobia in the workplace need not necessarily be directed at just one identified - or identifiable - homosexual, lesbian, bi-sexual or cross-

dresser. That targeting is, of course, shattering for the employee concerned, even if that Homophobia is misplaced and erroneous. That Homophobia is also a continuation of what somebody has already experienced in street, school, college, inn. However, a Homophobic *climate* at work is, in many ways, worse : maintained by banter,* jokes, innuendo, ill-concealed smiles, obscene gestures and graffiti - also chants, songs, and the aggressive masculinity of self-proclaimed heterosexual and "straight" men   *CAUSE / MOTIVATION*

HOSTILE   ENCOUNTERS   [HOSTILITY] 8
Workplaces are usually so restricted in space : one staff room, one cloak room, one floor, one office, one production line - that potentially hostile Encounters are very difficult to avoid. You cannot generally play cat-and-mouse. Contrarily, the oppressor becomes quite skilled making a hostile Encounter sound perfectly reasonable , indeed accidental; engaging in his Hostile Encounter when nobody else is around ; or asking the oppressed one to go just out of sight. Adverse face-to-face Encounters are not just the stuff of cinema and of drama.   *CAUSE*

HOUSEHOLD   TYRANNY   [..... CARRIED OVER] 7
Those who have been subject to domineering and tyrannical behaviour at home - from son, brother, boyfriend, husband - carry their fears and timidity into the workplace. That in no way *excuses* the tormentor at work - who will still come across as " more of the same"; but it could inform colleagues just why exactly someone is going under. *FACTOR*

HUMAN   CAPITAL 5
Human Capital is the sum total of all the skills and wealth and energy and inventiveness of all the workers in a workplace. So this Capital is just as important as financial Capital - maybe *more* important. So it ill behoves the employer who squanders his Human Capital - perhaps

during a long strike,° a walk-out,° a sit-in, a lock-down,° a programme of redundancy,° or an unresolved dispute. ° Conversely, awards, trophies, and photographs in the local - or national - newspaper, indicate "The 100 Best Companies To Work For."   *ASSOCIATION*

HUMAN RESOURCES 8

"Human Resources" is the novel, maybe *impersonal*, name for the alternatively labelled° Personnel Department / Recruitment Section / or "Staffing." The idea of *Human* Resources owes its origin to 18th. and 19th.Century "hands" ; later to Management Theory and Practice emerging from indigenous , also USA, Business Schools.

"Hands" were just that : hands and arms to work machines. They were not considered to be people : *individuals* with individual wants and foibles and anxieties ; rather they were treated as automatons : slaves° or serfs who were fully deserving of their bondage.

So it could be with valued Human Resources : were that Department ever to forget the *personal* part of Personnel. They must not view a *sentient* Resource on a par with (inanimate) computers, fax machines, photocopiers, desks,° warehouses, filing cabinets. *Real people* have hearts and minds. So it is that Personnel Officers and Human Resources' Departments are established to focus on *the whole* person : even where that provokes a clash with owners &/or P.R.   *RESPONSE*

HUMAN TRAFFICKING ...9

Human Trafficking is another huge subject that deserves a book of its own. One branch of Human Trafficking is child sexual exploitation; another, child sexual imagery ; another prostitution ; another economic migration ; another escape from civil war or civil unrest....usually within unsafe, overpriced, or non-existent boats and trucks. But all branches of Human Trafficking tend to overlap, and *all* are inherently exploitative.

The Government has a huge task identifying the Traffickers and the pimps and the slum landlords and the boat owners. Once identified, Traffickers have to be tracked down, halted, prosecuted. But Traffickers are always ahead of the pack. They receive considerable funds from piecework, sweat shops, ° drug dealing and cartels : funds they are very reluctant to lose. People in misery ° are the Traffickers' main commodity. As such, slaves ° and sufferers alike are *objectified*. They cease to be real people : only the means by which their owners are enriched. Sadly, the main reason Traffickers are rarely, perhaps never, apprehended is the uncomplaining, uncomprehending, though hardly willing, submission of their subjects. *CAUSE / MOTIVATION*

HUMILIATION   [MOCKERY]   [TAUNTING] 8
Humiliation sums up an extremely large segment of oppression in the workplace. The word means to "make humble" - by definition, *against* the wishes of the person being demoted° / ridiculed° / unfairly criticized. ° Many managers believe that one or more of their colleagues must decrease that they might *in*crease.   *MOTIVATION / RESULT*

HURRY 7
Generally the Hurried worker is an oppressed worker : Hurried *and* harried. There is even a condition called Hurry Sickness. Ridiculously, many days of Hurry, replete with tension and false time limits, are completely unnecessary. A far better job would be accomplished were it to take *longer* - even if that meant renegotiating a contract, a despatch date or a product specification. Act in a Hurry, repent at leisure. Many employees dread going into work - regardless of their dread of the final hour of the day - because of a disturbed climate of Hurry.   *FACTOR*

IDENTIFICATION WITH THE OPPRESSOR 6
Identification with the Oppressor is a complex unfolding of collusion, imitation, mitigation, even perpetuation. Identification with the Oppressor can easily be seen as a pathway to delaying defeat, reducing suffering. Not a few oppressed ones and their senior managers are nervous anticipating a bully's° total or ultimate elimination or humiliation .° After all, the bully° is likely to be a valued cog in his employer's machine " too good to lose." *RESULT / RESPONSE*

ILLEGALITY [CONSPIRACY TO ACT ILLEGALLY] ...7
Not at all uncommon is the invidious position of the employee forced - or persuaded - to act Illegally : probably against his or her desire, inclination, religion, or moral compass. Maybe someone is asked to work cash-only, or to remove a machine-guard, fiddle the figures, alter the tachograph, pay below the minimum wage,° adulterate food - or to use the Lump [labour only subcontracting].° And if you are looking forward to, or depending on, your next wage packet, you are very tempted to act Illegally - especially when you yourself are not the prime instigator or moral agent. *CAUSE*

IMITATION 6
Just as the worst and harshest management styles are Imitated, so Imitation can be highly effective where new, conciliatory, management aims or tools° are successful, and worth sharing. And, of course, Imitation is also flattery. It would be a pity if happiness in the team, or calm in the wider workplace, were *not* infectious. *ASSOCIATION*

IMMIGRANT LABOUR 8
It is far from automatic that a workforce dominated by Immigrants will be unhappy or unproductive. On the contrary, much Immigrant Labour is desperately needed and remorselessly hardworking. However, an

Immigrant Labour force comes unstuck when there is ghettoizatation of certain jobs or floors or outposts ; and places where the indigenous population feels it is excluded, even unwanted. Also when certain menial jobs are labelled : " Immigrant Only" - often to the detriment of Immigrants themselves. An Immigrant or "asylum-seeker" designation defines many imported workers as underlings°...so reviving their corporate memory - and direct experience - of slavery and the Empire. It should also be remembered that Immigrants are often paid less than the Minimum Wage:° partly because they are felt not to be worth anything more ; partly because they are very unlikely to complain ;° and partly because even when wages are fair, so much is deducted for introduction, transportation and accommodation (emoluments°); also because money is unjustly withheld for breakages and defects ; so that anything left over is next to worthless. Then, to add insult to injury, Immigrants are frequently overcharged for documentation, work clothing and (poor quality) food. As if things could ever get worse, Immigrants are then threatened with peremptory dismissal° - and the inevitable repatriation that is a consequence of being without work or work permit. *CAUSE / FACTOR / RESULT*

IMMUNITY 7

If ever a foreman or manager or section-leader gets it into his head that he is Immune from criticism° and redress,° he will have greater impetus and temptation to turn to bullying.° An owner or head office ° must make it crystal clear that nobody is Immune when it comes to allegations of mismanagement or unsafe practices.° *RESULT*

IMPOTENCE 7
Impotence can be both literal : not able to enjoy or benefit from sexual intercourse ; or metaphorical : inability to concentrate at work ; to face a task ; to complete an assignment ; to face colleagues. Impotence is not infrequently induced, and provoked, by workplace oppression.
RESULT

INADEQUACY 8
Inadequacy is usually a self-diagnosis for not feeling up to the task in hand. And that Inadequacy might originate in management's negative feedback,° a spouse's low estimation of self, a mountain of paperwork,° postponed housework, or simple unpreparedness ° for promotion° - or for new demands.° Wise Personnel foresee and reduce their employees' feelings of Inadequacy.
CAUSE / RESULT

INABILITY TO DELEGATE 5
People who work for somebody unprepared to Delegate soon get disheartened. Not only are they working for a self-styled martyr ; they are also given no rope or leeway or opportunity to shine on their own. To make matters worse, workers are often blamed by the workaholic for messing-up on what they have tried to do of their own volition. Exhaustion is definitely a *cause* of oppression as well as a by-product.
CAUSE / FACTOR

INCENTIVES 4
Incentives are innocuous when the employer merely wants his staff to achieve the best they are capable of. They become oppressive, however, when staff cannot attain Goals, and Goal-Posts Shift. We all experience disappointment in a Supermarket when we don't spend enough to be rewarded. How much worse for the employee in a tight labour market : one where her skills are in abundant supply.
ASSOCIATION

INCOMPETENCE 6

Incompetence is both an excuse and a pretence for bullying° in the workplace. Incompetence *sounds* incontestable - but in fact means whatever the oppressor wants it to mean. The trouble with the yoke of Incompetence is that it can never be thrown off, even if the oppressed one *is* competent. It might be worthwhile an employee challenging the diagnosis. After all, she wouldn't have been taken on if she was that incompetent! Perhaps alleged Incompetence provides the impetus for in-service training.° *CAUSE / RESULT*

INCRIMINATION 5

Incrimination in the workplace is a clear instance of scapegoating,° a ready resting-place for grudges° and blame.° Incrimination also smacks of the set-up. And once Incriminated, an employee can never prove her worth, however hard she tries. Incrimination is also a cycle : passed on to others, at home as well as at work. Personnel needs to be very astute not to *collude* with alleged, induced, or actual Incrimination.
RESULT / MOTIVATION

INDIGESTION 4

Digestion would not on the surface have any relevance to oppression at work - but it is high up the list of consequences of fearing° either the workplace or one individual within that workplace. Indigestion is sending all the wrong messages to the stomach and gut - with the stomach and gut sending all the wrong messages back. As with sweating and sleeplessness,° a harsh work environment is an identifiable culprit. *RESULT*

INDISPENSABILITY 4
Indispensability is a myth - but an attractive illusion, like 24/7 availability.° There should always be a deputy or shadow equally ready and able to step up to the plate. Indispensability can of course drift easily into overwork,° or at least presenteeism.°   *ASSOCIATION*

INDUSTRIAL "ACCIDENTS" 9
Despite the best or worst efforts of Safety Officers and the Health and Safety Executive, Industrial "Accidents" (calamities) are all too common, especially in construction, extraction, agriculture and machine maintenance. Also where just-in-time, prolonged overtime° or impossible targets° lead to car crashes. And although Industrial "Accidents" are often fatal , debilitating, or incapacitating, they are rarely investigated properly or compensated for. Routinely in certain organizations there is a culture or carelessness. Often forgotten is the over-representation of new recruits, casual labourers,° and apprentices in "Accident" statistics.   *RESULT / FACTOR*

INDUSTRIAL PSYCHOLOGY 4
The very much 1930s, 40s, and 50s.' discipline of Industrial Psychology is closely related to the study of Social Psychology °- much as Applied Economics or Economic Behaviour are offshoots of pure Economics. Industrial Psychology had its hay day with the Conveyor Belt,° and Time-and-Motion. ° An added asset was the academic sophistication that Industrial Psychology offered "simple" production lines. Better, perhaps, than Management Theory.°   *ASSOCIATION*

INEFFICIENCY 5

In an efficient organization, the *Inefficient* worker sticks out : especially to the next person on the production line, the next Duty Officer, the next service-user, the next employer. Sometimes Inefficiency is restricted to just one area of an employee's responsibility: paperwork , recording, returning telephone calls, tidying up or filing. Where Inefficiency is first suspected, sensitive management guidance° is one answer : guidance best given early on, not later. *FACTOR*

INFLEXIBLE ROTAS [ROSTERING] 8

Rotas are always contentious because - as with overtime° or shift working° - they exercise, or obligate, often unwilling employees : sometimes setting those called able-bodied at a disadvantage to those with a disability ; compliant workers at a disadvantage compared with carping co-workers; ° child-free ° workers at a disadvantage compared with parents. Rotas intrude upon travel, leisure, Sundays, sleep,° family responsibilities° and much else. By their nature, the dreaded Rotas *are* changeable, at a minute's notice, by management - yet curiously beyond challenge° by the actual workers charged with turning up at the requisite time !° Sometimes illogical Rotas improve with team negotiation.° *CAUSE / FACTOR*

INSECURITY 8

The word Insecurity is not always helpful. Many oppressors refer to a worker's Insecurity as good reason to come down hard, to get the oppressed one into line. Thus, with a good measure of irony, the thoughtless line manager imagines he is *helping* the victim of his crass behaviour to become more secure in herself.... much as the torturer desperately wishes "to help" the tortured one come to his senses !

Nonetheless, thousands of leaned-on employees *are* Insecure. Which comes first : the chicken or the egg ? The demonization or the demon ? A good and wise employer recognizes that *all* his staff are potentially Insecure : some days more than others - so guiding them through the bad times instead of making those times worse !

FACTOR / RESULT

IN-SERVICE TRAINING COURSES 4
Like most other Bullying° tools, In-Service Training Courses sound so innocuous. The trap is to surround the said Course with a ribbon of "Confidentiality."° A snout - not unusually the trainer herself - then faithfully relays back to co-worker° or line manager° exactly what the oppressed one said - or failed to contradict - on that Course : how little she learned. Negative Feedback° includes alleged Racism,° Sexism,° Homophobia,° or Dissent.° And the snout giving the Feedback shares a desire to paint the oppressed one in the most horrible light. While all the time, the victim° lives in Fools' Paradise : actually cherishing the fellowship ; the escape°; detachment from day-to-day drudgery. Occasionally, oppressed ones are actually sent under a cloud for more In-Service Training, in response to guidance° - or the annual appraisal.° *ASSOCIATION / RESPONSE*

INSIDER [THE INSIDE CIRCLE] 6
To be an Insider, "one of us," is the cherished opposite of being an outsider° - and a lot more comfortable a place to be. Maybe the Inside track is indicative of the face that fits.° *ASSOCIATION*

INSPIRATIONAL "PEP" TALKS 4

Many American or Japanese firms start their days / staff conventions with inspirational talks : the idea being to motivate staff benignly. Like the school assembly, these gatherings or exercises can be invaluable in setting a tone for the day ahead. They only become threatening when "underachieving" sales people are named and shamed to rapturous boos. *RESPONSE*

INSUBORDINATION 7

Insubordination is shorthand for an employee's failure to follow instructions or to obey one particular manager / panel of managers / management directive.° Within the Police,° Fire Service or Army,° Insubordination, " mutiny," might be an actual offence - even where an "awkward" recruit has been misunderstood. In local government, refusal to be supervised, or instructed, or examined, by a particular person is also called   Insubordination : gross misconduct.°   *FACTOR*

INTERNALIZATION OF GROUP PHILOSOPHY 5

The HOW we do not understand - but the repercussions we do. The Internalizing of Group Outlook / Group Philosophy allows us insight into unreasonable and insensitive management behaviour.° If a line manager or foreman or deputy head-teacher is cocooned, featherbedded, flattered, within a subgroup of uncritical colleagues, (s)he will act irrationally. That includes both bullying° and the issuing of immoral or illegal° orders - or legitimate orders to do illegitimate acts. And an employee who stifles doubts or inhibitions, to keep her job, is oppressed indeed. Ready-made teams of co-workers° are notoriously difficult for newer recruits to penetrate. See Silo. *FACTOR*

INTERROGATION 7
If an employee of whatever standing is going to be subject to an Interrogation - whether by a panel, supervisor,° or dynamic duo° - she fully deserves to be accompanied by a sympathetic colleague or union rep ; or have access to a note-taker whose notes she will sign before leaving the room.   *CAUSE / RESULT*

INTERRUPTIONS 4
Innocent interruptions happen all through the working day : power supply, visitors, telephone calls.   But many people experience a working day *consisting only of interruptions* - whereupon they fall behind with their own task allocation. Worse, when the oppressed one tries to explain / excuse herself, she might be verbally interrupted by her manager : unsettling, to say the least.   *FACTOR*

IRRITABILITY 6
Irritability is a known - but underestimated - response to isolation and oppression in the workplace. Where a loved one, co-worker° or line manager° sees someone Irritable (where that is not a one day wonder, or attributable to temporary stress° at home) the question should be asked : " Is current work experience *satisfying* enough for the Irritated / *Irritating* one ?"   *FACTOR / RESULT*

INTERNS [INTERNSHIP] 6
Interns are relatively new in the British Isles. These employees, crucially, are not *counted*, nor are they remunerated, as *real employees*. They are merely "observers" on work experience. So they do not have to be paid a Minimum Wage,° or offered any job-security.° Not a few Interns would starve were it not for the Bank of Mum and Dad. And some Interns do a lot more than simply sit there !   *ASSOCIATION*

INTIMIDATION 9
Intimidation is one of the best catch-all words to describe the flavour and outcome of workplace oppression. Intimidation means to make timid ; to belittle ; to make cower. And the bully° delights most in seeing a co-worker° crushed. She might then curry favour : favour and praise° immediately withheld, to be replaced by escalating Intimidation. *CAUSE / RESULT*

ISOLATION 8
Daily, the oppressor relies on his victim's Isolation. Isolation is the experience of utter despair° that you are alone in a hostile workplace.° Nobody is on your side. Nobody understands the misery.° Moreover, nobody will come to the rescue. Appeals° to higher management might get nowhere, should a "gifted" or "essential" line manager ° stand in the gap between you and they. Isolation then feeds of itself.

Isolation is one of the most pivotal strategies in workplace oppression. The idea is that the scapegoat,° the disgraced one°, the dissident,° will feel worse if Isolated.

Isolation can be enshrined and perpetuated by separating recalcitrants from otherwise-supportive co-workers :° redeployment.° At worst the oppressed one will be sent home on "gardening leave," effectively suspended.° And forbidden to communicate with her Workplace or with any former colleagues or with anyone she is accused of misleading/ill-treating/letting down.

Isolation can, of course, be a purely mental delusion : " I, even I only, am left;" "Nobody is on my side;" "They've all ganged up against me."

It is not unknown for the oppressed one to feel she is isolated - or told she is isolated - when many of her co-workers° are privily on her side, wishing her a better deal... if only they themselves were empowered.°

In the end, Isolation is only conquered by colleague solidarity, °
as opposed to co-workers° willingly - or fearfully - joining the fray.

CAUSE / RESULT

[THE] ISOLATED INCIDENT 5
Another form of Isolation is the Isolated Incident : usually incorporated in the charge : ".... and this was not an Isolated Incident." Whereas, wise managers will see what really *was* an Isolated Incident as *not* part of a pattern ; on the contrary : a valuable learning experience. *FACTOR*

JETTISONING WORK OR RESONSIBILITY 5
Particularly when we are depressed or overworked, the only path to survival° might be Jettisoning some tasks, some responsibilities: throwing them overboard. The metaphor comes from the sea : the impossibility of keeping a ship afloat in a storm , burdened with extra weight or crew ! Of course, a grasping management might not welcome the Jettison !   *RESPONSE*

JOB DESCRIPTION 4
Many Job Descriptions attract derision : " Dinner Lady must mix gravy;" " Successful applicant will be expected to be available to all guests;" "We are looking for a proven Child Abuse practitioner," etc. But Job Descriptions can be useful in a dispute. Oppressed ones might usefully offer to do no more than what is in their Job Description. Alternatively, one worker under stress° might reasonably point out that extraordinary demands° were not clearly laid out at interview stage. In practice, Job Descriptions contain a catch-all clause referring to : " any other duties your line manager° might require of you." Nonetheless, Job Descriptions should act to restrain the over-zealous, or unscrupulous, manager.   *ASSOCIATION / RESPONSE*

JOB INSECURITY 8
Whenever or wherever an employee feels her job or her prospects are blighted or threatened, she will not be able to perform at her best. She will always be looking over her shoulders. And in the Army or retail or the hospitality industry, it is very much in the interests of the employer to broadcast how perilous life is. You'll have far fewer absentees,° agitators, complainants° or troublemakers° if there is no post to come back to, nothing in the wage packet. In fact, in most "developed" countries, Job Insecurity accompanies zero-hours°, low morale and minimal pay : a figure not uncommonly far lower than the minimum wage.°
CAUSE / RESULT

JOB SHARING 4
Job Sharing is obviously an option, because it has already been granted and facilitated. That is where the problems begin. What if one of the Sharers subversively blames the other Sharer for anything that goes wrong ? What if the Team so led subtly exploits the situation ; finding they get more reward from one half than the other ? What if one face fits° and the other face doesn't fit ? Or could it be that *both* Job Sharers are marginalized° and isolated° within the organization that regrets it went down that route ? No two masters can serve a man.
ASSOCIATION

KANGAROO COURTS 7
Most sudden, unannounced, proceedings against errant employees are, Kangaroo Courts. How could they be other? Right under the noses of Personnel,° also the owners, Kangaroo Courts proceed unhindered. At first it sounds quite innocent : the oppressed one is invited along for "a quiet chat," or " extra advice " ;° and before she knows it, before she has chance to bring in a union rep,° or prepare her defence,° she is in front of Kangaroo Court. Very intimidating.° *CAUSE / MOTIVATION*

KEENNESS 3
A precious aspect of employability is Keenness : working so hard, or working so well, that the grateful employer quantifiably benefits. Nobody knows why some workers are Keener than others. Is it the money ? Is it the perks ? Is it the praise ?° Or does work well done bring its own satisfaction ?° Beyond dispute is the reaction of the oppressor when he does not feel that his team member or new recruit or stalwart incumbent is Keen enough ! *FACTOR*

KEEPING COPIES 5
Wherever and whenever a diligent employee suspects she is being bullied,° tracked° or downgraded, she could Keep Copies. That means Keeping Copies of all relevant notes, e-mails, memos,° letters, appraisals,° supervision sessions° and testimonials. These might all be needed at tribunal° - or when Personnel get round to tackling her grievance.° *RESPONSE*

KEEPING ONE'S HEAD DOWN 6
Keeping one's head down is a worthwhile strategy for avoiding present or future workplace oppression. It works best when redundancies° are under discussion. Also when there's an inspection.° So when senior management pass through the office or floor, they literally do not notice the employee who has done nothing to raise her head above the parapet. The downside of keeping one's head down is that it makes you less vocal in a purge.° The oppressor might come down more heavily on the silent one because she can so readily be picked off. *RESPONSE*

KEEPING A DIARY OF WORKPLACE OPPRESSION 7
Diaries of oppression are absolutely invaluable. They can assist first a spouse, second a grown-up child, third a line manager, fourth a senior manager, fifth a tribunal,° sixth - and perhaps most crucially, the oppressed one herself, to trace *a pattern* of bad supervision,° deteriorating staff relations,° continued victimization.° The Diary does not have to be exhaustive - in fact, too lengthy a Diary is impenetrable - but it does need to be accurate *and contemporary*. The bully° might be able to explain away one outburst,° one incident, one ill-thought-out memo, °but may feel threatened, momentarily daunted, by the well-kept Diary. The beauty of the Diary is that it is ever-accessible. A greater blessing would be absence of oppression in the first place. *RESPONSE*

KINDNESS 8
Kindness at work does not rule out firmness. Everyone from the MD to Personnel,° line management° and co-workers° can be Kind. And Kindness spreads its tentacles everywhere....just as its opposite : Unkindness° does. Moreover a Kind working environment° is one with a built-in attraction for those needing to earn a living and put food on the table. *RESPONSE*

LABELS [LABELLING]   ...5
Labelling (Labelling Theory) is an established approach to the understanding of victimization.° We all carry a label round our neck : black, female, gay, troublemaker,° due for the chop, angel, indispensable°...whatever. That Label allows lazy thinking. It is also very difficult to shed a Label. It is round her neck however long a worker works at that work station. *CAUSE / FACTOR*

LABOUR RELATIONS 8
This term is very old-fashioned : more 1960s than 2020. Labour Relations lumps all employees together as either having a very poor or a very good record of cooperating° with management. Workplace oppression is a symptom of *dysfunctional* Labour Relations; but, ironically, it is in the interests of neither union° nor management to address workplace oppression when other joint goals are more precious. Oppression is an embarrassment during negotiations. One oppressed employee is easy to sacrifice for "the greater good."   *ASSOCIATION*

LEADERSHIP   STYLE 7
Different Leaderships are labelled° autocratic °/ democratic / collegiate°/ absentee°/remote control / tight / task-centred / diffuse &c. Some Leaders delegate ; others retain all powers within their grasp. For good or ill, Leadership Style impacts on *any* potentially oppressed employee in the frame.   *FACTOR   / MOTIVATION*

[BEING] LEANT ON 6
Not uncommonly, oppression in the workplace is assisted - and perpetuated - by certain employees, even managers, constables, agents and subcontractors, being Leant On. It could be a quiet word exchanged before an important meeting *not to* raise a particular topic - or a stronger word exchanged after that meeting to retract, or not to repeat, an unwelcome contribution already made, but not necessarily minuted. Alternatively, a worker can be Leant On to take a short-cut, to do involuntary overtime,° to play with additional risk,° to misuse public funds, to act dishonestly,° - or indeed to Lean On someone lower down the pecking-order !   *CAUSE / MOTIVATION*

LEAPFROGGING 6

The key to mitigating oppression in the workplace is permitting, even encouraging, Leapfrogging. The most junior or insecure° employee *must* be certain from day one that there is a sympathetic ear somewhere high up in the organization who can crack open the bad egg of misery° at work. Grievance procedures° fail when a grievance has got to be processed first by the manager or team leader who might already be behaving in an arbitrary or unkind° manner. Better to go to the top, and keep going to the top. After all, the downtrodden° worker has little to lose by Leapfrogging. Who knows ? The ultimate owner of a business might be outraged by the presence and practices of the bully° perched some rungs down the ladder. *RESPONSE*

LEARNED HELPLESSNESS [LEARNED HOPELESSNESS] 8

Psychologists now accept that negative° attitudes and reactions are incremental, cumulative - rather than genuine stand-alone experiences. That means frustration° and oppression building on past encounters till the resulting mountain is both forbidden and forbidding. That totality then tethers the oppressed one ; hemming her in ; restricting her coping mechanisms,° till the totality wins. The totality is then a self-fulfilling prophecy. The reason Helplessness or Hopelessness is Learned is that it is all-too-clearly recalled whenever new danger looms on the horizon.

FACTOR / RESULT

LEAVE GRANTED [LEAVE WITHHELD] 5

Leave is so important, so heartily desired (often *out of necessity* desired) that Granting it is a treat; whereas *Withholding* Leave is an ever-present fear,° indeed, threat.° In emergency-response or sedentary jobs, in particular, postponing Leave or cancelling it altogether becomes management routine : the "only way" management can satisfactorily fulfil its mission, compensate for its understaffing°.... and make a profit.   *CAUSE / FACTOR*

LEAVE NOT TAKEN 4

Frequently, the oppressed one does not take Leave entitlement, ironically imitating the presenteeism° of her oppressor: for fear° of what scheming, what shortfalls, what complaints,° will be discovered, or not, while she is away. And Leave Not Taken feeds into further oppression, because the tired employee then becomes less confident° to face down, or survive, future oppression. *MOTIVATION / RESULT*

LETHARGY 5

Lethargy is induced by many factors: overwork,° underwork,° call cramming,° unrealistic targets,° improbable time limits, sleeplessness.° Lethargy is not the same as laziness.° Far more complicated than mere idleness. Lethargy might be a safety-, coping-, or survival °mechanism. Bullying° might be a cause of Lethargy as well as the result. And, needless to say, that same Lethargy is repeated once the oppressed one gets home after work.   *RESULT / RESPONSE*

LIABILITY [BECOMING A LIABILITY] 3

Liability is *a neutral term* - although almost every worker in the land wishes to avoid Becoming it ! Liability is a measure of technical as well as procedural responsibility in and around the workplace. And, in its less literal sense, many a scapegoat° is called " a Liability." The whole team is supposed to suffer, even to the extent of smaller payment by results,° because a troubled colleague has become a Liability. Again the label° needs challenging: simply because that employee *was* taken on by the interviewer(s) in the first place; therefore has a right to prove her worth ;° thus gaining more general acceptance.° *CAUSE / RESULT*

LIBERATION 7

The oppressed worker might find Liberation at home, at the gym, rambling, praying, at 5pm clocking off,° or on holiday. Or in the store room. Or in the filing room. Or at the water cooler / photocopier. *Or not at all*. Workplaces are perplexed by those sudden resignations° which might bring Liberation to certain hard-done-by employees. Or not. Most workplaces do not *set out* to be prisons - but imprisonment° is their workers' abiding experience. At its most gruesome, suicide° is Liberation...of a sort. Crucially, very low, or unrealistic, pay° *precludes* Liberation. Because Liberation often depends on strong spending power, high job satisfaction.° *RESPONSE*

LINE MANAGER [S] 8

The immediate supervisor (foreman) in any hierarchical° chain of management. He should be a friend - or at least a respectful and impartial colleague :° rooting for his team, his new recruit, his underling.° At worst : he is a power-hungry bully.° *ASSOCIATION*

LISTENING [THE LISTENING MANAGEMENT] 7

Management that listens is management that learns. It has often been said that, for all their training, Social Workers do not actually *Listen* to those seeking their help. So it is that Personnel,° human resources,°

need to be totally unshockable, also vigilant.° Nobody can depend on bullying° automatically coming to the surface. Its whole focus or *modus vivendi* is to remain secret.° The answer is to Listen to the person who knows most about oppression : the oppressed one herself ! Management can of course provide suitable *forums* for Listening : such as team meetings without agenda,° the genuinely open door, or the pro-active grievance procedure.° In the end, however it is the responsibility of *everyone* in the office, school, hospital, everyone on the shop-floor to look and to Listen. *RESPONSE*

[THE] LOCK-OUT 5
Being Locked Out of work premises is an extremely unpleasant - and humiliating° - experience. Lock-Outs might happen during or after a dispute,° or hastily announced redundancies.° Other forms of Lock-Out include being Locked Out of a bidding process, Locked Out of a supply chain, Locked Out of a labour auction - or Locked Out of meetings. *RESULT*

LOGS 4
Be vigilant keeping Logs not only in respect of work completed : letters/ faxes / emails sent, visits made, meals served ; but also where any worrying interview, or interchange of ideas, took place in the presence of a menacing manager. These will be referred to later - and respected. Most grievances° rely on a dossier. *RESPONSE*

LOSS OF ENERGY 4
A worker's Loss of Energy is attributable to numerous stressors outside the workplace : age, weight, sleeplessness,° depression,° whatever. But such Loss is also a result of being constantly taken to task and humiliated° at work. It's as if the body and mind are weary of fighting off bullying° - with no surplus Energy for the task-in-hand ! *RESULT*

LOSS OF MOTIVATION 6
A valued,° cherished, duly rewarded, employee sees work as a net gain to which she becomes highly committed.° In contrast, an undervalued, disregarded, enslaved° employee feels Loss of Motivation. "Why help the general cause if that is the thanks I get ?"   *RESULT*

LOW WAGES 8
Low Wages definitely contribute to workplace oppression. Usually, Low Wages are a strong indication of the skinflint regime. Low Wages commonly accompany apprenticeship,° internship,° traineeship, demotion,° exploitation,° unpaid overtime,° zero hours' contracts° - or unrewarded travel between assignments.°
Low Wages might be dispensed even if that makes a firm in breach of minimum wage legislation.° And there might be wage deductions° for lateness, broken crockery, damages, essential clothing, tips. Low Wages, non-living Wages, are key to how little an employer values° his employee and her assets ; or how shaky is the business ; or how wealthy is that employer on the back of his deplorable employment practices. Low Wages act as a disincentive to achievement,° commitment,° experimentation and ambition. On the other hand, and absurdly, some poor payers still inspire worker loyalty !   *CAUSE / MOTIVATION*

LUGGAGE 5
Luggage is the psychologist's way of describing a parcel, or parcels, of leftovers, manure, that now need leaving at *someone else's* door. And where better than to take one's Luggage and leave it outside the door of an already downtrodden,° marginalized° and oppressed employee ?
FACTOR / MOTIVATION

MACHO MANAGEMENT 9
No concept, no stream of ideas imported from business schools, has had such impact, such far-reaching consequences : consequences almost always deleterious, as so-called Macho Management. The word itself is assumed to be an abbreviation of the Italian *machismo*. The intention of Macho Management is an abrasive,° conflictive,° brutal style of man management ;° its reward, a smooth-working organization run solely for its owners / shareholders and their enrichment, regardless of the health and well-being° of its workers. Macho sounds so much more acceptable, responsive and respectable than bullying.°   *CAUSE*

MALICE 7
Pure Malice is both nurtured and omnipresent in the oppressive workplace : first, because employment is fertile ground for its uncontained growth ; second, because employees are caught off-guard. Especially within a church,° a charity° or local government, the oppressed one rules out Malice *or the possibility of* Malice. But never say never. The Devil is not kind-hearted.   *CAUSE / MOTIVATION*

MALICIOUS ALLEGATIONS 8
Employers and managers should always treat allegedly, or possibly, Malicious Allegations with great caution. Many people gain advantage by making such an Allegation : parent of naughty school child, scolded co-worker,° litigious customer, rival agency, underperforming contractor, jealous° line manager, aggrieved deputy overlooked for promotion.° The " beauty" of the Malicious Allegation is that it *does* achieve its desired result on far too many occasions. The complainant° is believed above the oppressed, victimized,° one. Worse, the subject of the allegation is sometimes sent home on gardening leave,

suspended,° *dismissed.*° And the best outcome : that the Malicious Allegation is found to be unfounded turns out to be either an unsatisfactory absolution, or a pyrrhic victory. Schools° and hospitals° are notorious for mishandling Malicious Allegations. Mud sticks. Often the exonerated employee or whistleblower° (whistleblowers do attract *far more* Malicious Allegations than anyone else) is paid off quietly, reinstatement deemed *too difficult.*   *CAUSE / MOTIVATION*

MALINGERING [MALINGERERS] 4
Malingering is a common managerial complaint° : sometimes associated with so-called lead-swinging. ° Undoubtedly, one or two workers, one of two departments indeed, are guilty of very low productivity,° very high enjoyment of optional activities - eg. gossip,° fundraising, Facebook, Google, Wikipedia, Porn, sleep. An organization's responsibility is to trim or control actual Malingering without blaming employees or subcontractors for lack of supplies, shortage of materials, power out-takes, and delays beyond their control. Simple blocks can be put on social network° sites. Or the manager could, discreetly, make more frequent visits to the team room or the shop floor. *Sometimes,* workers take a lot of unfinished assignments home, unpaid,° so should perhaps be treated indulgently when they book a Summer holiday from their desk !   *ASSOCIATION*

MAN MANAGEMENT 7
"Man Management" is a (sexist° ?) 1950s/60s' term for the organization and deployment of a male-dominated workforce. Shorthand now dated! But a *laudable* intention of that era was to decide how : beyond a body of work needing shifting, *the shifters of that work* needed close personal attention also.   *ASSOCIATION*

MANAGEMENT THEORY....5
Some say Management Theory is whatever "fad" has excited MBA and Business Schools in the recent past : hierarchy° / top-down / bottom-up° / bunker / silo° / black swan / just-in-time° / blue sky / joined-up or 360-degree thinking / streamlining° / whatever....Management Theory bears down on the oppressed one because she is less likely to be fully up-to-speed - or quite receptive enough - to change° or the advice° on offer. After all, she has not got an MBA.   *ASSOCIATION*

MANAGEMENT TOOL[S] 6
Any stick metaphorically to beat down an already browbeaten, downtrodden° employee. The literature of Management is bulging with Tools : Tools far more useful to those higher up the hierarchy° than those at the bottom. See targets° and appraisal.° *ASSOCIATION*

THE MANUAL [THE MANUAL OF WORKPLACE PRACTICE] 7
It is depressing that *any* workplace has a Manual in the first place. Good practice should be self-evident upon entry, or through experience - rather than enshrined on parchment. Take the anti-racism strategy or the anti-ageist strategy, or, tellingly : the anti-workplace bullying° strategy. Once it is " in the Manual," it is a given, not requiring further discussion! The cynic would say good practice exists in inverse proportion to its coverage within the Manual. Bankrupt Manuals are often the issue of bankrupt human resources° departments. See protocols.°   *ASSOCIATION*

MARITAL BREAKDOWN 6
Due leeway should be given to an employee who has suffered recent marital breakdown - even where she has requested no allowance be made, no reference to said breakdown be alluded to, in the workplace. It takes a mighty juggling act to split up one night, then come into work the next morning ? What if spouse or boyfriend was also main carer for young children ? What if spouse or girlfriend works in the same organization ? What if Police had to be called out ? It all needs sensitivity. And if an employee's performance *suffers* for a few days, there should be some mitigation. Many women in particular are afraid to refer to an estrangement lest they be pitied, patronized,° overworked,° cross-questioned, seduced. *RESULT / ASSOCIATION*

MASOCHISM 6
Masochism : suffering of self by self, is a huge topic. The word has entered the language burdened by levity or pornographic intent. Yet the central truth is important : that a downtrodden° one might be instrumental in her own torment - *or its inflictor.* Now it is quite possible that a saddened worker comes to expect the worst - and cannot visualize any alternative outcome. But she remains very unlikely to bring a load crashing down on herself. Indeed, beware of excuses for sadistic° bullying.° *ASSOCIATION*

MASCULINITY 8
Harsh regimes are often called macho° or masculine : on the assumption that *female* leaders might be more motherly, more compassionate °(not necessarily the case !). Masculinity is a primeval urge to throw one's weight around, to win at all costs. And at what a cost! See Macho Management. *FACTOR / MOTIVATION*

MAXIMIZING PROFIT 6
Most usually management's wish - sometimes its *obligation* - to Maximize Profits encourages and perpetuates oppression in the workplace. At such times employees are expected to be more than usually conscientious,° thorough, selfless and quiescent.... otherwise, *Profits* might go down the drain. Of course, cause and effect are difficult to prove. For instance, seconding senior staff to an overseas aid effort might *add to* a company's Profitability in the long run. The same is true of long and leisurely lunch breaks : counter-intuitively. Wise and kind employers do not consult their balance sheet daily. Such owners remain aware of that calculation in the background, but are never *bound by* net profitability.   *RESULT / MOTIVATION*

MAXIMUM EFFICIENCY 7
For Maximum Efficiency to be achieved - if that were ever possible - it could only be achieved by steamrollering° the oppressed one and her co-workers.° For Maximum Efficiency is *un*attainable except through mass redundancies,° zero-hours° contracting, de-unionization,° low wages° ....and the setting of impossible targets.°   *CAUSE*

MEMOS 5
Memos within offices (notices on factory notice-boards) should be neutral. But often they are not. The Memo as a management tool° has the advantage of getting straight to an employee when she may want or expect it least, ie. anytime. This can make her fearful° to pick up her post ! Memos are sometimes typed : originating from, or copied to, Personnel. They are perhaps most unwelcome in a shake-out. *FACTOR*

MENOPAUSE 4

Each year thousands of women in their late 40s / early 50s give up paid employment - or are forced out of their employment - due to the Menopause or Menopausal symptoms. This is a ridiculous state of affairs. If employers are not clued up regarding that important transitional phase in their employees' lives, what exactly are they expected to respond to ? There appears to be no earthly reason why women should not be kept at work - maybe slightly modified, shortened, or reorganized work - *throughout* the Menopause and beyond. And without being the least bit dismissive or condescending, line managers° need to recognize the onset of the Menopause and accommodate it : *not* treating it as a shortcoming, a sign of incipient mental illness.° Rejoice that all transitions are part of the natural way of things : a slightly prolonged equivalent to the premarital wobble, or morning sickness early on in pregnancy. *ASSOCIATION*

MENTAL CRUELTY 9

Mental Cruelty is another concept carried over from domestic violence° to oppression at work. Mental Cruelty is a none-too-subtle combination of fault finding,° sledging,° intimidation,° threats,° anger° and belittlement.° And because this form of Cruelty does not leave *visible* scars, it is extremely difficult to take to tribunal, °or even to Personnel.° Mental Cruelty is also very difficult to talk about at home : because family members do not always believe that things have slid that far. That employer might, after all, be a household name; *renowned*, even, as "the place to go if you want a job." *CAUSE / MOTIVATION*

MENTAL ILLNESS 5

Mental Illness is far too great a subject to cover adequately in a few lines. But taken at its broadest and most salient : absences from work due to labelled Mental Illness are likely to run to *30 times* those days lost through strikes° and industrial action.° Worse, many thousands of days sacrificed to psychosomatic conditions - mind on body - are simply entered as "flu," " lumbago," "diverticulitis," or "whiplash." A good and conscientious employer thinks about Mental Illness at breakfast, at lunch, at tea, and during the night : if only because this Illness consistently, or periodically, or occasionally, impacts upon one third of the entire population. And alert employers devote time and energy to supporting their severely depressed *or mentally oppressed* workers whom then they see more of ! One valuable initiative to address directly Mental Health in the Workplace is "Workways," in partnership with "Mindful Employer," the NHS Devon Partnership and the Nationwide Building Society: an experiment, also an early intervention worth copying. Nor should we forget the importance of bullying as an aggravating factor. *FACTOR / RESULT*

MENTORING 5

Mentoring is alive and well in the teaching profession and some branches of the armed forces. The idea is that a recent recruit is given a guide for the first 6 months or year of her employment. One of the Mentor's responsibilities is to identify other people in the organization who are making that newcomer's work life less fulfilling. Perhaps, and with the permission of the person concerned, the Mentor could approach in confidence the perceived tormentor. Mentors are very good fallbacks, sometimes friends, or friendly faces, also. *RESPONSE*

MICROMANAGEMENT 6
Bosses poor at delegation - unable to see the wood for the trees - resort to Micromanagement. That, in turn, de-skills° the workforce and leads to employees not thinking for themselves. Creative people are restricted to tram tracks - which is disheartening. *FACTOR*

MINIMIZATION 7
As with trivialization,° Minimization is management's default response to allegations of bullying.° "It can't be that bad!" " Not him!" "Must be all part of office cut-and-thrust !" The reason management or Personnel might not want to *counter* credible bullying° is that they are simply not listening.° Or else they fear° what might be uncovered ! *RESULT*

MINIMUM WAGE 8
It sounds improbable that paying the Minimum Wage could be considered *oppressive*. But the Minimum Wage is far too often accepted by employers as the *maximum wage*. Paying the Minimum is a powerful message to workers that they are not worth anything more ; that the employer is in a financially precarious position ; that the accumulation of dividends and returns for shareholders is priority number one. Additionally, many employees suffer privations on the Minimum Wage, a sum itself eaten away by travel, laundry, and the provision of specialist clothing or equipment. And none of this takes into account the thousands of migrants - or the dispossessed - who are never paid even the *Minimum* Wage in the first place. *RESULT*

MISCONDUCT [INDUSTRIAL MISCONDUCT] 8
Misconduct Proceedings do happen : regretted by most parties. But employers both can and should get together with Personnel and the unions° to ensure that everybody gets a fair hearing, prior warning, expert representation, and access to a McKenzie Friend.° No kangaroo court° should be tolerated : least of all where an employee is called in "for a chat," during which she is offered the chance to admit Misconduct - or simply resign.°   *FACTOR*

MISERY 8
Misery is an all-encompassing term for cumulative and continuing oppression in the workplace. That so many people are Miserable at their office, shop or work-bench is no tribute to Personnel, or, more generally, to senior managers and the overall owners.   *RESULT*

MISFIT [S] 7
Misfit is an uncomplimentary word borrowed from the worlds of fashion or jigsaw puzzle manufacture. The Misfit in the workplace is difficult to define - but easily recognized when she appears : the one whose appointment nobody can quite understand; the oddity; the one with those idiosyncrasies; the outsider; the non-joiner; the round peg in a square hole. And unless the alleged Misfit is an outstanding achiever in her own right, she is probably up against suspicion,° cyber-bullying,° even ostracism.°   *CAUSE*

MISSED MESSAGES 7
Missed Messages are probably nobody's *fault.*° Missed Messages might, at their simplest, be a telephonist's or a co-worker's act of omission.° Or manager and employee might simply Miss Messages by not hearing each other. Neither might come away from a meeting at all sure about the other's expectations° or time limits. In marriages, for instance, it is quite possible for couples to miss each other's cues for years on end. *FACTOR*

MISSION STATEMENT 4
Most schools° or hospitals° or departments of local government have slogans or Mission Statements : " Land of Opportunity;" " Confronting Illness Wherever It Appears;" "Making a Difference;"(unfortunately?) "A Good Place to Work;" " Everyone Matters;" or "All in it Together" - all of which ambitions risk failure to materialize. Some Mission Statements are obfuscating. Others originate in dreamland. Nonetheless, their *aim* is laudable : to give pride° and purpose to every worker from sweeper of the floors to MD. *ASSOCIATION / RESPONSE*

MISUNDERSTANDINGS 8
Simple Misunderstandings should be quashed, or squashed, before they get blown up out of all proportion. Misunderstandings are just that : understanding an issue - often a fairly trivial issue - in different ways. No panic. Most Misunderstandings are repairable. *CAUSE / RESULT*

MIXED MESSAGES 5
Mixed Messages in the workplace can be more serious than messages missed.° With the Mixed Message, an employer is saying opposites at the same time : " Cut down on petrol!" AND " Go check that out once more!" " Prepare to-morrow's starters before leaving!" AND "This kitchen needs a thorough clean before you go!" There are many other examples : where a line manager° wants someone to use their own initiative, then jumps down her throat for doing exactly that! *FACTOR*

MONITORING 6
Monitoring in the workplace takes several forms : sickness°/ punctuality°/ output / productivity° / telephone use° / mileage / internet access, whatever. Most Monitoring is benign. But Monitoring can be *a threat,*° or overpowering, for any oppressed employee worried about her performance,° indeed her future employability. It is Personnel's job first to make clear exactly how much Monitoring is happening ; second, who sees the results?- and why ? Any employee actually being bullied° is advised not to submit to any *ad hoc* Monitoring affecting only herself, and only her line manager.° See Tracking. *MOTIVATION / ASSOCIATION*

MOODS 8
All employers, all employees too, have Moods and periods of Moodiness. What separates the oppressor from everyone else is an inability to *control or modify* his Mood. A common cop-out is : " I can't do anything about it !" or " That's me,° so you'll just have to go along with it !" or "Maybe I got out of the wrong side of bed ?"

However, *adverse* Moods can and should be suppressed where human interaction strives toward a common end. Ironically, Moods spread : so the oppressed one soon gets Moody with her colleagues, spouses and children when she has experienced ingratitude, worse , harshness° at work. Eddies.   *CAUSE / RESULT / MOTIVATION*

MORALE 9

High staff Morale is a useful antidote to workplace unhappiness /° unpleasantness. Conversely low staff Morale is indicative of careless Personnel, tight targets° and deadlines,° and a top-to-bottom oppressive work regime. And when a report, newscast, inspection° or missed delivery has damaged Morale - or when Morale has plummeted over a botched, hostile or rushed takeover° - it is extremely difficult to rebuild. Managers should always be alert to low Morale in *one* particular outlet or department or team : not replicated elsewhere in the organization. Is that the locus of all the bullying /° intimidation ?°

FACTOR / RESULT

MORNING RITUALS 3

Japanese firms based in Britain have pioneered the use of Morning Rituals before actual application to the task in hand. Sometimes these look like Aerobics and sound like cheer-leading. Small Christian firms can start with prayer or a hymn. Secular firms can start the day with the sort of group hug (love-in) that imitates the rugby scrum. Schools° have traditionally had assemblies : not necessarily with religious content. The Morning Ritual could be as simple as bacon sandwiches all round.   *RESPONSE*

MOTIVATION TO CONTINUE 5
You have to be motivated to get up in the morning, to enlist, to volunteer covering sickness,° to put in for overtime° - or to maximize your talents. Happiness at work encourages Motivation ; and in turn Motivation results in happiness° and harmony at work. The other relevant meaning of Motivation in relation to workplace oppression is the bully's ° *own* Motivation. Is it fear,° pride,° sadism,° insecurity,° childhood memory,° baggage, ° or simple opportunity.° Even then, inverted sympathy for the bully ° should not lead to anyone *excusing* ° him.   *ASSOCIATION / RESPONSE*

MURDEROUS FEELINGS [MURDEROUS IMPULSES] 5
The temptation is to laugh off the suggestion sometimes made by an oppressed one that she feels like *murdering* her line manager.° But so great is the fear° and trepidation a worker might feel simply seeing the face - or parked motor vehicle - of her oppressor, that *harming* him, substantially harming him, cannot be ruled out. We know from the chronicling of domestic violence° that talk of Murder is far from empty hyperbole. More eddies.   *RESULT*

MUST IMPROVE [MUST TRY HARDER] 7
The word Must is so deceptive, also slippery. It is not a given imperative, as most people innocently assume it to be. Instead, it is rather like TINA (There Is No Alternative). The *Must* often dwells *within* the oppressor, not the situation. *Must* is also a disguised threat° and a goal post shifted,° truly unattainable target.°   *MOTIVATION*

MISOGYNY 7

Misogyny is a specific term for a hatred of women : very common in the workplace - especially where women form very few OR very many of the total workforce. Misogyny is easily disguised behind " jokes," including practical jokes, banter° and crudity. But Misogyny is also extremely unpleasant and oppressive. Moreover a few women are guilty of Misogyny too : for instance, lay-women in the Church of England. Combating Misogyny probably needs a fundamental shake-up in the office or factory - with clear recourse to grievance procedures.° What makes the fixed Misogynist disposition *worse* is that it has its origin and its best breeding ground *in the home* - so is part of the domestic violence° already too familiar to women coming to work outside the oppressive home. See Sexism. *CAUSE / FACTOR*

MYSTERY EMPLOYEES [.... SHOPPERS / PATIENTS] 5

Undoubtedly, Mystery is missing from much working life. Too humdrum by half for poetry ! Yet Mystery is *startlingly* effective. Visitations usually mean the factory worker / sales assistant / clerk / nurse has no clue she is being "set up." But this element of Mystery need not automatically be *threatening.*° The boss from HQ might actually share a joke with a junior when he is discovered / uncovered. The best aspect of Mystery is exposing the rogue foreman or team leader, once and for all. Exposure comes when the man from Head Office picks up the mood of despair° - or indeed mood of quiet satisfaction - on the floor, in the ward, within the team. *RESPONSE*

MY WORD AGAINST HIS 7
Lawyers and prosecutors the world over dread - or relish - My Word Against His. There are many parallels between the closed workplace, the closed prison° cell, the closed kitchen, the closed anteroom, or the closed convent : My Word Against His. The assumption throughout is that one person says one thing ; another person - the adversary ? - says something different. Either the truth lies exactly half way between both accounts - or, more often, one person has got the right end of the stick whilst the other clings to the wrong end. Seniority° is a distinct advantage in *he says, she says*.... Why *not* believe the manager or worker who has been around since time immemorial ? Surely that person would have no reason to produce false testimony :° intentionally or unintentionally. Which leaves the oppressed one *even more isolated.*° Time perhaps for a diary,° better still , a tape-recorder. *Witnesses* definitely assist an accused one's credibility. Also knowledge that the bully° has done exactly the same thing to someone else, perhaps in a different time, a different place. And *if* a manager cannot be trusted to use supervision° correctly, and *without* misrepresentation, then it is an employee's right and duty to ask for a third person in the room. *CAUSE / MOTIVATION*

NATURAL JUSTICE 6
Natural Justice is shorthand for a prevailing climate of fairness° in the workplace. And many sanctions or obstacles confronting honest, but oppressed, employees defy - or deny - Natural Justice. *ASSOCIATION*

NEGOTIATION 6

The word Negotiation used to refer almost exclusively to industrial relations, strikes.° But Negotiating can produce astonishing results further down the pecking-order. For instance, a prospective employee can Negotiate her terms before starting. Or a supervisee can Negotiate the place, length and intensity of her supervision.° Or an outside mediator° can be drawn in to Negotiate a solution prior to formal grievance.° *RESPONSE*

NERVOUS BREAKDOWN 8

Nervous Breakdown is an all-encompassing - and not very scientific - term for cumulative nervous tension (in this context, *in the workplace*): tension that cannot *in extremis* find expression except through floods of tears,° smashed computer, so-called "hysterics" or complete collapse. Many oppressed ones get drunk, but drunkenness° is far from being a universal manifestation of Nervous Breakdown. In fact, some of the most frightening Breakdowns are quiet, quiescent - with few if any external symptoms except hopelessness° and inertia.° It is a peculiarity of the workplace that it not only induces Nervous Breakdown, but holds within itself the capacity for repeating that Breakdown ; deepening or worsening it - because underlying bullying° or overwork° remains unaddressed ; then providing no escape from Breakdown except resignation° or retirement° - when both those options put pressure on the oppressed one's fragile financial status ; and where neither of those two options addresses the underlying stressors : later to trouble that worker's successor - or the next new recruit - or someone different in the team. *RESULT / RESPONSE*

NIGHT SHIFT 5
The Night Shift is often a happy hunting-ground for workplace bullies.° After 6pm, there are bound to be fewer managers or inspectors° around. So they can come down hard on those who do not work by command - or, conversely, those who work too hard, too thoroughly. If 8 of a gang take a regular kip during the night, or place bets on the gee-gees, a 9th. member who never sleeps or gambles on the job will be an outsider.° Night work is often different in location and emphasis from day-time work, even for the same employer. That might demoralize,° and de-motivate,° the Night Shift - whose staff have often been employed already, elsewhere, or in their own homes without a break, in the past 24 hours. And what if patients on hospital° wards or in care homes° become demanding, even incontinent, during the night ? Just being called out at Night is stressful.°   *ASSOCIATION*

NOISE [NOISE POLLUTION] 5
Unnecessary or unshielded Noise in the workplace is itself an act of oppression. Gas and electric engineers, studio broadcasters, road-menders and machine operatives are particularly at risk from Noise. As are administrators or social workers who work in busy team rooms, responding to sonorous telephones. Noise grates. Nor does it disappear at home time. It stays on in tinnitus - and rowdy neighbours ! *CAUSE*

NO   LUNCH 6
No Lunch is a bit like Leave Not Taken : a signal from the oppressed one that she is desperately trying to impress her co-workers° and management. She goes without Lunch, or hastily grabs a sandwich over the computer - because she knows that if she fails,° she will incur further displeasure. And she *dares not* fail.   *FACTOR / RESULT*

NON-CONFORMISTS [NON-CONFORMITY] 7
Although Non-Conformists are more closely associated with religious faith and heresy, Non-Conformists *can* pop up in workplaces big and small, as well. Non-Conformists do not swallow the group ethic.° They are not on-message. ° Thus they are to be feared or excluded. Furthermore, their Non-Conformity is a significant threat to any Team,° Team Leader, °or Line Manager °....people who all tend to play by the book. A few Non-Conformists see the error of their ways. Fortunately, a few do not. *FACTOR*

NON-JOINERS 5
Non-Joiners : employees who specifically do not join in the gossip,° in the charity appeal, in the tomfoolery, in the office outing, in the party, whatever, are not especially welcome in the workplace ; or else, contrarily, they are idolized as *superior* mortals. *ASSOCIATION*

OBEDIENCE 7
Though the notions of Obedience / Disobedience are associated more with naughty toddlers and restless scholars, they *are* carried over into adulthood : pointedly in the contexts of domestic violence° and strictly hierarchical° or quasi-military professions. *True* Obedience overrules independent thinking and selfhood.° *MOTIVATION / RESPONSE*

OBJECTIFICATION 7
Objectification affects women at work more than men - but *all* workers might be lumped together as "hands," "the workforce" - or "them & us." Women at work are also objectified by men's sexual desire / innuendo / chat-up lines. Some men meet a far greater number of women at work than elsewhere, sowing the seeds for inept approaches, and vulgar jokes. And women have more opportunities for task-centred (?) interaction with the opposite sex at work, than they may have at home.   *FACTOR*

OBSTACLES TO THE FULFILMENT OF POTENTIAL 6
Anything standing in the way of employees fulfilling their potential should be of concern to management : fear,° dread,° impotence,° paralysis,° narrowness of vision, the curtailment of ambition. Bullying° always stunts growth. It cannot *nurture* talent, only crush a person's capacity to display talent. Talent is even a threat to the tyrant.° How abiding are these Obstacles ? Research would seem to indicate they are *ever*lasting. Would that the impact of being flattened at work disappeared at home time, or at bath time, or in the commute, or after a good night's sleep° - or at the point of resignation° or retirement.° But the evidence is that man's inhumanity to man (and woman's to men and women) is never erased. That is the stuff of nightmares, literally; and an explanation of how the oppressed one often fails to regain her bearings - recapture tranquillity - in her *next* employment, or under a good alternative manager. Such frozen awareness° happens after domestic violence° as well. Who, we might ask, is ever in pole position to restore a damaged employee's confidence?°   *FACTOR / RESULT*

OBSTRUCTION [OBSTRUCTIVENESS] 8
It is one of the harshest things any manager can tell a worker that she is being Obstructive. Presumably, without her, or without her opposition, everything would be all right. Obstruction can easily lead to formal disciplinary.° So it essential that " Obstruction" is broken down into its constituents : incompetence,° lack of clear guidance,° risk, °safety,° time,° incapacity,° joint enterprise, fear.°   *FACTOR / RESPONSE*

OCCUPATIONS PARTICULARLY PRONE TO BULLYING AND OPPRESSION   [selected]   [and in alphabetical order]:

---

a) ARMED FORCES....10
Most informed people assume bullying° is rife in the Armed Forces - even where that assumption is based more on TV drama and hearsay than on hard-and-fast revelation. The Armed Forces are actually perfect breeding-grounds for aggressive° man-management° : closed organizations, secretive, often inaccessible to outsiders, strictly and ruthlessly hierarchical,° intrinsically violent,° predominantly masculine,° daily preaching the cult of obedience,° unquestioning compliance.
In these circumstances it is a miracle there are not *more* reported instances of bullying,° desertion and recourse to dispute resolution procedures.° Even here there is difficulty : because the very Admirals and Majors drafted in to sort matters out are themselves disciples of a

rule of iron. Instinctively, at courts marshal, they will uphold the *status quo*. The aggrieved conscript might then attempt leapfrogging. °
In the long run, most squaddies, sailors and air crew will never even whisper, let alone proceed with, dissent. ° The chance of reprisal is too great.. There is real fear° that service personnel will not be believed, let alone relieved of stress.° Also the Armed Forces have *extra weapons* of oppression at their disposal : weapons not available to most civilian organizations : lock-ups, glasshouses, returns to barracks, damning despatches, compulsory chores, kit inspections, march-pasts, square-bashing, rotted rations, press-ups and circuit-training are all to be dreaded.° Not forgetting dishonourable discharge. Absurdly, a superior officer can *allege* insubordination where that assumed insubordination becomes, in turn, justification for ever more persistent bullying !° "Mutiny" is not so much a wake-up call for the military as military's call for the firing-squad.
No outpost of Army, Navy or Air Force has yet offered assurances to root out the intimidation° of recruits, despite policies enshrined on parchment. And if *one* ruthless officer is caught out - even admonished- he or she is simply labelled "a bad egg," "a rotten apple." Would that one tribunal° carried weight sufficient to be a precedent for future redress of a repeat pattern : recruits ground into the dust.

b) CALL CENTRES 9
Call Centres are relatively new on the British work scene : only 30 years or so old. Call Centres boast row after row of telephonists and salespeople, each with his own computer and monitoring screen, working frantically, furiously, fanatically, to answer customer enquiries- or to fulfil a different defensive ° brief : completely detached from the face-to-face encounter that might formerly have been possible in a bank or an electricity showroom..

Call Centres generally do not welcome, let alone *facilitate*, quiet periods, rest periods, meal breaks,° toilet breaks. Nor are telephonists expected to show any flair or independent judgment in their work. Whole lists of FAQs are displayed. If somebody does this, or threatens to do that, this is your "personal" response ! Nor are telephonists or advisors expected to spend *too long* on an abortive sale, overdue refund, damage in transit or vexatious caller. For time is money - and forfeited commission.°
Added to verbal abuse,° long hours,° stuffy barns, tight schedules,° noise pollution,° caffeine withdrawal and bullying,° Call Centre staff are demoralized,° de-motivated,° by having all their work packaged up and sent to Scotland, India or Mauritius; facing displacement by synchronized speech, the answering machine - or the simple *abolition* of "Customer Services."!

c) CARERS PAID 9
Paid Carers experience considerable oppression because of their very special remit : whether visiting patients at home or assisting them in residential institutions. The profession is generally *very low* paid,° un-unionized,° fragmented, disheartened,° understaffed,° untrained,° and torn in all directions. Additionally, Carers Paid imitate Carers Unpaid° : often being one and the same person. Hourly-paid Carers are frequently denied any pay or recompense for long periods travelling between service-users. Then they are encouraged - ordered - to skimp or resort to "call cramming": ° that is, fitting 6 people into an hour where that agency's paymasters believe their one patient will have the benefit of an entire 55 minutes. And in Care Homes, nurses and auxiliaries are expected to work like slaves° for lots of extra hours, out of misplaced "goodwill." No wonder Care Home orderlies live only for their next tobacco break !° Amazingly, this largely casual° and unregulated work

is growing exponentially with a rising population, longer life-spans, and the increased infirmity of people visited / looked after outside of a hospital° setting. Worth remembering : were any Paid Carer to mutter a word of dissent, she would be dismissed° immediately, despite any plea that it is her meagre wage that feeds and clothes her children.

d) CLERGY 6

The last place anyone would look to discover, or uncover, workplace bullying,° would be the Church. Yet Church leaders, bishops and stewards can be terrible tyrants °: squashing the faith, hope° and good standing of newer Ministers, rookie organists and churchwardens alike. Nor is the Church free of the Free-Masonry° that might have actually been born on the lofty pinnacles of our great cathedrals. To make matters worse, a servant of the Church frequently faces reverse bullying° and verbal abuse ° from a section of their congregations. Yet if a priest under pressure ° is eventually denied his or her living and takes the Church to Tribunal,° a standard response is : "God is your employer, not man." !

e) HIGHER EDUCATION 7

It defies form that a world as ethereal and supposedly " liberal" as Higher Education should be a hotbed for bullying,° criticism,° backbiting, marginalization,° hire-and-fire°- all complemented with delicately-crafted webs of intrigue and sundry oppression. And, as in Nursing,° Probation, and the Caring° professions, bullying° is so unexpected in this hallowed setting that it goes unchallenged.°

f) JOB CENTRE BULLIES 9

Someone does not even have to commence employment to be subject to abject bullying.° Under pressure° - real or imagined pressure - Job Centre staff routinely impose upon jobseekers impossible conditions before they receive any benefit or support. Bullying° takes the form of: " you must improve your CV," " you must try harder,"° "you must send out 20 CVs a week," "you must be permanently available," "you are overdue for benefit sanction" - or " you must *prove* to us your casual° employability." And Job Centre Bullies cannot be confronted - less confounded - because they, literally, hold the purse-strings. Sadly, Job Centre Bullies are *also* workers, workers who once sought work : in this case workers who depend *on the workless* to earn a living ! Targets° for getting jobseekers off the books are probably too rigorous- and undoubtedly one or two Job Centre Bullies are themselves demoralized,° desensitized. Conversely, many oppressed staff on the right side of the screened counter become *over-zealous* in fulfilment of their briefs, grounded as these are on a universal belief those on *the other side* of the counter are malingerers.° The greater number of "benefit sanctions" the better ; the more pleasing to the Department of Work and Pensions. No matter that "sanctioned" claimants actually *starve*. Because there is now no official welfare safety-net. The attitude of Job Centre Staff *does matter* : not only for their own morale° but also because downtrodden° jobseekers will take into their eventual employment / relocation° all the worries and frustrations they have experienced *prior to* that employment.

g) NANNIES 9
Nannies, in common with nursemaids, governesses, housekeepers and *au pairs* are highly likely to be taken for granted, at worst enslaved.° In such closed situations, they are expected to work for way beyond a 40- or 48-hour week. Not a few Nannies have 168-hour a week responsibility. Exploitation is never very far from domestic servitude. Nor are Nannies likely to complain,° as their workplace is also their *home*. Naturally, the best Nannying Agencies operate at a far more superior, and professional, level. That is because good Metropolitan Nannies and housekeepers are in short supply.

h) NURSES [NURSING] 8
Surprisingly, Nursing - the *ultimate* caring profession - is not free of bullying.° That is because the activity of Nursing demands a person revealing her whole self and committing that whole self to the task in hand. That - and severe time° and financial constraints - makes Nurses far more likely to encounter bullying° Sisters and hospital managers than might crop up in a more secular working environment. To say nothing of the reverse bullying° that sometimes emerges from *beneath* pristine bed-sheets ; from aggrieved and vexatious patients.

i) POLICE [POLICE FORCES] 10
The Police are notoriously tough - even ruthless - employers (however unjustified that presumption in some of our better-run Police Forces). The very word "Force" is indicative of masculinity,° unquestioning obedience,° rigid hierarchies,° no tolerance of dissent. ° Why exactly the Police modelled themselves on the Armed Forces° remains a complete mystery. A more collaborative, collegiate° management structure would have yielded far greater rewards than the belittlement,

intimidation,° verbal abuse,° canteen culture, and climate of fear, now inextricably linked with the due maintenance of law and order.

j) PRISON OFFICERS 10
Bullying° is also rife amongst the staff of many of our prisons : private prisons, publicly-run prisons too. That is partly because prisons are (literally!) closed and "total" institutions : relentlessly hierarchical,° authoritarian,° and understaffed.° In the midst of unbearable tension behind bars, everyone is looking for a fall-guy : particularly the Prison Officer who is perceived as kinder° or more independent-minded than the rest. Nor will prisoners themselves hold back from complaining° about their warders !

k) PUBLICANS [PUB LANDLORDS] 8
Under the Beer Orders ; worse, under the sway, servitude and absolute dominance of a trinity of PubCos (Pub Management Companies), many Publicans are ruthlessly exploited. They are expected to sell only tied drinks. Additionally, they are called upon to cook only slightly profitable full meals morning, noon and night ; then to deal with complicated Licensing legislation ; still needing diplomacy to deal with drunkards, and customers inclined to be both obstreperous and confrontational.° As if that were not bad enough, the Publican's job - in a declining market - is over 100 hours a week in duration : with few, if any, holidays. No wonder the divorce rate on that side of the Lounge is sky-high.

1) SUPERMARKETS 7
Supermarkets can either be the very best or the very worst of employers. At their merriest, certain Supermarket chains provide excellent perks° and career progression : store manager by age 24! However, the overall situation is far from rosy. Dig under the surface and you uncover frantic and frenetic work schedules,° unrealistic targets,° moveable or inconvenient shifts,° family-unfriendly staff expectations, relegation of young women to checkout only, recorded announcements in the background 17/7 , adverse customer feedback,° perfunctory staff appraisals,° cutting colleagues,° insecurity,° zero-hours, ° - and overwork.° All proving that bargain-hunting trolley-pushers are exacting a very human price for their cut-price groceries.

Other Professions that could have been included in this Section of Occupations particularly prone to bullying° *are the Fire Service, Social Work, the Royal Mail, "Junior Doctors," Television Researchers, Door-to-Door Sales' Persons, Waiters, Waitresses, Charity Fundraisers - also the Cabin Crew of Airlines.... [and this is* **still** *not an exhaustive list !]*

****

[THE] OFFICE PARTY 6
The Office Party, by definition, should be an occasion of unalloyed joy. In practice it can become a hotbed of rumour° and resentment,° even oppression. *Any* Party suffers when it is alcohol-fuelled or rowdy. More subtle is the announcement of targets° and star winners at the Office Party. Tearful,° fearful,° employees might well shy off altogether, where there are points to be scored.   *CAUSE / FACTOR*

OFFICE POLITICS 9
Office Politics can be a euphemism for bullying,° intimidation,° dissent,° and other forms of oppression ; but *sounds* like fun, even rebellion. "Politics" overwhelms *new* or sensitive or collegiate° recruits in particular: no mere curiosity.   *CAUSE / ASSOCIATION*

OMERTA 7
The code of *Omerta* in the workplace - lips sealed - is often absolute. *Omerta* is actually *expected* in many work settings, pre-eminently in Police° Stations and Hospitals.° Sneaks, snitches and whistleblowers° are extremely unwelcome. Better to be ground down and say nothing. Better to treat customers shamefully and say nothing. Better to break the rules and say nothing. In fact, saying nothing becomes more prized than saying something. Management really should confront *Omerta* ; as should a team leader when the whole team or department clamps up. Dishonest employers and employees, also dodgy couriers, have their own special difficulties leading to, or arising from, *Omerta*.   *RESULT*

ON   CALL   [PERPETUALLY ON CALL]   [168 HOUR CALL-OUT] 6
In an unceasing, 24 hour-a-day, 7-days-a-week culture, some employees are expected to be On Call at all times - even when in bed, late in the evening, during holidays and business conventions. This employer expectation° is both unfair° and counterproductive. Nobody is indispensable. On Call makes some bosses lazy: not employing a Deputy ; crazy rotas ;° not managing without Call Out.   *FACTOR*

ON-MESSAGE [STAYING ON-MESSAGE] 5
All organizations have survival ° built into their ethos and operation. And employees are paid, in part, to Stay On-Message. It matters not in the least if that Message is absurd, ill-thought-out, impractical or unreasonable. It is incumbent upon junior management in particular - and upon any spokesperson - to Stay On-Message. Deviations cause trouble, worse, engender unrest.°   *ASSOCIATION*

ONE-TO-ONE TENSION 8
One-to-One Tension is a tighter description of personality clash.° Instant dislike of an employee, especially a new recruit, or a recruit recruited against the oppressor's wish, can result in day-to-day filtering out° of positive feedback.° Amazingly, senior management is not always alert / alerted to One-to-One Tension, even when it stares them in the face. That might be because the oppressor is also the favoured one ; or else the oppressed one is afraid to respond to oppression. Passing dissatisfaction *up the chain* does not look great on one's employment record.   *CAUSE / RESULT*

ONLY YOU 7
When management or a line manager wants to express profound dissatisfaction° with the oppressed one's performance,° the putdown : "It's Only You" follows as surely as night follows day. And once the struggler is convinced it *is* only her at fault° ; only her falling short of expectation ; her sense of isolation° and despair° increases.   *CAUSE*

OPEN DOOR POLICY 5
A number of bosses and line managers pretend that they have an Open Door Policy : " my door is always open." That usually means his door is *not* open. Contrarily, the device of the Open Door might threaten a team - because they have less chance for jest or subversion, less privacy.° Nonetheless, the *trumpeted* Open Door must remain Open !

RESPONSE

OPPOSITE SEX BULLIES 6
As stated elsewhere in this Dictionary, *women* are just as capable of grinding down male employees as are men grinding down the women under their control.° Even, or especially, romantic gestures : passes, innuendos,° flirting and seduction can actually *worsen* someone's experience as not being comfortable and content° at work. *CAUSE*

OUTBURSTS 7
Outbursts at work might be traced to personal problems (marriage, children, debt....) but more commonly, Outbursts are a powerful indicator of oppression : the oppressor flipping / ranting (privately, if he can rein himself in that long) - or publicly, in front of co-workers° and the team. This latter stratagem is very risky, unless it is cunningly used as a warning° to the rest.

Or the oppressed one *herself* flips : the last straw on this camel's back. Perversely, both the oppressor and unsympathetic co-workers° might find these Outburst highly amusing / satisfying. *CAUSE / RESULT*

OUT OF THE LOOP 6
Out of the Loop is another way of describing someone's relegation to the land of the unknowing. An oppressed employee might deliberately be kept in the dark as to what is happening and who is to be given more responsibility and for what. Knowledge is power.°   *FACTOR*

OUTSIDERS 6
Outsiders are always under threat : not only in the workplace but also in the Church,° in the golf club, in the market-place, even in the family. And the Outsider is either self-defined : she feels she is beyond acceptance, preferring instead her solitude, forced or "voluntary" ; or else the Outsider is *allocated* that status by co-workers° who see her as a menace,° a threat,° an interloper, charlatan or grass.

By definition, the Outsider at work can never come indoors. However hard she *tries* to win acceptance - and *because of* those efforts to win acceptance - acceptance is denied, week after week, year after year. That is partly because *insiders* need an Outsider in order to maintain group cohesion. Better the enemy beyond than the enemy within.
FACTOR   /   RESULT

OUTSOURCING 9
After months or years of stable Government / local government / Health Service / airport employment, many loyal and longstanding employees are told their work is to be Outsourced. Not only must they then apply for their own jobs. They must also face, or endure, slashed wages,° zero hours,° call-cramming, °unpaid travel, denied emoluments,° inflexible rotas,° cuts, and undercutting.° Outsourced work is rarely as organized or as dedicated or as secure as the patterns of "employment for life" it frequently replaces.   *CAUSE   /   MOTIVATION*

OVER-QUALIFICATION 4

At least half of all employees - maybe 70% - are Over-Qualified. That means their degrees and diplomas and certificates - though conscientiously acquired - are ignored by their (grasping?) employers who are only interested in the company's balance-sheet. Thus M.A.s stack shelves ; LL.Bs sit by telephones ; teachers drive taxis. All very good for work-experience ; less good for the raising of staff morale,° eliciting the best from a workforce. Again, Over-Qualification is a sign of too free or rapid a flow of available labour. *ASSOCIATION*

OVERTIME 8

Overtime impacts upon oppression in two ways : wanted and *not wanted*. Wanted Overtime might be allocated, or restricted, to favoured ones (who also "need the money"). Unwanted Overtime (working all hours) is often awarded to the oppressed one - and, here, this requirement to stay late / come in early is far more likely to be implicit, not explicit ; *un*paid, not paid : a means of wearing an already overburdened employee down / out. *FACTOR*

OVERWORK 9

Very similar this to unwanted overtime;° except that this expectation° of the oppressed one, and her less litigious co-workers° is very intense: a real burden, one to be dreaded,° 24/7 (literally). Managers may try to set a good/bad example by Overworking *themselves*. The eventual employer colludes often with such exploitation°/ under-payment of workers senior AND junior. *CAUSE   /   RESULT*

OWNERSHIP 4
The traditional model of organizing the workplace is a hierarchy° installed by Owners and / or shareholders. Other models of conducting a business include partnership,° teamwork, management buyout, cooperatives° - and the giving of a majority of shares to voting employees. Undoubtedly, oppression of workers is easier to achieve in a top-down fiefdom : where employees are to do as they are told.
CAUSE / FACTOR

PANIC [PANIC MODE] [PANIC ATTACKS] 7
Panic sets in when targets° are unmet, orders undelivered, families unvisited, other organizations not consulted. Additionally, Panic surrounds the inspection,° the downsizing,° or the crackdown.° To make matters worse, an oppressed employee often Panics when she is called in to see the boss; when a service user complains; or when she is behind with her paperwork.° Panic also accompanies I.T. failure or the accidental deletion of data. Medically-defined Panic Attacks should be addressed with some urgency ; also *mapped* in order to understand just when ? - perhaps why ? - they are occurring in the life of *one* employee, and not the lives of all her co-workers.° *ASSOCIATION / RESULT*

PARALYSIS 8
Paralysis is the inertia,° hopelessness,° helplessness,° the oppressed one feels when she has been criticized° and downtrodden° once too often. And Paralysis might be a harbinger of complete breakdown° - or sleeplessness,° uncharacteristic tetchiness with co-workers, °partners, children.
RESULT / RESPONSE

PART-TIME WORKERS [PART-TIME EMPLOYMENT] 8

On the surface, Part-Time Working should be an ideal antidote to stress° and oppression in the workplace. After all, the 20-hour-a-week worker should experience exactly half the aggro of her 40-hour-a-week colleague° - with *twice the time* to recover, into the bargain. Unfortunately, life is not as simple as that. Many Part-Timers are blamed for being Part-Time ! They are told they have not produced° enough in their fewer hours : with the barely-concealed expectation° that they should stay on, encroaching upon their *non*-contractual hours, "to make up ground," " to pull their weight," " to earn their crust," and to " help the sinking ship." This expectation,° more a *requirement,*° is as unfair° as it is automatic. The Part-Timer is fully entitled to quit when her hours are done. Hard cheese. Then she might be blamed° not only by a line manager,° but also by some of her full-time co-workers° who suspect she is malingering.° In other words, the team is distrustful and resentful,° envious, of the Part-Timer in their midst - especially if flexible working° patterns in that setting are novel.

ASSOCIATION

PASS THE PARCEL 7

Pass the Parcel is a childish game alive and well in the workplace. Two Parcels immediately come to mind : the assignment / report / visit / complaint /° confrontation /° filing, that nobody else wants to face . Alternatively, the Parcel is a *real person*, a real apprentice,° a real trainee, a real " liability "° passed freely between line managers° or teams, outlets or outposts.

CAUSE / RESULT

PATERNITY LEAVE 3
In recent years, Paternity Leave has been championed, also extended, by Government ministers. But paid or concessionary Paternity Leave is often an *option*, or treat, rather than *a right* or requirement.° Two consequences are clearly in opposition here : men bonding more with their offspring - at the same time doing more to support the woman who actually gave birth ! - and the workplace potentially bereft of a valued colleague° now called to the Maternity Ward when he might be more usefully engaged in the latest assignment, crisis,° conference, or target-reach° in the factory or office he has "deserted." *ASSOCIATION*

PATRONAGE 6
Patronage is a term more associated with the 1700s than the Millennium. But never believe anyone who says something has been banished. What has "disappeared" usually survives but in a different form, a different arena. So it is with Patronage. Every single employee relies on a Patron : maybe the person who appointed her; maybe her team leader ; maybe the boss himself. There is absolutely no chance of surviving in a hostile° work setting *without* that Patron. Patrons act as buffers against unjust criticism° or persecution.° The downside is the way a Patron might care little for employees outside his magic circle. On a mundane level, Patrons argue in favour of pay rises for those lucky - or unlucky - enough to be Patronized ! *ASSOCIATION*

PATTERNS OF EMPLOYEE DISSATISFACTION 7
It is not rocket science for wise employers or Personnel Departments to *map* dissatisfaction in their various outposts or workplaces. One sudden resignation° might be unfortunate, the second problematic. One

rumbling might be ignored. A *second* formal complaint° or rumoured uprising *cannot* be ignored. There really is no smoke without hint of a fire. And there really are a series of unobserved mini-eruptions prior to the spectacular explosion. No employer can prosper with a predominantly unhappy° workforce - or restless section of that same workforce. Warning signs include higher rates of sick leave,° lower rates of productivity,° teams without focus or direction. *Mapping* problems to some extent isolates the *cluster* of irritations that needs urgent address. *ASSOCIATION / RESULT*

PAY DIFFERENTIALS [PAY GAPS] [GENDER INEQUALITY] 6
Men are still paid between a fifth and a third more than women for doing the same - or roughly the same - job. There is also a Gap of 30 , 100, *1000, times,* between "rewarding" the new office messenger / cleaner and his Chief Executive. Unfair° Pay Differentials soon become a cauldron for dissent,° on the shop floor, or in the staff room. And American research shows such resentment° yields greater tension between 2 employees of *roughly the same* qualifications and ambitions° than between trainee nurse and consultant. *ASSOCIATION*

PAY SCALES [UNEQUAL PAY] 7
Almost every employee looks forward to a pay rise : in most offices or the professions, incrementally moving up an imposed, or negotiated, Pay Scale. The oppressed (disgraced?) one - sometimes in common with *all women* in that defined work setting - is very unlikely to climb the Scale as quickly as she deserves to ; maybe never. Demotion° often comes into play after "incompatibility" within a former role. *CAUSE*

PEER REVIEW 6
Assessment° or monitoring° by one's equals - more positively, cooperation° and joint endeavour *with* one's equals - is an excellent working model for getting the job done, then working out how well the job *has* been done. Ideally, home visits and writing up can also be done collaterally. Good Peers can even obviate the need for team leaders and hierarchical ° line managers.° Barriers between adjoining desks,° as within call centres,° are always to be regretted. *Why not pool* all *the talents* ? See Bottom-Up Management.   *RESPONSE*

PERFECTION [PERFECTIONISM] 8
The pursuit of Perfection by Perfectionists is all well and good, as long as that endeavour is self-motivated,° self-rewarding. Perfection is only a *millstone* when the employer or management *demands* it - or when, conversely, the employee herself cannot move towards completion of a task until Perfection has been achieved. The best and most efficient workplaces are frequently those where occasional failure,° though noted, is anticipated *and* forgiven. Even so, it would be absurd for a manufacturer of fine china to engage a glazier or a finisher whose reject- rate of £2500 figurines was more than 5 to 10 % !

Error ° can become a tool of learning, not of despair.° For instance, most employees incur damage to the company car at some point in their driving careers. Likewise, most employees innocently send the wrong letter to the right person ; or fail to sign out on each and every occasion they leave the office. Perfection may *never* be attained : least of all by the seasoned bully° himself ! Where management *can* help is removing the risk of catastrophic failure, ° perhaps through a sensible training manual.° Line management° can then be used for positive -

not negative or intrusive - double-checking ; also adherence to necessary prevention-of-disruption procedures. It is all about safety.° *Safe* workers feel safe enough to speak out and raise the alarm. Safe workers are committed° to their organizations enough to want good results at the end of the year, *if not the best ever.* Perfectionists sometimes need saving from themselves ! *ASSOCIATION / RESPONSE*

PALPITATIONS 5
Palpitation of the heart is both a specific and a metaphorical medical disorder. Should a partner or GP or sufferer see a possible link with stress in the workplace, that concern needs to be voiced. Palpitations are often accompanied, or caused, by stress,° sleeplessness, ° tinnitus, and unrealistic deadlines ° or targets.° *RESULT*

PERCEPTION OF OTHERS 7
Whatever Perception an employer has of an employee, employee of colleague,° colleague of manager, manager of new recruit,° it impacts on both contentment° and productivity ° within the workplace. So it is worth taking some time and effort to ascertain whether intra-workplace Perceptions are fair° and accurate. Throughout this *Dictionary*, the oppressed one is *further* oppressed by *mis*conceptions: Misperception of her ability, commitment, contribution, *intent.* *CAUSE / FACTOR*

PERFORMANCE [PERFORMANCE INDICATORS] 8
It is interesting how central to employment *Performance on the job* has become. The very word Performance comes from Theatre. And work is nothing if it is not theatrical. *Measuring* Performance through

indicators - much as an undergraduate or trainee teacher's capability across the board has to conform to 100, 300! indicators - is one way of sorting out the wheat and the chaff. The only trouble is : the "chaff" are *real people* who are probably Performing quite satisfactorily already! See Targets.°   *FACTOR / ASSOCIATION*

PERKS 4
Perks, short for Perquisites, bungs, bonuses, rewards, emoluments,° are far more likely to be claimed by, or awarded to, favoured ones° than their sick or underworked,° neglected or bullied,° cowed or downtrodden° colleagues.° See Emoluments.   *ASSOCIATION*

PERSECUTION 9
Persecution is a very ancient word, not immediately used - or imagined relevant - in the UK. In fact, the word only really survives in its *passive* sense : the Persecution Complex. Yet Persecution is not necessarily an exaggeration when describing the red- hot- poker end, the searing repercussions, of bullying° and tyranny° in the workplace. And *women* are more persecuted than men ; immigrants more than the indigenous population ; doormats more than feisty fighters. Persecution can be *mental* as well as physical. Also many men and women subject to Persecution whenever and wherever they are working, face it when they get home, until it's time to clock in° again. *CAUSE / MOTIVATION*

PERSONAL DISINTEGRATION 8
At its most deleterious, workplace oppression leads directly, or indirectly, to Personal Disintegration: sometimes mislabelled° (?) nervous breakdown.°   *RESULT*

PERSONALITY PROFILING [PERSONALITY TYPE] 5
Personality Profiling is as old as Time-Motion° and Carl Jung. All sorts of blueprints or tests or group exercises or research are employed to divide staff into Conformists/Rebels, Divergent/Convergent Thinkers, Introverts/ Extraverts Fixers, Solidifiers, Doers, Talkers, whatever. The only trouble is : the process of labelling° or, more pertinently, *shedding a label*. Say if Team Study Day° identifies you as a Natural Leader, reinforced by your getting the whole team finishing a jigsaw in record time, what happens when yout want to pass in a difficult discussion - or when you fail to apply for a vacant Senior post ? Most employees, thankfully, are a *rich mix* of Personality Type. *ASSOCIATION*

PICKED OFF [BEING PICKED OFF] 7
Here the oppressor silences/dismisses° one employee at a time. The remainder then become more worried, more fearful.° For is it their turn next ? Like dominoes : one collapses, all collapse. The process of Picking Off is also closely related to racism,° sexism, ° isolation° and marginalization.° And ironically, whilst purging, °the oppressor clings to the falsehood : " It's only you."°. The opposite of Picking Off is *Buying Off*. *CAUSE / MOTIVATION*

PIECE WORK [PAYMENT BY RESULT] 8
On the surface : Piece Work is more equitable than standard wage. The woman who picks more plums, packs more boxes, despatches most parcels, is rewarded more than the slow coach. That leaves the slow coach feeling guilty° that she is not fast or dextrous enough. Worse, if a

whole team's output depends on joint productivity, ° the weakest link risks persecution, °sub-minimum wage, °even dismissal. ° *FACTOR*

PINCER MOVEMENT 6

In theory, Pincers are ideal : why not complain° about the oppressor to *both* a trusted co-worker ° and the oppressor's line manager ?° Better still : make a complaint to both Human Resources and senior management *at exactly the same time* ? Still risky, however. The whole Pincer Movement depends on management being *alarmed* that there is an oppressor in their midst : soon to be caught in between a rock and a hard place. Please do not bet on it. *RESPONSE*

PITY FOR THE BULLY 6

Amazingly, certain workers under pressure - not least because they are subject to bullying° in the workplace - is that they take Pity on the Bully. And men falsely imprisoned have been found to take Pity on their gaolers. Also those subjected to *torture* nonsensically take Pity on their torturers ! The oppressive manager might even spin a yarn that *he himself* is under attack ; expected to produce° more with fewer workers; has been dumped by his wife; has been staying at his desk° late at night, etc. All this woe attracts Pity from she who should herself be pitied. And Pity is best seen as tacit permission for the Bully to continue his incompetent or ruthless° management style. Key recognition should be given to the analogy of domestic violence° - where the bully also elicits Pity, often accompanied by begging forgiveness; and earnest assurances that nothing like that will ever happen again ! Tell me the old, old story. *RESULT / RESPONSE*

POINTING 5
Universally, Pointing is taken as aggressive.° Pointing can also indicate victimization.° Fellow employees Pointing should be reported straightway : definitely *not* a harmless gesture.   *MOTIVATION*

POOLING IDEAS AND KNOWLEDGE AND EXPERIENCE....4
Instead of the bunker, the silo,° or " every man for himself," some agencies, cooperatives° and outposts have opted for the Pooling of Ideas and Expertise. This is a direct challenge to the purely competitive° instinct - where if you've made some inroad or some progress; or if you've found a solution, you keep it strictly to yourself so that you alone get the credit. Far better that everybody joins the learning curve and that *everybody* reaps a dividend.   *RESPONSE*

POSTERS 6
Posters prominently displayed in the workplace have a disproportionate effect exposing - or mitigating - oppression along that same corridor. Posters might warn of the respective dangers of fast food, drinking,° smoking,° pilfering, the office party,° the social media° or taking a taxi home. And coming straight to the point, *some* posters exhort passers-by to use the Samaritans, go to Relate, have zero-tolerance of domestic violence,° consult Human Resources, join a Union° - or even take up a grievance.° Posters do, of course, need *refreshing* and updating. They also need to be *clever*. And in no way condescending. See Publicity.   *ASSOCIATION / RESPONSE*

POST-TRAUMATIC STRESS DISORDER 8
Several oppressed teachers, doctors, social workers, producers, soldiers,° find the pressure° they experience at - and because of - work akin to Post-Traumatic Stress Disorder. The two can go together. Where work Trauma differs from sudden flood, fire, bereavement, catastrophe, car crash, is that it is far more likely to be *cumulative*. That in no way depreciates from the severity of Post-Traumatic Stress Disorder : manifest in shivering,° tearfulness,° sleeplessness,° nervous breakdown, °panic attacks,° absenteeism,° domestic violence.° See Mental Illness. *RESULT*

PRAISE 10
Praise is astonishingly rare in most workplaces. Which is counter-intuitive : because the Praise Dividend is *huge*. Employees *glow* when they are Praised. They then either work harder - though not requested to- or else they Praise their co-workers° and underlings,° in a chain of positive feedback.°

Managers, especially oppressors, *withhold* Praise, for fear it will make workers more complacent. What better than that the striving worker works a bit harder NOW in order to win *future Praise* ? A future that, significantly, never happens - because of moving goalposts.° So Praise taken to be most *detrimental* to management represents a *direct transfer of power* ° from the Withholder of Praise to the taken-for-granted one hitherto starved of Praise. On the other hand, recent research indicates that florid Praise should not be excessive or undeserved. If Praise goes over the top, it is discounted by its receiver as phoney or condescending. Better in those circumstances for Praise to be directed at *the effort* put in, rather than the finished product. At the same time, proper Praise does still generate a more relaxed and collegiate° working atmosphere. *RESPONSE*

PREFERMENT 7
Preferment is an indication that one employee is Preferred above another ; and perhaps put on fast-track progression up the ranks. Sometimes, this elevation relies on merit ; at other times, on blatant favouritism.° *FACTOR*

PREGNANCY 6
Pregnancy is a potentially worrying time for many employees : morning sickness, biological changes, possible relationship difficulties, abortion, altered plans, excitement, expectation - and the bringing to the surface of buried demons. Yet whilst many employers are good providing formal maternity leave, they frequently fail in their hidden responsibility : to show a Pregnant worker tender loving care (different from patronizing her). Employers who *do* get it right actually benefit from enhanced performance,° stronger loyalty. *ASSOCIATION*

PREJUDICE 8
Prejudice is a vast subject, again better dealt with in a book of its own. At its simplest Prejudice means pre-judging someone by the colour of her skin, her self-presentation,° attitude or sexuality - or according to any other measure of perceived shortfall.° By now, Prejudice should have been eliminated from companies, shops and offices. Wish that it had been. One of the worst aspects of Prejudice is the ignorance of the oppressed employee that she has been pre-judged, even before opening her mouth or proving her worth. *CAUSE / FACTOR*

PREMATURE ADULTHOOD 7

Where an employee or soldier° or apprentice° is aged 16, 17, 18, 19, or 20; or where a local authority allows for even earlier employment, it is quite likely the younger worker will be exposed to bad language° and high risk,° wide responsibility and heavy obligation: far beyond her tender years. At the same time, she is very *unlikely* to be supported in her judgment, her decision-making or her task fulfilment.° At the same time, she is very *likely* to be criticized° and/or ostracized.° Yet she will not wish to jeopardize her status and earning capacity by rocking the boat ; nor will she necessarily confide in mother, father, brother, boyfriend, flat-mate. *FACTOR / or ASSOCIATION*

PRESENTEEISM 7

A fairly new term for coming in early and leaving late : to prove to management your commitment° (Corporate Man / Organization Man). Ironically, Presenteeism might be just a jacket on the back of a chair at daybreak: how impressive ! Job insecurity° worsens Presenteeism :the incessant, unsleeping, I- Phone® its adjunct. *RESULT / RESPONSE*

PRESSURE [PRESSURES] 9

Pressure is an all-encompassing term for stress° or oppression at work. And it is usually the newer or younger employee° who goes under first of all. Pressure tends to come from below, beside *and* above wherever you happen to be placed in the organization. Luckily, most workers develop coping mechanisms° (tactics) for deflecting or ignoring pressure. Early studies in prisons called this process : adaptation. Prisoners - like workers - literally could not get through the day without releasing themselves from unbearable pressure.

Pressures as a plural serves to recognize *the amassing* of lots of different individual Pressure-points in the day : typically: a quarrelsome breakfast + a disrupted or uncomfortable commute° + supplier delays + new tasks + negative feedback° + a troublesome co-worker° + snow + whatever = *the last straw*. FACTOR / RESULT

PREVENTION 10
Prevention is an all-embracing term for manuals,° team strategies,° employee safeguards,° and locally-drawn procedures ° = a stemming of bullying° and wickedness *at source*. *Vigilant* management bothers about the consequences of a tarnished name, a detrimental ethos ° and-more positively : an exemplary approach to staff welfare.° RESPONSE

PREVENTION OFFICERS 7
Some very large organizations can afford to provide a bullying° Prevention Officer, though probably not called that. The Officer concerned might be called an Anxiety° Prevention Officer, Stress° Reduction Officer, Staff Welfare° Officer, Staff Counsellor - or Status Equality Officer ; or simply be based, without portfolio, in Personnel.

RESPONSE

PRIDE 8
Pride is not a sin in the workplace. Instead, Pride is our guide and goal until the bell tolls for our exit. Pride involves both self-image° and self-belief.° When workers are proud of their skills, crafts, and output,° they carry that Pride into their next assignment - and even take it home with them. Yet Pride is not always *an economic good*. Many employers rely on their staff having *little or no* pride in their day-jobs in order to *increase* output, thereby maximizing profits.° That is why ruthless managers have to dampen Pride down : for Pride takes too long! And Pride does not permit the cutting of corners. RESPONSE

PRIVATE USE OF COMPUTERS   [.... SOCIAL NETWORKING] 6
More employers are now restricting use of work computers - even *personal* laptops or tablets - during work time. Additionally, certain pornographic or social networking sites are automatically blocked. Nevertheless, everybody accepts that work computers *are* used for personal need, personal auction, personal messaging, personal surfing, etc. . There are even buttons on work computers that conveniently allow an employee to return to task immediately a supervisor comes through the door ! The only antidote to the Private Use of Computers is to have a crystal-clear workplace policy on the issue. That policy might well ban all forms of pornography and Tripadvisor whilst agreeing to Wikipedia and Facebook. Twitter might be permitted for keeping up to speed ! Maybe Private Use will be granted in lunch hour.° Or else line managers° may ask someone to stay later if she had used the Computer for her own ends. In other settings, the use of *all* Computers is forbidden for gossip surrounding strange co-workers,° inept managers and out-of-touch head office. *A fine line has to be drawn*. If management is too hard on Private Use, restrictions will be circumvented, defied or openly resented. On the other hand, if management is too lax about Private Use, it risks getting nothing done !
ASSOCIATION

PRIVATIZATION 7
Before 1979, the word Privatization hardly existed. Then there was a four-decade long explosion of it - and of its two close neighbours outsourcing° and Private Finance Initiative. Governments and municipalities used to boast good wages and salaries, exemplary working conditions, excellent pensions. All on a not-for-profit basis. Then came along agencies, targets,° the internal market and arms-length governance : sometimes called light-tiller administration.
Soon, previously secure °workers found themselves competing for their own jobs, working to a short-term contract° or zero-hours,° placed

outside previously negotiated wage settlements, hired and fired.° Were Privatization *benevolent*, it would be a valued enemy of oppression in the workplace. But Privatization often looks only at the bottom-line: *a race to the bottom.* See Low Wages.   *CAUSE / FACTOR*

PROBATION [BEING ON PROBATION] 7

Being a Probationer is not a very powerful° position. Many firms take people on for 3 months' approval, 6 months' approval, or 23-month contracts. In such circumstances, it is vital that Probationers are adequately protected from summary dismissal° after, before or after formal appraisal.° Maybe the Probationer could be offered a mentor° or a sympathetic line manager ;° even offered a second chance. So it is not unusual for Probationers to feel vulnerable° and under pressure.° After all, they are always on thin ice - and hugely dependent on their reference.   *FACTOR*

PRODUCTIVITY 8

Most conveyor belts, and most sections or departments within an organization have either a Productivity goal or a Productivity measure. However, like all targets,° these objectives should be achievable without overdue exertion. One does not have to be in a busy cafe, a clothing sweatshop or a hospital's A&E for long before concluding many expectations of Productivity are entirely unrealistic. In such conditions, overworked° employees sacrifice tea- and lunch-breaks° - even toilet ! - in case they can't keep up. Meanwhile *stress*° levels are both stupid and dangerous. Also, failure° to meet Productivity goals can lead to more or less instant dismissal,° especially for the newer worker still on probation.°   *CAUSE / FACTOR*

PROTOCOLS 5
Every now again, management systems - particularly beleaguered, or rapidly expanding, firms- issue Protocols : edicts to be adhered to, from now on. Maybe the new rules are incorporated in the Manual° as well. And one of the most valuable Protocols is the anti-bullying° one. Also that Protocol that lays out how apprentices° and new recruits are to be inducted, and how treated thereafter.   *ASSOCIATION*

PSYCHOMETRIC TESTING 5
From time to time, sociopathic and Psychometric measurements come back into fashion. Pre-employment questions include : " Do you have a wide circle of friends ?" ; " Are you usually calm ?" ; " Do you like to help people with their problems ?" However, a Test is only as good as its creator, its fairness,° its elimination of rogue scripts, an adjustment for *double-guessing* - and the delicacy with which its results are extracted, then transmitted to manager or management. Psychometric analysis intrudes into team away-days° when everybody is invited to come up with their strengths and weaknesses.   *ASSOCIATION*

PSYCHOPATHIC TENDENCIES 7
Perceived Psychopathic behaviour must be treated with extreme caution. Like all dangerous labels,° it is a label that sticks. However that does not rule out the line manager° - or vicious co-worker °- with Psychopathic Tendencies (*defined as a personality disorder making antisocial behaviour, violence° too, more likely*) tormenting° the oppressed one, unprovoked, *especially when unprovoked*. In several instances of domestic violence,° Psychopathic Tendencies have been identified relatively late on in the bullying° cycle : so when these

characters (usually male°) turn up in their workplaces, but in a *different* role or outpost, they are extremely unlikely to abandon their predilection : manifest in unashamed pre-meditation.   *CAUSE*

PUBLICITY [PUBLICIZING WORKERS' RIGHTS] 6
There is no point having extra benefits for part-time workers° : sickness° and holiday pay, or an anti-bullying° protocol,° if no Publicity attaches to management's revised approach. Nobody should rely on "word getting round." It often doesn't - in the process saving owners thousands, even millions, of pounds. Most workers *do* take No for an answer if they have the temerity to ask for something extra. So it's back to posters° and those informative team meetings.°
ASSOCIATION / RESPONSE

PULLING WEIGHT 6
The expression " Pulling One's Weight" has its origin in herding, husbandry , heavy haulage and ice-bound travel. In times past, every worker, every burly serf, *had to* be able to stoke coal, lay stone, tow wagons, lift bales of hay- or shift barrels of beer, all without outside assistance . So any slackers° were immediately identified as lily-livered parasites: people ready to *benefit from* food and drink; and from a crude wage ; without ever doing their bit for the common good.
And in *modern* times, the Weight to be Pulled is frequently more metaphorical than actual. Oppressors and foremen alike wish to dole responsibilities out : first and foremost those tasks perceived to be awkward or unpleasant. Then, at annual appraisal,° *non-contributing* workers are called upon to explain themselves. Unfair° it is that mums with young children - or heavy caring responsibility at home - are still reprimanded for not Pulling their Weight at work.   *FACTOR*

PUNISHMENT 9

Punishment in the workplace is an all-embracing term for everything from thrashing a child worker in a back-street factory to crude wage deductions ° or unjustified dismissal.° Punishment sounds simple, but it is anything but. Punishments can be given out according to a tariff *without* an employee being aware of that tariff. Or Punishment, redundancy,° might be arbitrary, even random. Alternatively, *internal* Punishment might overlap, or conflict with, *external* Punishment : the full weight of the law. Certain professions like the Police° are past masters of using this overlap to their advantage : " I have been absolved by the law therefore I should not face internal disciplinary procedures,°" - or : "I have been demoted° / dismissed,° therefore I should not also be prosecuted." To muddy the waters further, an employee might *think* she is being Punished when she has "merely" been subject to the shake-up,° turn-around, or policy of last in, first out. Whatever the exact circumstances, Punishment is always upsetting and unwelcome. It is also an unsettling evocation of far-from-idyllic childhood. *RESULT / MOTIVATION*

QUANGOS 7

Quangos are nearly always fertile breeding-grounds for bullying.° The word Quango stands for a Quasi-Autonomous Non-Government Organization (more accurately : a Quasi-Autonomous *National* Government Organization). Oppression flourishes in the Quango - as it does too in many a charity or social services' department - because it is *least expected* there. That catches the oppressed one unawares. Worse, redress° is less possible here: because normal Personnel safeguards don't apply to Quangos. Nothing does. Even Quango Heads : the great and the good, are parachuted in ; sometimes drafted across from dismal failure° in other Quangos ! Moreover, Quangos are intensely *secretive.*° And how could great appointees be *bullies*?   FACTOR

QUASI-DISCIPLINARY PROCEDURES 8
In many ways, the oppressed one has more to fear from Quasi-Disciplinary Procedures - appraisal ° called advice,° formal guidance° or professional guidance° - than from the real thing. Quasi-Disciplinary takes power° from senior management and deposits it in the hands less safe of first or second line manager. ° If led into Quasi like a lamb led to the slaughter, certainly get a silent witness, a McKenzie friend,° or union rep.° The seasoned bully° definitely does not appreciate shining lights.   *ASSOCIATION / MOTIVATION*

RAMPAGE 6
A Rampage usually takes place when there has been an unfavourable inspection° / accident / incident / report°/ conviction / visitation. And the Rampage is open season for oppression : on the pretence that management is extremely unhappy. ° Management wants change,° and wants it quickly. Management also wants a tightening of all procedures.° From this moment on !

This purge° - and the preceding Rampage - is a fortuitous excuse for selective oppression.° Most people have been pulling their weight° and following the book ....*except* for a few renegades.

The oppressor further down the chain might wish to save his own bacon at the expense of an underling.° And the Rampage provides him with ideal cover for tools of oppression that might not be permitted at other times of the year. Whereas secure, °collegiate,° workplaces have no need for a Rampage.   *CAUSE   /   MOTIVATION*

RATTING [DROPPING IN BOILING OIL / STEAMING MANURE] 7
Since time immemorial, cavemen have dropped fellow cavers in the doldrums. Line managements° and cultures of bullying° are fertile breeding-grounds for Ratting / being Ratted on / being sold down the river. Thus a new or insecure employee becomes *more* insecure, more fearful,° because she knows only too well a bucket of manure is circulating : just ready to drop on her unprotected head. And scheming, unco-operative co-workers° are not beyond gleefully letting that cauldron of Boiling Oil pass them by !   *CAUSE   /   MOTIVATION*

REBELS   [REBELLIOUSNESS   ] 7
All too easy it is to dismiss dissenters,° or those tempted to complain° about harsh management practices,° as "Rebels." And in many fields of employment, Rebellion or mutiny is sufficient *of itself* to merit instant dismissal,° demotion,° or punishment.°   Worryingly : the target of oppression, the "vexatious" complainant° is unlikely *to see herself* as a Rebel, merely as one hard done to. See Troublemaker.
FACTOR   /   MOTIVATION

REDRESS 6
Redress is not normally an option for the oppressed one. By the very nature of her dilemma, she has very low self-esteem ;° very little reason to upset the apple-cart ; very little status in the organization ; and very few allies.° She might try grievance° - if Personnel publicizes that there is such a recourse. But Redress might still be bitter-sweet. *She* will be re-located° or given a generous pay-off - whilst the bully° merely continues his browbeating° behaviour on her successors, unimpeded.   Worse, Redress might merely be a mealy-mouthed statement that there has indeed been a regrettable Personality Clash° -

with attendant shortcomings on *both* sides: " We know this is not the response you may have wanted....but Mr. X sincerely regrets any disappointment you might have felt...." RESPONSE

REFUSAL TO PAY WAGES   [WITHHOLDING PAY] 9
One cannot imagine an act more reminiscent of slavery than Refusal to hand out Pay Packets. Many cruise cleaners and caterers, for instance, are only paid after disembarkation, if at all. And in back-street factories, weeks might elapse with mere *promises* of reward.° Withholding pay - withholding emoluments° - on the flimsiest pretext ; after the merest hint of insolvency - ought to be illegal in all circumstances. After all, it is exploitative, a breach of trust, and an act of stealing : stealing people's time, dignity, toil, goodwill ; also *their livelihoods*. Instead Withholders of Pay go forward to the one-sided tribunal,° or powerless Small Claims' Court : with no guarantee that expensive litigation can be averted. The empty pay-packet is a *fait accompli* : the hardest of hard cheese.   RESULT / MOTIVATION

REJECTION 6
Constant Rejection is an occupational hazard for freelance journalists, commercial travellers or interviewees on the circuit. But Rejection *is* avoidable to some extent. Would that more firms would not call people for selection where the successful candidate has already been anointed. Nor do Redundancy Procedures° need to be as harsh or unsympathetic as they are frequently experienced to be. Repeat Rejection: *in work*, as well as out-of-work, is demoralizing° and dispiriting ; for many people, a self-fulfilling prophecy. We all yearn for the opposite : Acceptance, ° and inclusion.   CAUSE

RELAXATION [RELAXATION EXERCISES / TECHNIQUES] 9
Any decent employer or Personnel Department will tell a worker how to Relax, even Relax on the job ! Relaxation is critical to good performance. In other words, a Relaxed worker gives freer rein to her potential. One thing workplace bullying° or stress° *never* achieves is Relaxation, an aspect that makes it far more deleterious. Relaxation Exercises at work or at home include self-massage, soothing music, time out, entry into the secret garden, wish-fulfilment, lying down, lying back and puzzle-solving. Deeper Relaxation comes with a colleague-to-colleague heart-to-heart talk, a walk round the block, or the controlled inhalation of breath, even a bit of piano playing.
RESPONSE

RELIGIOUS BELIEF [RELIGIOUS ADHERENCE] 7
Whilst *most* Workplaces accommodate turbans, Sabbaths, Friday Prayers and total abstinence, a few do not. Conflict° arises when the line manager° holds a different perspective on Religious Adherence than the oppressed one - or when her co-workers° are mocking. Ironically, it might be *only* her Religious Belief that enables a carer° or Probation Officer or nurse° or Secretary to get through the day : so the contradiction or denial of that Belief leaves her in an infinitely worse position than if she was agnostic. In supermarkets,° for instance, there is often enormous pressure° to work Sundays - and co-workers who do the Sunday shift tend to resent the excused one.
Occasionally, Religious Adherence persuades an employee to speak out against malpractice, unethical trading, or short cuts in the workplace. Other areas of Religious debate are gay rights, same sex marriage, abortion and cross-culture adoption. *FACTOR / RESPONSE*

RELOCATION 6
Personnel traditionally turns to Relocation where an organization is big enough for this to take place without too much *dis*location. Relocating the oppressed one is easier than making changes,° addressing the grievance° properly - or *Relocating the Bully* . Never forget : Relocation is not a *neutral* outcome. It leaves the oppressed one without her former allies,° often with a longer commute° - with the label° of past troublemaker° into the bargain ! And, needless to say, the concurrent survivor of *domestic violence*° is hardly ever offered an attractive or achievable option of Relocation. *RESULT / RESPONSE*

REMOTE CONTROL OPPRESSION 6
It is a mystery as to how a bullying° manager or co-worker° can exercise his tyranny° by Remote Control. How can the oppressed one feel oppressed when he or she is ill with what seems to be something else, on a training course - or taking a holiday ; even *promoted* ? The answer is : very easily! Bullies° do not require *physical* presence to continue their control° and control freakery. A well-placed, targeted, phone call during supper, before bed time, or on a day of working from home - a day off even - can be *explosive*, and have the desired destabilizing impact.   Thus the oppressed one is never allowed to forget her oppressor.

Or the bully° can operate via colleagues,° memo,° form-filling, or the social media.° Not a few bullies° have been so dominant face-to-face, during appraisal° and supervision,° that they cannot be put aside when they are seated upstairs in the managing director's office, or out on *his own* home / retail visits. Indeed, the oppressed worker might see his *absence* of itself as a threat:° requiring much sweeping up, and catching up, before he returns to do the sums and settle scores. *CAUSE*

REPEAT ABSENCES 6

Absenteeism,° sickness,° oppression, in the workplace: *which comes first ?* Whatever the answer, any present Personnel Department and any *future* employer wishes to know about past Absences, especially *paid Absences* from work. Tellingly, Repeat Absences are frequently attributable to workplace bullying° - yet this never comes to the surface. Easier to write down on a form: stress,° dyspepsia,° anxiety,° indigestion,° depression, °chronic fatigue. That is because the grinding down of an underling° is both an acceptable deficit and something beyond investigation / redress.° Sickness monitoring ° *can be* humane and sensitive, as well as overdue ; but it should not be a line manager° who is entrusted with that monitoring.° *CAUSE / RESULT / FACTOR*

REPRIMANDS 9

Formal Reprimands are more common in the Police° or Armed Forces° than in less hierarchical° work settings. Nevertheless, a Reprimand sits uneasily on anybody's work record. So an oppressed one is recommended to ensure which warnings° - what advice° - are also counted as Reprimand / dishonourable discharge. Also she needs to have a friend or colleague° or union rep° in the room at the same time. *And* to request sight of her Personnel file. *MOTIVATION*

RESIGNATION 9

Someone's Resignations can be considered neutral : the happy decision to move on, to have children, to bid for recruitment by a rival...or simply looking forward to retirement.° However, many Resignations are forced, suggested, *even encouraged.* The oppressed one might resign when the last straw has broken the camel's back. Or Resignation is used to lift the cloud that prompted the leaving under a cloud. The *other* meaning of the word Resignation is Resigning oneself to whatever torment° is currently being experienced ; yielding to the temptation to *give up* the good fight.   *RESULT*

RESPECT 8
Respect is hard won and very swiftly sacrificed. Respect- or lack of it- permeates all corners of the workplace. Not uncommonly, deference and strained Respect is shown to one or more managers / section leaders/ foremen° in their presence, face-to-face - whilst those figureheads are *ridiculed* behind their backs. Respected managers, Respected stalwarts, are actually very difficult to take to task or take to tribunal.° Then there is the *Disrespect* shown by an oppressed one's customers, shoppers, passers-by, service users, cleaners and visitors. A *wise* employer will nip this Disrespect in the bud : to the extent of calling in the police,° providing a panic button, excluding offenders from all future treatment, or favour, or attention. Remember : workers Disrespected by their own hierarchy° are noted down by the public. Especially in restaurants, schools and waiting rooms, customers do have ears ! Conversely, *accumulated* Respect, very deserved, is harder-won than Disrespect.   *RESPONSE*

RESPONSIBILITY 6
Responsibility can be a task, a grade at work, or a state of mind. Responsibility reveals, or results from, degrees of autonomy.° And one means of bullying° a worker is to take Responsibility away from her ; conversely, to endow Responsibility on her, *knowing* she cannot cope; or setting her up for something to go wrong that will not possibly be her fault.°   *MOTIVATION / RESPONSE*

RETRAINING 4

Retraining should be offered - or imposed - on any line manager° or co-worker ° who transgresses into bullying° or oppression. For it is the bully° himself who has fallen short, *fallen down*, not the oppressed one. *RESPONSE*

RETURNING 5

Returning to a place where you have been humiliated,° stressed,° marginalized,° discriminated against,° or sent to Coventry° is never going to be an easy transition. Particularly where co-workers° and line managers° alike are hostile° or suspicious.° This is more so when emerging from a home overshadowed by caring responsibilities° or domestic violence.° This places a burden on Personnel to ensure that any re-entry is thoroughly panned...*and gradual*. There is no point Returning to bullying° unless the bully° has been removed or relocated.° Nor , if there has been nervous breakdown, °should the issues that might have led to such incapacity remain unchanged. The best Returns are treated as planting for florabundance further down the line. *RESULT / RESPONSE*

REVERSE DISCRIMINATION 7

As mentioned elsewhere in this Dictionary, black employees might persecute white; female employees turn against male; junior recruit make life more difficult for team leader.° Where there is a downward spiral of distrust,° anything is possible. And Personnel has a fine line to tread not damning an alleged bully° when, perhaps misguidedly, he is simply doing his job alongside somebody embittered by somebody - or somewhere - else. Oppressed ones might be internalizing aggression° and dishing in kind....or simply be backtracking. *FACTOR*

REWARDS 7

A Culture of Reward is the opposite of the culture of criticism.° Also, not all Rewards are *tangible*. A job well done might bring its own Reward and satisfaction.° Non-monetary Rewards include words of praise,° certificates and trophies, bottles of wine, weekend breaks in the country, or overseas, the eventual gold watch - or a team buffet! Realistic Rewards are always more beneficial than punishments.° Suitably Rewarded employees *glow* - and tend to work *even harder* in the future - if only because they are appreciated by their boss or firm or agency.° Just a word of caution : Rewards should not be so enmeshed with targets° that the *Un*rewarded are *jeered* by their co-workers, °and despised by their managers.   ASSOCIATION / RESPONSE

RIPPLES 7

There is nowhere ebbing is more consequential than in the intolerable workplace ; and, conversely, in the *welcoming* workplace. When a manager tears a strip off an employee, she becomes unhappier, less secure in herself, more damaged in the image she has of herself, until, very soon, she seizes up at work *and at home*. This devastation can be immeasurable. How many stressed employees do we hear saying of their team leaders° and line managers :° *"If only* they knew what brutes they are!" " If only they could see....!" Yet, on a happier note, Ripples work splendidly in *the opposite* direction in the positive shop/ branch/ floor/ office/ school - where everyone is collegiate.° FACTOR

RISK 8
Risk often has its own set of proper procedures within the workplace. Risk is taken seriously if only because of insurance liability, occasional employee liability ;° also due to traceability to a dedicated manager prepared to take responsibility° as opposed to wanting *pay* for responsibility.° Even so, thousands of employees - especially in construction , transport, and manufacturing - are daily put at Risk by careless, lazy or unscrupulous employers. The Bully° should also be attentive to the Risk he is running in respect of juniors, or employees less secure° than himself.　　　　　　　CAUSE　/　RESULT

RIVALRY 9
Rivalry can be *constructive*, in childhood as in adulthood. The best sort of Rivalry enriches sporting and other levels of achievement. Good
Rivalry gives us a measuring rod against which we can match our own ambition. ° However, tendentious Rivalry is alive and well wherever there are targets,° grades,° promotion,° status differentials,° blue-eyed boys,° or bright sparks. And intense Rivalry is *far from* innocuous when worker and co-worker° tear each other apart ; when Rivalry splits a team or a floor in two ; when the oppressed one and her immediate line manager° are bitter Rivals ; when Rivalry is stirred up my management in pursuit of higher output; ° and when Rivalry defeats workplace harmony. ° Ironically, the best or worst Rivals are more likely to be our otherwise well-meaning co-workers° than the most senior autocrats° in the organizations joined up to.　　CAUSE / MOTIVATION / FACTOR

ROBUST [ROBUST MANAGEMENT STYLE] 9
I thought I was totally alone, unique, hating the word *Robust*. In the 1980s, the word seemed to come from nowhere : usually accompanied by terms like efficient management, employment advice,° annual appraisal,° necessary measures, strong leadership,° consistent practice, or maximum efficiency. Very soon, in a climate of fear° and streamlining,° people began to complain° about the Robustly rumbustious . If targets° were not met, or if manure was ready for dumping on somebody's head,° the dread weasel-word *Robust* was employed to embrace intractable intransigence. Thus *Robust* lingers on as word born of the bully° - *for* the bully° - who dares not speak his real name. All too often only the steamroller° is Robust. Cue to leave this particular word unsaid.   *CAUSE / MOTIVATION*

ROCKING THE BOAT 5
The easiest way to criticize° a potentially oppressed employee is to accuse her of Rocking the Boat : not being one of us.° In this climate of fear,° the troublemaker° has to be thrown *overboard*.   *MOTIVATION*

ROGUE EMPLOYEE 7
To call one particular employee *Rogue* is not automatically a reference to Criminality or Professional Misconduct. The Rogue might simply be a nuisance or troublemaker.° Otherwise the so-called Rogue is an employee whom management bitterly regrets recruiting / conscripting / transferring. See Scapegoat.   *FACTOR / MOTIVATION*

ROGUE MANAGER 9
The Rogue Manager is really a contradiction of terms. How could somebody have been appointed, then promoted, ° eventually taking charge of a whole team / floor / department / office / conveyor belt: all this being without having displayed fitness to lead, or leadership skills°? Unfortunately, as the Police° have discovered, and at great cost to their reputation, it is possible to have a Rogue Manager not just at one level but at almost every level above that grade, right up to Deputy-Commissioner. Such rampaging and all-pervasive corruption° makes it impossible to pursue grievances,° or even to introduce checks and balances. Power° may not question Power.°   *CAUSE / FACTOR*

ROUND-THE-CLOCK   [ROUND-THE-YEAR]   WORKING 8
Times was when most workers could clock off° at home time, at the bell, at the whistle, or at 5pm. No longer. Many office, sales' and professional employees, in particular, are contactable 24/7, 364 days a year. Such flexibility° even applies if wage-slaves° are on leave or on holiday or asleep !° Or in the cloakroom ! That omnipresent availability can itself become oppressive: because there is no rest, no escape.° And managers or co-workers° alike are extremely unlikely to rock the boat° if everything is remunerative and hunky-dory. The very act of perpetually being in contact is not neutral. *CAUSE   /   FACTOR*

RUTHLESSNESS 6
Ruthlessness is perhaps not as common at work as is sometimes supposed. Yes : bullies° are definitely Ruthless - as are some schedules° and management practices.° but, thankfully, there are more checks and balances than there used to be : *if* those restraints can be made effective. The very word Ruthlessness sums up the tyrant.°
CAUSE   /   MOTIVATION

SADISM 7
The topic of Sadism deserves a book all to itself. Suffice it to say : many workplace bullies° are also Sadists : Sadists on the road and at home as well as at work : delighting in enslaving° folk, then grinding them down ; standing back, with satisfaction,° to see a writhing bundle of humanity, a wreck. *CAUSE / MOTIVATION*

SADO-MASOCHISM ...7
Many treatises, not a few of them pornographic, have been written about the phenomenon of Sado-Masochism. The term means cruelty° both dispensed and received by a single sufferer. At work, the *receiving* of the cruelty° is uppermost - and the fact that the beating is willingly (?) endured does not excuse the beating in the first place. Some bullies° say, without a moment's hesitation : " She asked for it!" others : " Well it's brought her into line." In sport, the police service,° and the armed forces,° in particular, Sado-Masochism is rife. See Cycle of Oppression. *RESULT / MOTIVATION*

SAFETY [SAFE GROUND] 7
Ideally, all employees would feel Safe at work : Safe metaphorically, Safe literally. But oppressed ones, self-evidently, feel definitely Unsafe; unsure where they stand ; or where the next load of trouble and complaint° will come from. Maybe there is Safety in numbers : in the Team / Staffroom. Maybe not. *RESPONSE*

SARCASM 8
Many people take Sarcasm for granted : wit, harmless fun. But that only appertains if the targeted worker's self-esteem° is already high. She is

then in a position to brush off vibes and jibes alike - or at least not to internalize them. A good guide is to count Sarcasm as noxious. *CAUSE*

SATISFACTION   [SATISFACTION SURVEYS] 7
It is a truism that a Satisfied workforce is also a happy workforce. Company profits might not go through the roof; yet that time will come. If workers are Satisfied, they will smile more, meet the needs of more of their co-workers° and customers more effectively; also spread the word an organization is worth supporting. Many Satisfaction Surveys do actually reveal or uncover Dissatisfaction! But no panic ! Minor Dissatisfactions can swiftly be dispelled beneath a benevolent umbrella. Just because a Survey might yield uncomfortable truths does not make the exercise worthless.   To the contrary.   Is a place on the *Sunday Times'* list of *The 100 Best Employers to Work For* beckoning ?
ASSOCIATION /   RESPONSE

SAYING   "NO!" 7
Saying "NO!" *sounds* easier than actually saying it. Most foremen and line managers° neither expect nor welcome the word "NO!" In fact, they expect the response : "YES!" to requests for extra writing, visiting or unpaid overtime.° To say "NO!" therefore takes courage, and is a useful survival strategy.° *RESPONSE.*

[THE] SCAB 4
The charge of being a Scab is damning: so damning few workers ever recover from this disgrace. Scabs are those who go into work by crossing a picket-line or ignoring an instruction to strike.° And memories are long. Scabbing is one of those rare instances where aggrieved colleagues are encouraged to intimidate *each other* instead of standing united against a different foe. *CAUSE   /   MOTIVATION*

SCANDAL 6
A Scandal at work might well not implicate a particular person, but if her luck is already stretched, she might be blamed :° unfairly. *FACTOR*

SCAPEGOATS [SCAPEGOATING] 8
The Scapegoat is a Biblical figure : the *goat* prepared for the slaughter instead of the child / messenger / detainee otherwise condemned to die. The *attraction* of the Scapegoat is his anonymity, also dispensability; he conforming - or not conforming° - with some hated stereotype.° Once the oppressor stops *caring about* the Scapegoat, the Scapegoat can take upon herself the woes of the entire system - because she no longer qualifies to be a valued constituent of that system. Scapegoating is the process of selecting one person to bear the sins and troubles of everyone else....doing nothing to assist the self-esteem° of the chosen one. Scapegoating is particularly detectable in the literature of racism.° Where the white employee, a longstanding employee, might be too risky, too costly to act as Scapegoat, the black worker, the asylum-seeker, the outsider, °makes an ideal candidate.

The Oppressor is often *praised* for his Scapegoating : for keeping a tight ship.° And Scapegoating is a popular enterprise because it can provide welcome cover for favoured ones,° allowing them to stay on board, amply gratified that they have kept their heads down.°
CAUSE / MOTIVATION

SCHEDULES [PUNISHING WORK SCHEDULES] 8
Schedules come in three main forms : the work-allocation Schedule, the work-completion Schedule, and the time-allotment Schedule. If any one of these Schedules is too punitive° in relation to individual or group expectations ; in relation to time devoted to a job; or time

allowed to travel° or prepare oneself between jobs : then employees will feel pressurized°, bombarded, ° or inadequate.° *CAUSE / RESULT*

SECRECY 8
Secrecy is the greatest friend of the bully,° the greatest enemy of the survivor.° The bully° *has to be* fairly secretive, lest his own superiors discover and disown him. Equally, the survivor needs to keep the degree of her oppression Secret : because of pride° and her desire to arrive in a better place; one day to be free of the bully.° Ironically, breaching Secrecy is a big no-no in many areas of employment : releasing a key ingredient for further oppression. The talking employee becomes the walking employee. Even grievance procedures° are kept secret. And Secrecy perpetuates domestic violence° too. *RESULT / ASSOCIATION*
.

SECURITY AT WORK [SECURITY IN THAT CAREER] 7
Ideally, most employees would feel Secure at work ; therefore able to look forward to a long and stimulating career. Unfortunately: temping short-term,° and zero-hours' contracts,° also mass redundancies,° make Security of employment a distant ambition° for all too many. On a one-to-one level, a line-manager's° relentless criticism ° makes the single beleaguered° employee Insecure - where her co-workers° might feel perfectly Secure (or pretend to be). *ASSOCIATION / RESPONSE*

SELECTION PROCEDURES 6
In one respect, Selection Procedures cannot be oppressive - because, except after a spouse's promotion°/ relocation,° nobody is usually *forced* to apply for a new job (although restructuring° might put you in a position where failure to re-apply becomes constructive dismissal°). In real life, some Selection Procedures *are* however patently unfair,°

leaving some applicants demoralized,° worse humiliated.° Much depends on interviewers, and the organizers of trust games / group discussions, putting candidates at ease ; also never asking one candidate to upgrade or downgrade a rival.° *ASSOCIATION*

SELECTIVE SURVIVAL [SELECTIVE   OPPRESSION] 7
The bully° or the ruthless° manager actually *selects* who should survive - and who should not. This choice is not just a matter of who should be made redundant° - or promoted °- and who should not. The choice, particularly where conflict° is brought to the employer's attention, is between who should get the high-jump and who should not; who should be speedily silenced; and who should be allowed his voice. Obviously, the trusted and long-term branch manager / foreman / assessor / team leader° is going to score higher in the Survival stakes than the apprentice,° the powerless° complainant,° the "troublemaker"° - or the new recruit. Whatever the dossier of evidence, it will be ignored if its findings are inconsistent with a defendant's good reputation. Ironically, the fatter dossier, the *more* likely it is that it will be laid to one side, unread. See Filtering. *CAUSE/ RESULT   /   MOTIVATION*

SELECTIVE   REDUNDANCY 5
Redundancy is not always a carefully thought-out business. It may actually be *a Receiver* who wields the axe **,** not even the old owners**.** Selectivity shows preference for the higher-paid employee to go before the lower-paid ;° the woman to go before the man ; the favoured one° to go before the one out-of-favour ; the immigrant before the native. Pregnant° women, and perceived troublemakers,° are definitely in line for the chop. *RESULT   /   MOTIVATION*

SELF-APPRAISAL 5
By consenting to Self-Appraisal, an employee shows enormous trust in her line manager° or employer not to use its results oppressively. Personality profiles / tests° are notoriously unreliable - as is any questionnaire that can be answered tactically. *ASSOCIATION*

SELF-ESTEEM 10
Self-Esteem is arguably *the golden key* to all human endeavour. Often taken for granted in the positive, Self-Esteem can never be discounted in the (more frequent) negative : when it is depleted, or at risk of disappearing altogether. Self-Esteem lies at the base of all eating disorders, much guilt,° most domestic violence,° many instances of bullying, ° incapability, rivalry,° heads-to-head, target fulfilment,° energy....everything. Take Self-Esteem out of almost any equation, and nothing's left. *ASSOCIATION / MOTIVATION / RESPONSE*

SELF-EXPLOITATION 7
On the surface, Self-Exploitation sounds like a contradiction of terms. But several prostitutes, drug addicts, students, strivers and self-employed operators *do* exploit themselves, or work unpaid overtime,° or sell themselves short. Quite a few enterprising entrepreneurs actually pay themselves nothing until their shops or businesses are established. Relevant here is the "planting" of Self-Exploitation. To be a good masochist,° the masochist must have been taught by a role-model : a parent or husband or work partner or stakeholder or trafficker.° So that low remuneration and those long hours are not entirely *accidental*. It might well be a past employee was so oppressed and undervalued° that she carried over her damaged self-worth° into self-employment.
CAUSE / MOTIVATION

SELFHOOD 9

Selfhood is a very useful term for self-confidence,° self-respect,° self-regard,° or self preservation.° Attaining Selfhood in the workplace is aided by autonomy° and degrees of trust.° Selfhood also prospers in, and through, a happy home. Selfhood, in turn, counteracts defeatism.° See also Self-Esteem. *RESPONSE*

SELF-PRESERVATION 9

When the oppressed one feels strained to breaking point, she will either resign, or bury her head, or keep her head down,° or call on co-workers,° or fall back on coping mechanisms. Her aim, not unnaturally, is Self-Preservation. Conversely, the co-worker° who considers herself at risk of being next in line of fire will also aim for Self-Preservation, discreet silence , *even where* that is to the detriment of the oppressed one. At the same time, the closely scrutinized, or guilty,° or incriminated, or inefficient line manager° - sometimes also the office bully° - will *also* aim for Self-Preservation : not wishing to be complained° about or found out in any whilst on holiday ! Whole managements are tipped - or coerced - to the extremity of Self-Preservation : very successfully so in the face of many a news report, court judgement, strike°- or damning inspection. *FACTOR / MOTIVATION*

SELF-REGARD 9

If the employee sacrifices Self-Regard - or is robbed of it - she will not be able to work at her best; nor bring about the advancement, enrichment, and ultimate satisfaction° of her employer. *RESPONSE*

SELF-RESPECT 10
Self-Respect is so important that it is key to any examination of, and all discussions around, workplace oppression. Self-respect is a delicate flower, easily squashed by bullying,° overwork,° banter,° gossip,° marginalization,° scapegoating, °whatever. *RESPONSE*

SENIORITY 7
As mentioned elsewhere in this Dictionary, the notion of Seniority is everso prevalent in the workplace : Seniority by age, date of employment, status,° rank, bonus, salary, responsibility° - or even Union old-staging. This only serves to *highlight* the person being leant on : the new recruit, or person transferred over, who can definitely *not* claim Seniority. As always, power° holds the balance in any complaint° or dispute° or protocol° or target° to be achieved. And raw power - like being assailed from on high - is quite intimidating.°
FACTOR / or CAUSE

SEXISM 9
Sexism in the Workplace is so vast a topic, it demands a book (or a series of radio programmes) all of its own. Suffice it here to say that Sexism should *always* be taken into account and raised in any discussion of oppression, whether at work or anywhere else.

Sexism is just as much a problem - maybe *more of a problem* - where woman supervises man ; woman supervises woman ; man supervises man ; only men work in a department ; *only women* work in department....but it does have a page in the manual !°

The biggest gender gap, at home just as much as at work, remains man overseeing woman ; powerful° man employing younger / powerless° woman ; or male organization employing just one woman. *CAUSE / FACTOR / MOTIVATION*

SEXUAL HARASSMENT 9

Sexual Harassment is far wider - some would argue far more *widespread* - than sexism,° although the two are related. Harassment includes homophobia,° lewd comments, unpleasantly sexist jokes,° assessment of the beauty or ugliness or potency or sexual history of colleagues,° touching, groping,° molesting - *or asking too many intimate questions*. Whether or not certain behaviours were considered normal, even amusing, in the past, in the present climate, Sexual Harassment is likely to be against the letter and the spirit of employment practice, employment law. It might even qualify for a couple of pages in the manual.°

Male co-workers, even male managers, often protest that innuendo° is fun and that women in the workplace should be broad-shouldered enough both to tolerate it - and join in ! That naivety ignores where women have already come from. What feels threatening° *is* threatening. *CAUSE / MOTIVATION*

SHADOW [SHADOWING] 7

The psychological theory of Shadow is that each person guards her Shadow with scarcely conscious vigilance : so that nobody impinges upon it / takes it up / stalks.° Many customer service points now have privacy lines painted on the ground, all because of Shadowing. Bullies° are notorious for gobbling up the Shadows of their victims . But hope is at hand. The *oppressed one* can secretly gobble up her oppressor's shadow : to his immediate chagrin. A useful - possibly overdue - turning of the tables, turning of the screw. *CAUSE / or RESPONSE*

SHADY DEALING 7
Wherever there is Shady Dealing in an organization, it taints all employees : even those not at all complicit in those transactions ; even those actively seeking *to expose them*. Shady Dealing is oppressive because it places extra burden on all workers ; also extra risk.° And denies them pride° at the end of each working day.　　　　FACTOR

[THE] SHAKE-UP 6
The problem with inspections,° visitations, crack-downs,° and Shake-Ups is that they tend to impact upon innocent employees as well as those guilty of some shortfall.° They also tend to be panicky, and rushed. Shake-Ups afford no space or consideration to diligent employees who have steadfastly attempted to steer a course away from Shake-Up ! Then there are redundancies° to bring into the unwelcome equation.　　　　　　　　　　　*ASSOCIATION / MOTIVATION*

SHIFT WORKING 6
Shift Working was one of the earliest repercussions of time-and-motion° studying. Managers realized they could increase output,° decrease energy costs, *and* meet delivery targets,° through 24 hour working : in some professions an absolute essential. Shifts do not, however, sit easily with family commitments,° leisure,° fitness, or sleep patterns.° Nor are Night Shifts always very well governed.
　　　　　　　　　　　　　　　　　　　　　ASSOCIATION

SHORTFALL 5
Shortfall comes in many guises : falling short on the till, on performance, on conveyor-belt output - or, at its most complex, not being or becoming the employee one's employer once hoped for. Wish that Shortfall was dealt with straightway, and in a conciliatory° frame of mind. More usually, Shortfall is an nasty undercurrent.°　*FACTOR*

SHORTLISTING 4
Shortlisting - sometimes called "longlisting" - for internal promotion is quite a carrot. Yet that carrot is definitely *not* dangled in front of the unfavoured, or disfavoured, employee. Crucially, Shortlisting is not as scientific - nor as logical - as it is made out to be.   *ASSOCIATION*

SHORT-TERM   CONTRACTS 8
In a flexible° labour market - particularly one over-reliant on working women with dependent children - the Short-Term Contract does have a role to play. After all, much contracting° by definition has to be Short-Term...otherwise jobs would last forever. Even so, Short-Term wages are not a lot of good for those with *long-term* ambitions° or caring responsibilities.° Additionally, a firm or shop or school or hospital employing mostly Short-Term Contractors risks undermining staff solidarity ;° and not treating their transient employees with sufficient respect.°   *ASSOCIATION / MOTIVATION*

SHOULDERING   RESPONSIBILITY 6
It sounds so harmless, good hearted indeed : a line manager° or co-worker° |Shouldering Responsibility : in order to "get everything done." With the clear implication that someone, somewhere, is *not* pulling her weight : thus leaving more on the Shoulders of someone else!   So this very masculine° metaphor is yet another excuse for bullying° and intimidation.°   *MOTIVATION*

SHOUTING 8
Shouting at work is only justifiable and excusable - though *not* unavoidable - where there is heavy machinery is operating, or extraction

happening, nearby. Shouting can all too soon become negative. Shouting is also the last resort of the irritated foremen or upset line manager.° Forget not that oppressed ones *also* Shout- when they have lost their grip / lost the plot. Shouting sounds bad ; frequently causing upset. Some people say Shouting is even worse *behind closed doors*. And what's the difference between Shouting and the raised voice ?
CAUSE / RESULT / FACTOR

SICK BUILDING SYNDROME 6
Research is still at an early stage into Sick Building Syndrome. A dysfunctional building can cause the unprepared employee untold extra stress :° whether through asbestos, concrete-sickness, low ceilings, poorly-maintained air conditioning ...or beneath the far too bright fluorescent lighting so favoured by local government. Recirculation of viruses is also a probability in the badly designed office / annexe/ finishing room. CAUSE / ASSOCIATION

SICK LEAVE [ABSENCE THROUGH ILLNESS] 8
Sick Leave impacts upon Workplace Oppression in many ways. Many are the Illnesses that have a psychosomatic component - or result from accident / self-neglect / self-harm. Therefore there is an element of guilt° in Illness : especially Illness that might have caused co-workers° a lot of grief, many unwanted extra hours° or unexpected tasks.

So : *returning*° *to* work after Illness is not a neutral act either. Co-workers° might express far more anger / relief than they do sympathy. In fact the whole organization might be covertly hostile to the oppressed one disgraced° further by illness. In such circumstances, sickness monitoring° may not help either. In the longer term there is here a perfect circle : workplace stress° leads to Illness which in turn leads to further stress.° Tribunals° now recognize that if ill employees return° to the same place that caused their Illness, without vast improvements, reinstated employees cannot function at their best. The root causes of Sickness must be addressed impartially - and not just by the line manager.°   RESULT / FACTOR

SICKNESS MONITORING 7

Local and central Government welcomed with open arms the USA practice of Sickness Monitoring. Many other large employers quickly followed suit. The logic was impeccable : no absence is entirely random : an Act of God. In fact absence happens more often on Mondays and Fridays ; some absences through "Sickness" neatly coincide with industrial action ;° and not all absentees take the same amount of Sick Leave each year, let alone conform to equal patterns of absence due to Sickness. Answer : why not Monitor Sickness on a graph ? And compare employee with employee, year with year, department with department, profession with profession ?

Human Resources however are not always as subtly as they are statistically inclined. Many boards are known to go at the returning° employee (still ill ?) like a bull in a china shop. " When were you first ill ?" "What were the exact symptoms?" " What did the doctor say?" "When did you first feel well ?" "Was your husband ill at the same time?" "Were your children off school at the same time?"

Questions are typically fired at the returnee° so fast that there is no space for her to protest° at her manager's assumption: that she is a malingerer,° a pragmatist, a skiver, or an exceptionally conscientious parent ! Worse : if she returns symptom-less, as after a bout of mental illness.° Some pressure.° *Extra* pressure. FACTOR / MOTIVATION

SIEGE [THE SIEGE MENTALITY] 8
Feeling under Siege at work is an uncomfortable place to be. It's like a bombardment :° one assault after another - until the oppressed one thinks she has nothing more to give. The Siege Mentality also eats into staff morale,° their coping mechanisms,° and productivity.° To be Besieged is a state of learned helplessness ° not inducive to happiness° and relaxation. In fact an employee under Siege is constantly on edge, if only for fear° of what upset° will happen next. See Defensiveness.
FACTOR / RESULT

SILO   THINKING 5
Silo Thinking is a relatively new term for an old phenomenon : listening only to people who are highly likely to agree with you ; more important, people who will not challenge you. Silo Thinking is remarkably self-perpetuating. Only the elite or Gang of Four° have a voice - and that voice is as comforting as it is pleasing. Anybody: any " rebel" or "troublemaker"° or "outsider"° - expressing a *different* view of an outfit or its prospects is automatically expelled from the Silo (if they had ever been allowed anywhere near the Silo!). And whistleblowers° are, of course, considered the lowest of all pond life.   *FACTOR*

SLACKING 7
Slacking is one of those catch-all terms for the suspicion° that various employees are not pulling their weight.   An obvious, though intimidating,° response by management is to track° a worker from dawn to dusk, spying° on her, double-checking her output, asking for extra time-sheets and evidence that she has done what she was asked to do.   Again, the alleged Slacker faces a conundrum. Once the label

malingerer° is round her neck, she cannot shed it, however hard she works ; however assiduously she makes amends !   CAUSE

SLAVERY 9
Because the British are convinced Slavery was abolished by William Wilberforce, they are no longer on the lookout for it. Worse, nobody counters or prosecutes it, because it is *so far* from the human imagination that any human being should stoop to Slavery. Exploitation:° yes. Trafficking:° yes. Low Pay:° yes. An atrocious work environment : yes. Servants :° yes. Slavery : no !
Yet Slavery exists and flourishes in cottage industry ; in some gypsy encampments ; in the employment of illegal immigrants and asylum seekers ; within the servants' quarters of rich mansions ; upstairs in backstreet factories ; whilst cockle picking; in the lifting potatoes and turnips; where children work laboriously for parents or uncles ; during internships.° Nobody suspects Slavery. Why should they ? Nor is it in anybody but the Slave's interest to go to the Police°? And that's exactly what no Slave is allowed - or empowered - to do. All Slavery is oppressive, and continues more or less unabated, *despite* the feeble provisions of a new Modern Slavery Act.   CAUSE /   MOTIVATION

SLEDGING 9
Sledging is a term borrowed from the Australian cricket-field. Sledging is the opposite of secret briefing, because Sledging is very open. The co-worker° or line manager° doing the Sledging *wants* to be heard, but only at the level of whispering. Sledging undermines° the oppressed one because it is half-heard, intuitively picked up - not broadcast. Frequently, the Sledger pretends his words are *in*audible. Advanced Sledging involves heavy sighs, exaggerated gasps of disbelief,

disingenuous merriment. The aim of Sledging is simple : to knock someone off her perch and *keep her* humble. ° *CAUSE / MOTIVATION*

SLEEPING ON THE JOB 5
Sleeping on the Job is both a metaphor and a reality. People Sleep at work because they have had to work beforehand for a different agency or outpost. Lorry drivers, frighteningly Sleep-deprived, also Sleep at the wheel - and with disastrous consequences. A few standby jobs *demand* that an employee sleeps in a bunk-bed or on bare boards: with the important proviso (s)he can be woken at any moment for the next "emergency." This all puts pressure° on the employee or contractor° in dreamland. And paid carers° routinely go to Sleep, unwillingly, because they have been up all the night before by their charge suffering upset stomach or dementia. *ASSOCIATION*

SLEEPLESSNESS 8
Sleeplessness or insomnia is directly related to bad days at work past; more crucially, bad days at work still *to come*. The oppressed one is very unlikely to sleep soundly, *or* to sleep 7 hours. Instead, bad dreams, forebodings, will crowd in upon wanted unconsciousness. At the extreme end, a tyrannized° employee will sleep barely at all. Ironically, when she then turns up at work, "next day," she will perform *worse* because of her weariness and wariness. That gives her employer excuse enough to persecute° her more. *FACTOR / RESULT*

SLIGHTS 7
The trouble with Slights is that they are often more imagined than real. Slights conform to a tally. A score is kept by employer and employee alike of what has gone wrong - which words have been carelessly spoken ? - so that this score can be dragged up whenever. Similar Slight-counting happens in marriage. If only all workers were as adept

keeping a tally of achievements° and positive results ! See Sledging ; also Quiver Full of Arrows. *FACTOR / MOTIVATION*

SMOKING 5

Smoking is yet another of those factors which is the cause as well as a result of some oppression in the workplace. Smoking is usually forbidden at work, indoors - but is still sometimes permitted *outdoors*. That makes for a "Smoking Club" which being outside° of might not be very clever. Or else, the Smoker is marginalized° because of time lost whilst Smoking. Knowing that a colleague° is longing for a Smoke might encourage some managers actually to prolong meetings/tasks where that Smoker has to be present ! *CAUSE / RESULT / ASSOCIATION*

SOCIAL PSYCHOLOGY 7

Social Psychology is a discipline - now a hundred years old - concentrating on the ways people react in company; how entrprises or clubs interact with their members and each other ; also how families experience and contribute to the outside world. Social Psychology literature, primarily originating in the United States, is extensive and enlightening where the workplace is concerned. Industrial Psychology° is a kindred discipline : again deserving a book all of its own. Some of Social Psychology's best insights relate to groups,° group dynamics, and behaviour analysis. *ASSOCIATION*

SOLIDARITY 5

Solidarity can be rather a fraught and troubled word : not unrelated to strikes° and scabbing.° One out ; all out ! But Solidarity does have a more positive connotation : where co-workers° stick or stand together against the common enemy : bully,° line manager,° quality-controller, tyrant,° whoever. And the oppressed employee also subject to domestic violence° needs all the Solidarity she can get. *RESPONSE*

SPARRING 7
As with two little boys play-fighting, the simulated struggle all too readily turns from joy to tears.° So it is in the workplace. The oppressor, if not always the oppressed one, comes to accept Sparring as a healthy constituent of staff development.° Sparring - as also sledging° - is *fun*. " I'm just sounding you out;" " I'm just teasing out your position;" "I'm just testing the temperature;" "I'm only providing the feedback° you requested..." Some banter° is both acceptable and part of the job. But when *does* that joy turn into tears° ? *FACTOR / MOTIVATION*

SPITE 8
We forget Spite at our peril. It seems so obvious : a bully,° oppressor, or line manager,° has acted out of "pure" Spite. We can never divine *the origin* of that Spite - envy,° rivalry,° past *sibling* rivalry,° slights° - but we know it when we see it. Co-workers° can - and do - also operate out of Spite. *MOTIVATION*

SPLIT SHIFTS 9
Shift° working is hard enough without the Split Shift. The latter demands of an employee that he or she takes just two or three hours' break between rostered° assignments. Typically, a hotel worker will live on the premises and do breakfast 6 till 10, lunch 12 till 3, dinner 6 till 10pm. Or else a cleaner will come in until 11am and after 5pm. The result is a period of time that *cannot usefully be used* for anything else: due to clockwatching, flitting, pottering, dozing, recovery, preparation. The world is upside down, leisure impeded. *FACTOR*

[THE] SPONGE 8

Images of the Sponge are everso useful in our understanding of workplace oppression. Because a Sponge recalls she who will absorb all the pressures° and humiliation° - all the sledging° - she is subjected to, often without complaint° or revenge.   *RESULT / RESPONSE*

SPOUSES IN THE WORKPLACE 4

Generally, the smaller, or larger, the Workplace, the more likely Spouses will be employed : not unusually, one technically answerable to the other ! And, with the probable exception of brother/mother/father/daughter outfits, Spouses can be bad news. It's all a question of loyalty and solidarity;° also how to separate home and work life. Spouse *bans* are not unknown. Nor is dual oppression : bullied° initially by woman, bullied in the repeat by husband of that woman! Looking in, as one unattached : not an easy place to be.

FACTOR

STAFF DEVELOPMENT 7

Staff Development is a management term for all Staff Relations, all in-service training courses,° all assessments,° all appraisals,° and all promotions° that makes a workforce more cohesive,° more productive° - and, hopefully, more loyal. Therefore Staff Development is an inherently *neutral* term. Problems arise when commitment to Staff Development is *absent* ; worse, when bullies° take control° of the process.   *RESPONSE*

STAFF TURNOVER   [HIGH STAFF TURNOVER] 8
Staff Turnover is not an Act of God. It always has a reason : ideally promotion,° pregnancy,° advancement or retirement.° Where Staff Turnover is *high*, especially if it is high in one department, one workshop, one team, that should cause alarm to senior management, awakening them from slumber.° Is one defined outpost unhappy,° unsettling ? Does that one outpost have an insecure° manager : perhaps newly appointed, inexperienced, less qualified on paper than his underlings.° Have there been any complaints° or grievances° emanating from that single work setting - where other sections are not causing equal concern ? Staff Turnover is actually quite *expensive*. Recruitment and re-training do not happen overnight. Maybe time to *recall* a rogue° - or struggling - leader and re-train him ! FACTOR/ RESULT / ASSOCIATION / MOTIVATION / RESPONSE

STAFF WELFARE [STAFF WELL-BEING] 10
Staff Welfare is an all-embracing term for worker harmony,° prosperity, advancement, general Well-being. It is not *automatic* that Staff Welfare will be a priority within any organization ; but, counter-intuitively, and despite extra fuss, extra expenditure, extra resources, it does help if Staff Welfare *becomes* priority number one.   RESPONSE

STALEMATE 7
Stalemate is rather an unpleasant word for rather an unpleasant state of affairs : where there has been no conciliation° or mediation;° less so constructive negotiation ° within the context of a collegiate° working environment. Stalemates leave an oppressed one with nowhere to go. She is preoccupied enough with her damaged status;° also worries at

home, without having to contend with either her union's Stalemate or the Stalemate reached in her own grievance.°   *CAUSE / RESULT*

STALKING 7
Stalking is a particularly nasty form of harassment at work : one that affects women more than men. It need not always have *sexual* overtones - although that is what the public understands best; more fascination, objectification, infatuation. The term Stalking is also used at work to express dissatisfaction° with an immediate line manager° who is always on your back ; never trusting you to do the job without close supervision,° unremitting appraisal.° The oppressed one feels she is being tracked,° literally *and* metaphorically.   *MOTIVATION*

STANDBY....6
Standby Contracts are another way round minimum wage° legislation. The arrangement is for an employee to be perpetually *available*, but only *paid* as and when. Standby only operates justly within the context of long-established self-employed status *and* at a worker's explicit behest.   *FACTOR   /   RESULT*

STATUS   DEGRADATION 10
In his work on stigma,° Erving Goffman uncovered Status Degradation: a process later developed by Harold Garfunkel as : "Communication between persons whereby the public identity of the Actor is transformed into something looked on as *lower* in the scheme of social relations." The Actor often then endures a " Status Degradation Ceremony" - where his / her *emasculated identity* is confirmed with cheers, jeers and laughter.

Garfunkel was not alone among sociologists in attributing Status degradation to *motivation* - the motivation of the socially valid - not behaviour : the alleged behaviour of those declared socially in-valid. In other words, the Degraded worker has not under-performed. (S)he has simply failed to live up to the categorization, the preferences, the understanding (misunderstanding) *and the approval ratings* of her superiors / inferiors.

In the workplace, Degraded Status might be so systemic that it has gone unquestioned for decades. Here, Central Management keeps tight control° of budgets, planning, the design of products, also the corporate knowledge-base, leaving their demoralized,° de-skilled° workers to operate the machinery, until it breaks down, to take down messages, and to do pre-programmed tasks : always conforming to a laid-down routine, in strictly laid-down working conditions, timed by the clock.° In other words, Management manages, workers work.

Goffman's Status Degradation, being a "total" procedure, was far easier to translate within a total institution : a setting such as battalion, battleship, squadron, prison, psychiatric hospital, boarding school, where ordained leaders/scoffers held total sway. Degraders not only recognize but also *welcome* the submission that comes with entry to a place where hierarchies° and external controls are both accepted and acceptable. Many total institutions are thus ready-made tyrannies.°

That still leaves, however, a great number of Degrading measures that can be brought into the ordinary factory, the unsupervised outpost, the busy, but lonely, office, the giddy shop or to the uninterrupted conveyor belt. First : " show them who's boss." Second : give out the orders. Third : read out the punishments. Four : parade some poor employee recently punished / sanctioned. Five : get the barber in. Six : yell at the late-comer or the clown. Seven : insist on silence. Eight : humiliate° any joker / non-conformist° in front of all his or her work-mates / co-workers.° Nine: drag out the lead-swinger° who has not met the target.° Ten : make no secret you are firing° the recalcitrant.

Status Degradation therefore does what it says on the tin : it crucially lowers an employee's self-regard,° pride,° self-respect,° reputation,° selfhood,° *identity*, until (s)he is quiescent. *CAUSE   / MOTIVATION*

STATUS   DIFFERENTIAL [S] 8
Status Differential is sociological shorthand for a gap in the ranks. Because most organizations are still rigidly hierarchical° - as opposed to egalitarian or collegiate° - it stands to reason that Status Differentials (salary differentials° too?) matter enormously. Woe to the new recruit who forgets that ! And all the research points to *greater tension* between close, approximate, or adjoining, ranks of employee, than between bottom and top, floor-scrubber and MD, houseman and consultant. The UK generally is still class-ridden° : awarding plaudits to favoured ones,° those who have risen most elegantly from fairly privileged° beginnings.   *FACTOR   /   MOTIVATION*

STAYING   LATE 8
Presenteeism°: Staying Late to satisfy / please / accommodate management is detrimental to overall health and the oppressed one's resourcefulness the following day or week. Staying Late also raises child-care° issues ; also delaying or detracting from family celebrations / treats. Reasonable overtime might be requested / sought out by employees, but *routine* Staying Late (quite often without remuneration / or thanks) is indicative of a dysfunctional workplace. Best if the line manager° herself disappears at exactly 5-15pm. to set a good example to the rest of the team or office or shift.°   *RESULT*

STEAMROLLERING 9
Many employees feel Steamrollered by their employers - or by a single employee of that employer. Steamrollering is the wilful oversight of employees' well-being ;° more generally, not acknowledging the added value workers can contribute within their work settings. Steamrollering often accompanies the purge,° the rampage,° or the new order.° It is no tribute to an employer when employees lurch from crisis° to crisis, feeling constantly besieged.° Nor does the Steamroller aid productivity° in the long run - whereas that is often its self-justification. *CAUSE / MOTIVATION*

STEPPING BACK 7
"Why don't you simply stand back from the fray ?" is the standard, and simplistic, advice given to someone going under at work. And there is some logic in that stratagem. Become a member of the audience, not the protagonist. And *when* we stand back - perhaps at the weekend or on holiday, or even during lunch° - the situation does ease slightly. Maybe there is an ally° somewhere, even a sympathetic senior manager. Or maybe there is a mitigating factor, a way out. Standing Back, or Stepping Aside, is never a wasted exercise. More than once, the person looking in from afar suddenly finds inspiration in a past memo,° or one clause in her contract, a witnessed understanding, a special letter sent, approval already given. Such a forgotten lifesaver then translates into a realistic get-out-of-jail card. Because oppression in the workplace does resemble imprisonment! *RESPONSE*

STEREOTYPING 6
Everybody carries round in his or her head Stereotypes of other people: (usually derogatory) images of those considered inferior - outsiders.° The beauty, or curse, of the Stereotype is that it is not only long-lasting,

but also a pastiche. And where a more powerful° manager adheres to his Stereotype of *sexy secretary*, *militant unionist*, *lazy shift-worker*, *dozy night-watchman*, *woman on maternity*, or *towel-wearing Sikh*, he robs that human being of actuality, potential - and reward.° CAUSE / MOTIVATION

STIGMA   [STIGMATIZATION   ] 8
The bestowing of Stigma is an enormous topic. Surviving° it is equally fraught. Originally a medical term, Stigma is now more sociological. Oppressed people, *oppressed workers*, all carry a Stigma, maybe based where they live like in a ghetto, a prison,° a trailer site or a council estate ; maybe the way they look or dress.° Stigma helps people who want to stereotype° other people. So one human ideal is to bear no Stigma. Needless to say, returnees° from battle or sickness or nervous breakdown° are Stigmatized - as are *ex*-jailbirds. Ironically, in some one-industry villages, *where you work*, as sole provocation, might be Stigmatizing. CAUSE / RESULT

STORM 7
The meteorological metaphor of Storm is always relevant to the workplace : Storm brewing, Storm overhead, Storm abating, the Perfect Storm. Yet there does not *have to be* Storm, nor the expectation of Storm, at work. There is no requirement for a climate of fear° and turmoil. Storms, then, are a sign of an unstable, maybe unsafe,° work setting. CAUSE / RESULT

STRESS   [STRESS   AUDITS   ] 9
Stress is one of those words so ubiquitous in the context of paid and unpaid employment that its very use can be meaningless. Better words are humiliation,° disempowerment,° unfair criticism.° Also Stress at

work is not easily detached from accompanying Stresses as a spouse or a driver or a parent or a daughter - or indeed, as a consumer.
All organizations should hold Stress Audits once every 6 or 8 weeks : in order to nip *avoidable* levels of Stress in the bud. Stress-releasers include : early going-home time, reduced targets,° managers labouring alongside their teams, light music, trust games. *RESULT / RESPONSE*

STRESS COUNTERS 6
Modern research tools allow Stress to be counted. Stress Counters - or contributors - include tight time limits,° productivity targets,° pulsating background music, light pollution, the sick building syndrome,° parking, hot-desking,° loud telephone conversations and expected, but unwanted, overtime.° Once an employee scores 70 out of 100 for these Counters counting, a wise employer might begin to address some of those factors.   *CAUSE / ASSOCIATION*

STRUCK OFF [LOSING LICENCE TO PRACTICE] 8
Being Stuck Off by one's professional body or royal college is the ultimate ignominy. But it might be one cure for persistent bullies.° Those tyrants° are far too often idolized by senior management. Yet bullying° and intimidation are most heinous crimes where other employees are relying on their work for personal and financial survival.
                    RESULT / RESPONSE

STRATIFICATION 6
It is often said that the 6-storey company headquarters is like an angel cake or a Cliffside made up of several layers of different rock : bosses and executive dining-room, top floor ; administration, fourth floor ; production, second and third floors ; packing and despatch, first floor ; Reception, lockers and workers' dining-room, ground floor; janitors,

cleaners and waste-disposal, basement. Other work settings will not necessarily conform to this pattern - but the truth is not far off. We are used to hierarchies° in Britain. And bosses have traditionally been remote from the workforce. But there are other models of partnership.°

ASSOCIATION

SUBCONTRACTING [LABOUR ONLY SUBCONTRACTING] 9

The beauty of Subcontracting for Government departments, arms-length entities, rogue agencies, docks, cleaners and franchisees is that nobody can be held accountable for acts of omission or commission ; nobody can be asked awkward questions ; nobody can be blamed for shortfall;° with normal workplace procedures easily circumvented. Nor can any worker complain° to, or about, the gaffer whose identity is rarely unmasked. Labour Only Subcontracting (the LUMP) is even more perilous. Workers come. Workers go. With no awkward paper trails.

CAUSE   /   FACTOR

SUBORDINATES 9

Sadly, hierarchies° *are* alive and well in most workplaces - despite other models of staff deployment proving themselves more beneficial, more productive.° Certain workplaces like the police station,° civil service, or barracks° cannot be understood deprived of stratification.° One by-product of ranking is the Subordinate. And Subordinates, even when called interns,° apprentices,° NQTs, trainees, rather than *Subordinates*, feel subordinated. And that is an uncomfortable place to be. Especially where a harsher foreman or line manager° gloats over the prospect of Subordination, alleged *in*subordination, victimhood.° And it should be taken as read that bullying° is never justified *because of* status.°

FACTOR   /   MOTIVATION

SUBSERVIENCE 6
Subservience is a general term for malleability : for obediently falling into line. Unctuous bowing and scraping. Not unexpectedly, the bulldozer° does not worry about the rubble any more than the slaughter-man feels for the fated lamb.   *CAUSE / MOTIVATION*

SUCCESS 9
It is very hard, seemingly contradictory, to talk of bullying,° tracking° or hounding ° in terms of Success. Yet bullies° *want* Success. That is why they bully° : to see the tears° -with the added incentive they have moved the goalposts° before underlings° can do better. At its worst, the oppressor's Success leads to transfer request,° resignation,° or personal disintegration.°

On a more positive note, Success can be *an antidote* to humiliation° in the workplace. If sceptical colleagues° or line managers° sniff Success, they might want to share in the reflected glory. Also, it raises that one, Successful, worker's self-esteem° a tonic: Success against the odds.   *RESULT / or RESPONSE*

SUICIDE 10
Suicide is such an important subject that it cannot usefully be covered in such a short space as this. Suffice it to say that hundreds of employees each year *do* take their own lives *for work-related reasons*. Some of this "prompting" must be due to bullying° or workplace oppression. Yet Coroners are far more likely to cite *home* worries or disturbance of the balance of mind as more significant factors than tyranny.° One wonders what the bully° might, or might not, be thinking when he hears of the ultimate sacrifice, that most conclusive letter of resignation.° Better that *every* Inquest covers recent employment.   *RESULT*

SUPERIORITY COMPLEX 6
One must treat the term : *Superiority* Complex with some caution, as it is too easily attached to somebody who is simply a bit unworldly ; at the same time, very good at her job. It is also a cop-out for racism,° because the term frequently alludes to the "reverse racism" of black people "rising above their station." Ironically, the term Superior is still willingly used in the workplace to denote *anybody* of higher rank; anybody further up in the pecking-order, where status-differentials° have such a bearing.. As such, "Superior" is an expression of admiration ; of conferred honour, due deference...implying somebody sits below, somebody who is *not* quite so exalted !   *ASSOCIATION*

SUPERVISION 8
Supervision *ought* to be a neutral activity, welcomed most by the apprentice° or newest recruit. Unfortunately, in workplaces under severe pressure,° like charities and social services, Supervision risks becoming a tool° of oppression : somewhere the oppressed one can be taken aside, criticized° and put back on the right track. The oppressive Supervisor is quite often also foreman and line manager;° thus the cowed employee is not empowered° to put her side of the argument. Nearly all Supervision is intensely private, even secretive.° At its most intimidating, the session is like a fireplace into which all complaints,° shortfall,° and unreasonable demands are cast as fuel.   *FACTOR*

SURVIVAL   [SURVIVAL STRATEGY] 9
Addressing, even conquering, oppression in the workplace really is a matter of Survival : Survival as an employee, Survival as a co-worker, Survival in that Department, Survival in that Company, Survival as a parent/or partner, Survival as a well person, *Survival alive.*

Maybe the oppressor : be he owner, MD, line manager, or computer whizz-kid, detaches oppression from the chance of Survival. Maybe he blames° the person who is going under *for* going under! Or maybe he writes his next testimonial or funeral oration without delving any deeper. It sounds ridiculous that anyone should take work so seriously as to let it get at him or her: threatening their very Survival. But if you are in a position of despair,° you do not see the wider world. You do not count life's blessings. Because daily work, daily volunteering, daily earning, daily humiliation,° act in concert to obliterate all other considerations.

It follows that Survival in the workplace must be top priority for a good employer - and indeed a good employee. A bad or thoughtless manager may well not have an employee's Survival at heart. Perversely, it might actually *suit* him to *get rid of* someone he sees as a thorn in the flesh: an alleged outsider° or troublemaker.°

Gaffer magnified, worker belittled,° means anybody under pressure would be wise to develop a Survival Strategy : one that includes allies,° coping mechanisms,° time out,° complaint,° grievance,° jettisoning workload, answering back, pincers,° whatever. Such a Strategy is not selfish, rather self-enhancing, self-preserving,° philanthropic if it serves to rid an organization of tyranny.° *RESPONSE*

SUSPENSION 9

Suspension - thankfully, still a fairly rare disposal - is an *extremely* ambiguous, delicate and uncomfortable place to be. Suspension usually happens after a complaint,° a mistake,° misconduct,° a criminal enquiry, an unbalancing of the books or a "personality conflict."° Sometimes Suspension is accompanied by conditions : *Do not go into work* ; *Do not contact the complainant(s)* ; *Do not contact former colleagues* ; *Do not make any public statement.*

It is not uncommon for Suspended employees to be stuck at home, lonely and isolated° for weeks and months on end. Nobody visits - not even Personnel or Occupational Welfare, the very people charged with reaching a resolution! Also mud sticks. No children or staff in a school, no typists, no fellow doctors, no one else on the tills, really believes the Suspended worker is *innocent.* Which worsens the position. And if anything else could deteriorate, Suspensions very rarely result in reinstatement to the same position as that which the employee left. Management is quick to codge together a leaving-package : a pay-off, a no-detriment testimonial, some back-pay, a gagging clause, compensation. Little of this lifts the morale° of the person Suspended who knows he or she is blameless;° alternatively, the scapegoat° for *somebody else's* failings. That low morale,° that destroyed self-belief,° that total distrust° of management, is then carried over into new employment, *if ever that eventuality is made possible* through a new employer's clean slate. RESULT / MOTIVATION

SUSPICION [CLIMATE OF SUSPICION] 9
The original suspicion might be quite justified : a missing handbag, an unbalanced ledger, an unvisited customer, some unpaid fines, a few deliveries not delivered, a court case thrown out. Cause for real alarm is semi-permanent Suspicion; and Suspicion that falls first on the *weakest* employee: the newcomer, the Scapegoat,° the outsider,° or the oppressed one herself. CAUSE / FACTOR / RESULT

SWEATING 7
It is almost a biological certainty that the employee under pressure or under fire will Sweat profusely, sometimes shivering uncontrollably. Unanticipated arguments,° complaints,° discussions and setbacks° at

work (not infrequently accompanied by bad news from home) lead to the Sweat, which in turn might lead to frozen awareness° or subsequent substandard driving, underperformance.° Best to have a quiet room at Reception where employees can go before being overwhelmed. Also : relaxation exercises. RESULT

SWEATSHOPS 8
By definition, Sweatshops are oppressive and exploitative. Sweatshops come in many guises : anonymous industrial units, back-street factories, cellars, garden sheds, remote farms, post-rooms - *or people's own homes*. Sweatshops would not be attractive to their owners if they were capable of exposure. Furthermore, thousands of Sweatshops exist behind - *or within* - respectable concerns. Such front organizations are paid handsomely to disguise their less reputable offshoots and interests.
CAUSE   /   MOTIVATION

TACTICAL   INTERVENTIONS 6
Provided an employer is alert and sensitive, he will intervene - or else Personnel will Intervene on his behalf - wherever an employee or shift is struggling. Such intervention is risky : because, in order to save one low-status person disappearing in the quagmire, a *trusted* manager might deservedly attract criticism° or relocation .° That is why most employers hesitate to do anything whatsoever in response to suspected or reported bullying.° The junior employee is far more expendable, much less to be trusted, than the known quantity.

Of course, there is nothing to stop co-workers° making Tactical Interventions. They can befriend the oppressed one, express allegiance - or even go to senior management and say the existing situation is intolerable. Management tools° are plentiful. But they need picking up in the first place ! RESPONSE

TAKEOVERS 7
Many workers, even managers, feel fairly content and secure° : *until* the day of Takeover. Takeovers are unlikely to be entirely seamless or harmonious.° The new owner might have come in during a fire-sale, or financed his Takeover through debt. So the new regime is anxious to avoid the extra cost or burden of employees they do not take to be quiescent, conformist,° productive,° let alone valued. ° So the exodus begins. Plus unplanned redundancies.°   *FACTOR / ASSOCIATION*

TAKING HOME WORK 7
For many decades, teachers, commercial travellers, office workers or office-based workers, have taken a portion of their work home. Some even work at home through holidays or illness° - or during that part of the week, or the night, when they are not on duty at all.

Expecting employees to take home logs, filing and computer programming, unpaid,° unrecognized, unrewarded, is definitely oppressive. That even applies where a worker "volunteers" to finish a report, or do the books, by her own fireside : that, where they are not already designated as home-based employees. An act of goodwill soon becomes *an expectation.*   *FACTOR / MOTIVATION*

TAKING ORDERS 8
The ability to Take Orders is elementary if you have joined a hierarchical° organization ; less expected where an employee is semi-autonomous - as in Probation, Advertizing, Public Relations, Architecture, or the Law. Squaddies° are not alone in being bawled out when they do not Take Orders. Yet a new recruit *ought* to worry about Orders. Not only might those Orders be arbitrary, unreasonable - or even illegal. Orders, as opposed to requests, might be irregular - or out-of-place where adults aim to work harmoniously with other adults.

Reluctance or *refusal* to Take Orders is actually counted as gross misconduct° or insubordination.°   *CAUSE / MOTIVATION*

TALKING THROUGH SITUATIONS & PROBLEMS 7
Provided that always the act of talking through an issue is *non-threatening,*° non-menacing, and non-judgmental, it is always worthwhile - even where there is a difference in rank° and salary between the two or more employees who are doing the talking through.

RESPONSE

TARGETS 10
Targets have many disadvantages, yet surprisingly few detractors. I first became aware of Targets in the school classroom : better GCSE results, higher attendance, quicker transfer of class, clean sheets on the football field. Schools even began to have Target-Days where each and every pupil was set a unique six-month Target. Before that, but vaguely off my radar, came *Sales' Targets*. Commercial travellers were paid commission° according to what they actually sold. Not unusually, many sales' staff came to be paid *only* commission. No sale : no food.

It was not long before shops paid their assistants on a part-commission, or commission-only° basis. No problem when the Minimum Wage° came along : simply make sure Commission earned is more than basic hours times Minimum Wage° rate, and make up the difference.

By the 1970s and 1980s, banks, offices, estate agents and, crucially, call centres° were all rewarding, incentivizing, staff with pay-by-results; and customers, investors even, were rarely told about this arrangement. Remarkably, a financial advisor might receive £2500 outright for selling a savings' plan worth £50000 : good money for half an hour's spiel. By Year 2000 - often long beforehand - Targets were *published*. Travel agents had them on the wall : "Sally sold 8 holidays yesterday, Simon 18!" Soon, Targets were announced in staff-meetings, with

everyone cheering or jeering when sales' figures were announced - with all the pregnant pauses you'd expect in Britain's Got Talent.
Needless to say, many employees are tearful,° and humiliated,° on learning they are bottom of the class. There has to be a *lowest*: fertile ground for bullying,° hire-and-fire,° "must-improve-most-improved-performance°," motivational lectures. *CAUSE / FACTOR / RESULT*

TEAM-BUILDING 6
Team-Building days, Team-Building exercises, are extremely useful, provided each member of the Team trusts° its leader / facilitator / joiner to speak and act honestly (but not too honestly) - and confidentially. Team-Building should never be used for humiliation,° marginalization,° or a ganging-up against the struggler, or someone struggling on that particular day or week. *RESPONSE*

TEAM LEADERS [TEAM LEADERSHIP] 7
Team Leaders, Team Supervisors or heads of department are not usually autonomous.° Although their ranks include many workplace bullies,° *most* Leaders are benign, conscientious and hardworking. For the small extra they are paid, these Leaders face sniping from above and below. In the end they can placate neither the Team they manage nor the senior management which granted their preferment. Caught in pincers,° the Leader might *himself* feel oppressed. *ASSOCIATION*

TEAM MORALE...8
Team Morale is as fragile a vase as individual Morale.° Not all employees, of course, work in Teams or cohorts or rooms. But many *do* rely on their co-workers.° Then come the Team meetings, Team targets,° Team scapegoats° - and, crucially, Team leaders.° Team Morale is most damaged when Targets° are missed, phone calls go

unanswered, orders are lost - or when complaints° flood in. Teams also suffer after harsh inspections° and crackdowns.° Team Morale is best seen as a potentially leaking basin. The oppressed one can be *lifted* by a magnificent Team, or *further ground down* within a dysfunctional Team.   *ASSOCIATION / RESPONSE*

TECHNOLOGICAL SKILL [TECH SAVVY] 6
For the next two decades, minimum, one cohort of recruits will have measurable and transferrable Technological Skills whilst some of their colleagues° approach computers / robots / systems with extreme nervousness, even fear.° Inevitably, this results in a two-speed floor on which managers must gently coax "old-stagers" into the sort of in-service training° where mistakes° are allowed.   *ASSOCIATION*

THANKYOU 9
"Thank you!" is a relatively rare response to excellent performance in the workplace. "What did you think I was paying you for ?" Yet when a key manager or co-worker says Thank you! sincerely, that one word transforms the oppressed one's day and her image of herself:° a similar glow to that left by praise° and positive feedback.°   *RESPONSE*

THEM & US 6
The Culture of Them & Us is age-old shorthand for confrontation,° and stalemate:° the detachment / entrenchment of managers and defeat of / contempt° for workers. In traditional and extractive industries, it may take many decades more to forget Them & Us.   *ASSOCIATION*

THIN SKINNED [THICK-SKINNED] 8
Whenever someone says they are having a hard time at work, perhaps with a wretched line manager,° they are told they are far too Thin

Skinned. They ought *to grow up* and be a bit more resilient. " Nobody would speak like that to you !" " Perhaps they were joking ?" " Let it be water off a duck's back !" "His bark's worse than his bite." "You maybe caught him on a bad day!" Needless to say, none of these platitudes uplifts the downcast nurse, harassed teacher, maligned local government officer or exiled machine operative one little bit. You'd proverbially need the hide of a rhinoceros to withstand the barbs of an office or canteen bully° on the rampage.°   *FACTOR / RESULT*

THREATS   [THREATENING ATMOSPHERE] 9
Overt threats are a bit like bad language° in the workplace : best suppressed, kept secret, or held back ready for the future firing of a torpedo° at a colleague° or an underling,° effectively to sink her career. *Veiled* threats are as different again. The oppressor here normally draws on power° and seniority.° He is in a position to hire-and-fire,° to suspend,° to redeploy,° or -" best of all," to make day-to-day life an absolute misery.° Many workers, sadly, feel constantly under Threat, especially of redundancy.°   *CAUSE / MOTIVATION*

TIGHTENINGS OF PROCEDURES 5
Selective Tightening of Procedures is a contradiction of terms. Surely the famed "crackdown"° - natural outcome of an inspection, or the publication of half-yearly results - would lead to a Tightening of Procedures for *all* employees. Not so. Line Managers° ensure that only disgraced° employees face the rocket. After all, it is their inefficiency°/ carelessness° that caused the stink.° Favoured ones° are exempt. Tightening is just one consequence of filtering,° and one symptom of scapegoating.° Thankfully, no crackdown° lasts forever.
    FACTOR / RESULT

TIME AND MOTION   [TIME-MOTION STUDY] 8
Time-Motion was popularized by Frederick Winslow-Taylor in 1950 - though Henry Ford can also be credited with the notion of Time and Motion in the workplace. Needless to say, Time-Motion's impact upon a workforce is enormous.   Modern call centres ° and sandwich production-lines are foremost, this Century, in honouring the concept that input / and throughput are strictly mathematical. The oppressed one is correctly nervous having her every contribution, her every distraction, measured. Because Time-Motion is all about tangibles, not intangibles ; output per hour, not those hours of rumination or navigation or reassurance or negation that *defy* calculation. *FACTOR / MOTIVATION*

TIME OUT 6
Taking Time Out is as important for the oppressed one as for her bully°/ supervisor / conveyor-belt operator. Maybe the oppressor needs anger management° too. Whatever conflict° has happened, or will happen, Time Out permits a re-assessment of the situation. That Time Out could take place at filing, during a walk round the block, at mediation,° or with both parties deciding to postpone further confrontation° for a week or so. Time Out, ideally, calms things down.
RESPONSE

TIME TO PROVE YOUR WORTH 5
One of the advantages of apprenticeship° or probation° or NQS (Newly Qualified Status) is the Time they allow both to acquire skills and to Prove Your Worth. A wise line manager° will be very generous and circumspect for the first few weeks and months : forgiving minor lapses ; ever-ready to offer guidance.° Conversely, the bully° usually makes no allowances whatsoever, whether driven by envy,° seniority,°

sadism,° or power° for power's sake. Many humiliated° workers, struggling to keep going, recount how their bosses never even gave them one chance : "thrown in the deep end." FACTOR / RESPONSE

TOILETS [TOILET BREAKS] 6
Many factories and call centres° actually restrict or time Toilet Breaks. Other workplaces count the number of times an employee might go to the Toilet ! Whatever the frowns and sighs about Toilet calls, one thing is certain, all employees *need* Toilets for different reasons : diarrhoea, upset tummy, food poisoning, menstruation, stress,° incontinence, hygiene, whatever. In such circumstances, coming down hard on Toilet Breaks can be deemed oppressive. In these days of No Smoking in the workplace itself, it is highly unlikely malingerers° would regularly take advantage of any degree of latitude where the Toilet / bathroom / sick-bay was concerned.   FACTOR

TONE   OF   VOICE 9
The voice is itself a musical instrument. And oppressed ones have learnt from birth, or from the first day of their employ, to pick up the Tone of Voice and its meaning. But beware. A bully° can be falsely tender and kind to catch his subject off guard. A bully might even show compassion° for a recent setback or bereavement. And if two bullies° act in consort - not at all unusual in a hierarchy° - one will elect to be hard man, one soft man. Be aware. Observations of great gravity can be spoken casually. Equally, quite *trivial* observations may be spoken with undue gravity. It goes without saying that the oppressed one might fear° her oppressor's voice *whatever is said or not said*. To get through the working day, she might be well advised to know every register of her oppressor's voice, every mannerism, every repetition, every implication, every deceit. Also noting whether a manager is nice to

some employees, horrible to others. Whether he changes tune, literally, when *his* manager walks into the room; whether his Tone of Voice is *perpetually unnerving*, even when he has stated he is anxious to repair broken bridges. See domestic violence. *FACTOR / MOTIVATION*

TOO BIG TO LOSE 6
If the workplace menace, the workplace bully,° is accepted as Too Big To Lose, he will become unchallenged° and unchallengeable. And the longer he remains immutable, the more crazy his trail of destruction. The organization, in turn, has to become bigger than any one appointee in its employ. A trusted warrior goes to war the next day as well.
FACTOR / MOTIVATION

TORPEDO [IN FOR A ROCKET] 8
The language of Human Resources is violent : no more so than with the Rocket freely set off, the Torpedo launched so accurately from Management's armoury. What better way to destroy *an already unsettled* employee than shattering any outward shell of defiance ? And when to do it ? Just *after* a particularly good report , sale or assignment delivered ; the downturn of an even plateau in her career. Maybe the Torpedo (a past error ? a complaint ? a discrepancy ? an aggrieved co-worker or customer?) was *always* there in preparedness. For a propitious launch, timing matters.   *CAUSE / MOTIVATION*

TRADES UNIONS [TRADES UNIONISTS] 8
This is a vast subject, much better covered elsewhere. But Unionization impacts upon workplace oppression in two key ways : first, *the best* Trades Unions are there to stand up against tyrannical° management and to stand by individual employees whose careers and composure have been irretrievably wrecked by bullying.°   Second, *the worst* Trades Unionists are so anxious to appease management and to hold the

party line that they *collude* with oppressive practices : reinforcing those practices and further isolating their own loyal members. That even - or especially - includes vilification of suspected or actual whistleblowers.° Fortunately, some modern Trades Unions are more independent of management; less backward-looking ; more proactive assisting some of their more depressed and downtrodden members. And who better to act as a McKenzie friend° than a sympathetic Union rep ?   *ASSOCIATION*

TRANQILLIZERS 5
Medically-prescribed Tranquillizers, or over-the-counter equivalents, should *always* be a warning sign of possible stress° at work- or unbearable stress° at home carried into the workplace. Of great concern, certain modern sedatives induce suicide° rather than helping to avert that terrible outcome. See Sleeplessness.   *RESULT*

TRANSFER OF JOB   [NEW JOB DESCRIPTION] 8
Larger employers are quite likely to have vacancies in totally different departments, floors or teams.° Furthermore, the employer might be quite sympathetic to internal applications for new or recently vacated positions. But again there is a snag: as with Transfer of Manager, an internal move might well reawaken all the ghosts of an oppressed one's past. In other words, she moves under a cloud. Better perhaps to consider resignation,° though it might be preferable for *the bully* to resign.° See Relocation.   *RESPONSE*

TRACKING   [LOGGING EXACTLY WHERE YOU ARE] 9
Tracking is not a new phenomenon. What is new is the arsenal of weapons modern management has to do its Tracking : GPS, mobile phone, pager, ringback, laptop log. And *new* Tracking devices are becoming available yearly. Old-fashioned telephoning-back-to-base can

itself be oppressive, particularly from someone else's home, or after hours. One elderly recipient of a care agency's° call-cramming wryly observed she got no actual help because all "her" 10 minutes was used on admin. Tracking at its worst is Big Brother; or slavery.° Management gets much more for its money because it knows exactly where every employee is situate and for how long: often far fewer minutes than the contract. And if a Social Worker conscientiously spends a *whole hour* on a suicide,° she will undoubtedly face the high jump. And logging on itself is unsettling. Half way through a job, the harassed employee panics that she is spending longer than she has been authorized to. Tracking also interrupts people's holidays! CAUSE / MOTIVATION

TRANSFER OF MANAGER 6

A stressed employee might well request transfer to a different team° with a different Manager. Except that her reputation / workload°/ vulnerability° might accompany, *even precede*, her. Far trickier for an organization is the moment it must Transfer the actual Manager - oppressor - to a different shop or hospital or outpost, rather than Transferring the employees he will manage in the future. And there is some reluctance to move a stalwart.   RESULT / RESPONSE

TRANSFER OF CASE RESPONSIBILITY OR WORKLOAD...8

Management Transfer of Cases or files or Areas of Responsibility is an invaluable handle or tool° of oppression. Again, the employee might actually *request* that this happens. But it still represents failure:° failure to cope, failure to hack it. And how humiliating° for the juiciest, most prestigious work to be Transferred...as punishment. ° In many fields of sales, commerce, travel or caring, there are such inherently satisfying assignments the withdrawal or Transfer of which represents defeat.°

Worse, these attractive assignments then go to a less-qualified co-worker,° or to the favoured one !° The bully,° needless to say is fully attuned to the impact of lost Workload, and the nonsensical use of *under*work° to put someone down.   *CAUSE   /   MOTIVATION*

TRAPS   [ENTRAPMENT] 8
Traps set in a workplace *can be* benevolent : an attempt by management to combat theft, short-changing, misrepresentation, employees' use of social media°- and fraud. However, Entrapment of *a good* employee in order to achieve her punishment° or dismissal° is distinctly *un*ethical. Is there any future in Trapping a bullying° foreman, head teacher or care home° manager by sending in a disguised management spy to see what is really going on ? Perhaps. *FACTOR / or RESPONSE*

TRAUMA 7
We associate Trauma more with accident or hospital operation than a day in the office. But Trauma is a foreseen and inescapable consequence of bullying°- whether at home or in the workplace. That Trauma makes the springs of resentment unquenchable ; fear of criticism° perpetual, even to the extent of self-fulfilment.   *RESULT*

TRAVEL   TIME   [COMPENSATING THE TRAVELLING] 7
Iniquitously, there are still employers, traders and care agencies° who refuse to pay their workers for Travelling between jobs. No way is Travelling to one's next appointment *an option*. One cannot usually get there by helicopter ! And what about horrendous traffic jams ? So the correct - *and just* - way to pay itinerant employees to pay them from the beginning of a working day / half-day / shift° right through to the end *including Travel Time*. Otherwise, employers would have both incentive and reward to evade minimum wage° legislation. And is

tracking° being used to find out the exact minute an agency no longer has to pay someone ?   FACTOR / MOTIVATION

TRIVIALIZATION 8
Dreadful instances of oppression in the workplace are frequently Trivialized. "You'll get over it !" "He's always like that!" "His bark is worse than his bite!" ° etc. Like all minimization,° Trivialization further isolates a bully's victims.°   FACTOR / RESULT

TROUBLEMAKER 7
Labelling° someone a Troublemaker is conclusive : an irretrievable, irreversible state of affairs. And the label° sticks. Manager or management now know the rookie, the old-stager or Union lackey most likely to cause grief in past, present or future. You can be deemed a Troublemaker simply for taking a grievance° forward.   MOTIVATION

TROUBLE-SHOOTER 6
A Trouble-shooter is sent in when a business or organization faces labour unrest, fierce competition,° underperforming management - or complete demise. Usually, the Trouble-shooter will get a concern back on track. Where this intervention impacts on oppression is the creation of an atmosphere of distrust,° suspicion,° scapegoating.° *RESPONSE*

TWO PEOPLE ON THE JOB 6
Allocating *Two People* to a job sounds Heaven-sent. No more isolation;° somebody to work with to get the job done ; someone to do half the driving ; someone to share responsibility for an unforeseen event or hiccup. What could go wrong ? A *great deal* can go wrong. What if those Two Workers do not get on ? What if they have completely different approaches to a task / assignment / day away / meeting / sale ? What if one of the Two is senior to the junior ; or is

there to tell tales ; or is planted to inspect° how the oppressed one is coping° / not coping. Mixed blessings. ASSOCIATION / RESULT

TYRANNY [THE TYRANT] 10
Tyranny is a broad and very expressive term for a culture of fear° in the workplace. Crucially, Tyrants are unstopped - unstoppable ? - whatever their employ ; wherever they are redeployed ;° and in whichever *household* they are king. Tyrants usually carry within themselves all the devices required for their survival° and the continued exercise of unbridled suzerainty. And it is not always in management's interest to demote° or dismiss° the Tyrant. Far easier to turn a blind eye and to marginalize° or relocate° *the oppressed one.* CAUSE / RESULT

UNCHALLENGED   BULLYING   AT   WORK 9
How desperately sad that Bullying° at work - that climate of fear° - so often remains Unchallenged. That draws in a parallel straightway with domestic violence° Unchallenged. There are several reasons for everybody - or nearly everybody - looking the other way : disbelief, guilt° that *someone else* is going through the mangle, envy,° unwillingness to be seen unco-operative° - not a good team player;° ignorance, actually being the favoured one,° actually liking that particular oppressor, actively disliking both the bullying° *and* the bullied° worker, contamination, whatever. But as long as the Tyrant° is allowed to perpetuate his Tyranny° - even praised° for his tight ship° - his casualties will mount. CAUSE   / RESULT / MOTIVATION

UNDER- AGE   WORKERS 7
So strict are the rules surrounding the employment of children still attending school that one wonders if there is any room left for child labour. Even paper rounds are checked up on ! Yet the employment of

Under-Age Workers continues unabated : piecework° in the evening and weekends ; keeping the shop ; packing goods ; unpacking goods ; looking after a lot of younger children without reward - and, of course, illegal shifts° in a back-street factory / sweatshop. *FACTOR*

UNDERACHIEVEMENT 8
The cowed, bullied,° humiliated,° exploited° worker is unlikely to achieve her best. Loss of productivity° as a result of oppression in the workplace does not attract nearly as much comment as it ought. Happy° workers are good for their bosses. *RESULT*

UNDERCURRENTS 9
If Undercurrents were immediately understood, they would not be clandestine - which is entirely their purpose. Few employees are in their workplaces for long without detecting those Undercurrents. The *very word*, taken from deep, unfathomable, waters, sounds mysterious and vaguely threatening.° On the other hand, work would not be as intriguing *without* Undercurrents ! See Gossip. *CAUSE / FACTOR*

UNDERCUTTING 6
Often, after the tendering of new contracts, or outsourcing,° the workforce is deliberately Undercut - or else their wages are Undercut. Anybody expressing discontent° is invited to resign.° Sometimes Undercutting is passed off as useful competition,° slimming-down, or rationalization.° *Immigration* can be a factor. *CAUSE / MOTIVATION*

UNDERLING[S] 7
Underling is no great role allocation - but is the actual role allocated to most employees, whatever their skills and wherever they are based.

The very word smacks of strict hierarchy,° also of class.° And being an Underling gives extra credence to the potential bully.°

FACTOR / MOTIVATION

UNDERMINING 9
Like harassment° or torment,° the word Undermining is an ideal description for *the process* of being oppressed in the workplace. The metaphor comes from mining or excavation. If you dig too deep, too hurriedly, the trench, prop, wall, or structure which depends on a firm foundation, collapses. And it can be argued that far too many workers experience an Undermining of their wills, skills, integrity, health, every single working day from 9 till 5. Learned hopelessness° / helplessness° is about as good as it gets for the office bully.° *RESULT*

UNDERSTAFFING 8
Some Understaffing at work is inevitable : as when someone suddenly rings in sick. Most Understaffing, however, can be accurately *predicted*, therefore generously compensated. A contingency plan should always exist : " What would happen if...?" Contrarily, some businesses and hospitals and outposts actually *rely upon* an incomplete establishment, for survival. That is because Understaffing is superficially *economical.* The wage bill is lower than it would have been. On the other hand, a saddened, strained,° stretched° work force, subject to suddenly cancelled leave° - will sooner or later rebel° or resign.° False economy? *FACTOR / CAUSE / or RESULT*

UNDERVALUING OF EMPLOYEES / VOLUNTEERS 8
Undervaluing those who work for organizations is a constant bugbear - yet one that can so readily be rectified. It stands to reason that the Valued worker will also be a happy° and productive ° worker ; also a

better parent and spouse. The whole is a virtuous circle. And the firm or school or local government department benefits from far fewer resignations° and the consequent expenses of recruiting, inducting, and training a replacement. Valued workers both glow and grow into their new settings.   *FACTOR / MOTIVATION*

UNFAIR DISMISSAL 9
The joy of Unfair Dismissals by unscrupulous organizations and outlets is that the damage is *already done*, whatever any tribunal° says. The Unfairly Dismissed worker will, in reality, never get her job back later - she is far more likely to be paid off or charged with a counter-allegation° - and if she does slot back in again, there will be a cloud, and she'll be sent to Coventry.° In a way, *the majority of* Dismissals are Unfair. Because Dismissal, as opposed to relocation° or redundancy° or re-training, is a very blunt instrument. A few outfits actually pride° themselves on hire-and-fire.° Absurdly, Unfair Dismissal is sometimes called "Constructive" Dismissal.   *CAUSE*

UNFAIRNESS 7
Every young child at some stage says : " It isn't fair !" - and much of life is Unfair anyway. But there are aspects of time spent at work which are *patently* Unfair, trying the patience° of a Saint : not paying the minimum wage,° not sharing out gratuities, not paying emoluments,° not taking into account travel time,° asking for 24/7 availability,° blocking promotion,° sacking someone because they're on a higher salary,° denying holidays, time off, or freedom from messaging during time away from work.° The list of Unfairnesses goes on and on : so much so that very little of working life appears fair at all ! That is partly because of power° and status° differentials, and historical inequalities.   *FACTOR / RESULT*

UNFINISHED BUSINESS 8
Psychologists refer to any pent-up grievances,° unresolved problems, grudges, envy,° past disappointments as Unfinished Business. The oppressed one at work is most likely to suffer because hers supervisor keeps a whole pile of criticisms° to bring out *bit by bit*. He also willingly passes on, down the line, any unwelcome luggage° left at his door by *his* managers. The trouble with Unfinished Business in the workplace is its abundance, literally and metaphorically ; also its usefulness as a management tool.°   *FACTOR / MOTIVATION*

UNPREPAREDNESS 6
If a new or existing employee feels Unprepared for a transaction, hospital operation, report, or journey, he or she is about to embark upon, for the benefit of an employer, then oppression is a distinct possibility. That Unpreparedness is rarely *outright refusal* ; more usually a founded conviction that going through with it would be somehow detrimental to her employer. And a worker risks the charge of gross misconduct° for not following orders. Wise managements *stretch* workers without throwing them in at the deep end ; without disregarding qualifications and experience ; without, at worst, setting them up to fail.°   *FACTOR / RESULT*

UNPROFITABILITY 6
Unprofitability in one particular outlet or division might be an early alert to low staff morale° and a high degree of oppression. Maybe neighbouring sectors *are* profitable, working efficiently for the benefit of the organization as a whole. Or maybe the presently unprofitable outpost *used to be* far more remunerative, before the accession that one chosen leader, that one tested bully.° *ASSOCIATION / MOTIVATION*

UNREST IN THE WORKPLACE....9
When a Captain says his troops or mariners are restless - worse, mutinous - the whole edifice could come crashing down. Sometimes this Unrest is referred to, militarily, as trouble in the ranks ; or geographically, as natives on the point of uprising. Happily, murmurings of discontent° rarely amount to outright insubordination.° But *that very spectre* threatens good order and discipline.° It is a measure of transformed industrial relations in Britain that fewer Trades Unionists° now call for strikes° or walk-outs. Alarmingly, there *should be* Unrest around bullying°- but *isn't*. RESULT / MOTIVATION

UNWANTED WORK 7
With low wages, significant unemployment, and potentially lucrative shifts° or assignments on offer, Unwanted Work would seem to be the very last problem on anyone's mind. But many job-seekers on JSA are forced into a type of Workfare for as little as £1 an hour (work experience); or are taken off stimulating voluntary work to go on a hopeless trek for unstable fast-food opportunities. Then there are the hundreds of workers who are employed to do one area of work, then are dumped with "other duties." Then there are *more* thousands of workers forced to do overtime° they didn't put in for. Some honest employees are even expected to do dodgy deals.° FACTOR / MOTIVATION

UPPING YOUR GAME [PULLING OUT YOUR STOPPER] 7
Upping your Game is *un*helpful advice given to the struggler and the oppressed one. Were she able to fulfil her potential, she would probably have done so already. And she was appointed in the first place because she was Up to the Game in the best possible way! Also if you are tired, underpaid° and overworked,° you have nothing left to

give. The cupboard is bare. Why not tell a 15-year old bare-footed Um, asylum seeker, in a strange land, to pull himself up by his bootlaces ? See Targets. *RESULT*

UPWARD ASSESSMENT 8
Upward Assessment is possibly the most useful corrective to oppression in larger businesses, government departments or retailing concerns. This way, even the *most junior* employee has the chance to comment on her line manager's° attitude and performance.° Some Upward Assessments are anonymous; others verbal only - so as to preclude a bully° getting hold of the file all about him! Very occasionally, oppressive managers wanting to improve their working relationships actually *instigate*, or cooperate° with, Upward Assessments. It is vital a nonconformist° or outsider° is not persecuted° further due to her honest appraisal.° Few workers Assess out of spite.° *RESPONSE*

UPWARD BULLYING 7
By no means all bullying° behaviour is downward. It is a possibility that a recently-promoted° team leader, ° foreman or section head will be bullied *in reverse* by envious,° scheming, or underperforming° employees still on basic grade. This is part of the "restless° rabble syndrome": backwoodsmen and women determined to unseat a middle manager who might actually be blameless.° Employees justly criticized° in the present or the past might be quite glad of a scalp. And delight in a manager's downfall to the same degree that *a different* manager once delighted in their own. *FACTOR / RESULT*

VALIDATION 9
Validation is a psychological term for self-belief° so strong that it upholds a person daily : through thick or thin, in the midst of crisis as

well as in the green pastures of life. We all long for Valid passports, Valid documents, Valid debit cards, Valid routes. So why not seek the *Validation* of every employee *in her own eyes* as well as those of her managers and her ultimate employers ? Validation regardless of her race, her looks, her dress,° her political opinions, or her sexuality.

ASSOCIATION / RESPONSE

VALUES 8
Organizations of any size have stated Values as part of a mission statement or Personnel manual.° However, because these Values are printed *on parchment*, they are *more* difficult to implement ! The greatest Value of all is an employer Valuing his workers and their varied talents. Because - as stated above - no business is stronger than its weakest worker(s). Good, positive Values should permeate every level of a hierarchy,° right down to basement. Thereby, employees feel secure° enough to raise their concerns ; and their ideas about how they might work better ; also be enabled, encouraged, to look forward to their employment in an organization they can be justifiably proud of. The alternative to this Elysian field is disguised *anarchy* - restlessness° - and a very fractious atmosphere in the ward or on the factory floor.   MOTIVATION / RESPONSE

VICTIM [VICTIMHOOD] 8
The word "Victim" has, quite understandably, fallen out of favour of late. Terms such as survivor,° litigant, narrator, and differently-abled are far more positive. But we still speak of the Victims of bullying° in the workplace : those in the wrong place at the wrong time, in line with the "innocent party" involved in a road crash.

"Victimhood" is an even more troubled word : alluding as it does to one who makes a living, goes out to dinner, on her mighty misery. No leeway is given to the Victim who still has many issues to address. She is called *vexatious* as if she wears her Victimhood with pride;° whereas all she wants is recognition, redress,° relocation,° or some other form of restitution.   And nowhere is Victimhood bestowed on someone's wilting shoulders than on the *serially* oppressed one : this in common with the survivor° of repeat domestic violence.° "Why didn't she walk out the very first time?"   *CAUSE / RESULT / MOTIVATION*

VULNERABLE [VULNERABILITY] 9
The word "Vulnerable" is one of the most pejorative political buzz-words of the 1990s and Year 2000s. In the 1960s and 70s it was probably a socio-medical, almost scientific, term for a way in, a way of breaking down the body's normal defences. Then, in a climate of so-called political correctness, it was grabbed by Statists as an alternative to words that were definitely out-of-bounds: words like "the handicapped," "battered wives," "cripples," "slow learners," etc. But then, not for the first time, the *replacement* word became worse than many of the originals! A bit like "client" or "job-seeker" or "hard-working family."

No news bulletin is now complete without at least half a dozen references to "the Vulnerable" - whether that mass refers to payday loan-debtors, schoolgirls using a dark alleyway to get home from school, or elderly citizens who cannot afford astronomical fuel bills.

At work, "the Vulnerable" can definitely be taken to include someone oppressed or depressed° by the office bully,° those who haven't reached their sales' targets,° those left out of a takeover° bid, those who have defied their union,° and those who have taken at least six of the past twelve months off, ill.   *CAUSE   / MOTIVATION*

WAGE   DEDUCTIONS   [STOPPAGES   ] 9
Many employees struggle to make a living or to keep their heads above water, financially**.** Therefore a harsh deduction of wage - and most

deductions from an already *minimum* wage° are definitely alien - throw a disempowered° worker into total confusion. The deduction might be designated for food, drink, accommodation, tips, uniform, insurance, breakages, the till roll, lateness, halted output, a seat in the minibus, industrial action° - in fact *any* pretence that allows an employer to retain *at source* what reward should rightly accrue to the worker. *CAUSE / MOTIVATION*

WAGE SLAVES 10

" Wage Slaves " usually work in very low-paid,° insular, unskilled, part-time,° commission-only° jobs on a zero-hours contract.° Additionally, Wage Slaves are over-represented in the "hospitality" sector : flipping hamburgers, drawing pints, collecting in dirty dishes, brewing steaming hot cups of coffee, frying fish. The term immediately alludes to a Minimum Wage° rather than a *living* wage ; acting as zombie rather than deft operator. Wage Slave also brings to the fore the image of a fettered Slave here fobbed off with a few shillings : much fewer shillings than amassed by the ubiquitous - multinational? - *chain* binding them to sink, shelf or counter. In other words, the Wage Slave looks forward only to going-home time. *In the opposite camp* however are many commentators who defend Wage Slavery as giving students an excellent overview of "real life" - at the same time instilling in young people the value of income honestly earned - albeit in gruelling circumstances; then honestly, and liberally, spent ! And nobody should decry the Saint who cooks an elderly gentleman's breakfast, cleans his shoes, fetches in his pint of milk. Wage Slaves are human beings too : smart, conscientious, mostly friendly, very attentive, amazingly *un*complaining° - with many of them enrolled on the social media into the bargain. How they actually *get* their smart-phones and i-pods® on such long shifts,° and low Wages is a miracle ! *CAUSE / RESULT*

WARNINGS 9

The oppressed one is certainly not short of Warnings : formal° or informal : some Warnings coming from a concerned, and parent-deprived, family; others from frantic co-workers° who have already brushed against, perhaps clashed with, the bully.°
Managerial Warnings, in particular, are unequivocal expressions of an organization's power.° And you don't argue with power.° Nor is there any point ignoring, let alone challenging,° a Warning. The Warning, then, constitutes a Sword of Damocles : an extra weapon for the bully° who always warned you a Warning was on the cards !   RESULT

WEAKNESS 8

Weakness is an all-embracing term for not being up to the job. As such, Weakness covers everything from a handkerchief full of tears° to a home life full of woes or a tumbler full of paracetamol. And, in the context of oppression in the workplace, Weakness could mean everything from nerves to laziness, malingering,° an indulgence, groping,° an acceptance of bribes, or - quite tellingly - an employee's perceived inability to stand up to banter,° to stand up and be counted, to stand up for her rights, *to stand up to the office or store-room bully.*°
         CAUSE / FACTOR / RESULT / MOTIVATION

WEAKNESSES 7

Weaknesses *in the plural* is a word very much in vogue : "interpersonal weaknesses," "transactional weaknesses," "IT system Weaknesses," "Weaknesses in the competition," "areas of Weakness," " Weaknesses in performance"....and, daringly : " institutional Weaknesses," a sure cousin of "Weaknesses in governance." Some managers sweeten the pill by speaking of their workforce's corresponding *Strengths,* and

"Playing to their strengths" - but it is definitely not 50:50. Long live the weakest link.   FACTOR / RESULT

WHISTLEBLOWERS 8
In the 1970s, a disturbing BBC Documentary introduced viewers to "Whistleblowers" for the first time; with prescience explaining their probable fate : that fate including demotion, ° dismissal, ° or being sent to Coventry.° Viewers discovered how big organizations are so defensive,° so self-deferential, they do not want to hear any narrative but their own. The threat° is not the shortfall,° or the alleged wrongdoing ; not the rogue employee° but the Whistleblower herself ! Whistleblowers soon learnt to shut up - or to smuggle their findings out, anonymously, to a friendly newspaper ; or publish them on what later became social media sites. And any Whistleblower who naively thought going to the MD was the answer had the rudest of descents to the abyss ! Facts became immaterial, reputations unimpeachable.

One or two less cynical outsiders° fondly believed at least one boss worth his salt would be glad, gratified even, to be informed of corporate, or Lone Ranger, malpractice. Nothing could be further from the truth. The Whistleblower became enemy Number One: a messenger blamed,° felled, for bearing bad news....leaving the culprit acquitted to rounds of raucous applause.

Totally unexpected : it was publicly-funded hospitals, quangos and government departments who revealed themselves the least tolerant of Whistleblowers in their midst, now charged with contravention of the Official Secrets' Act. But then schoolchildren have always hated snitches.

If, to-day, Whistleblowers dare to speak out, they are served with gagging orders and told they will lose everything if they keep rocking the boat: salary, pension, reputation, savings, home, *liberty*. Moreover, nobody else will ever employ them. And if matters could get worse, the

Whistleblower herself becomes object of a malicious allegation° or suit of defamation. No garlands. No rewards. Just suspension°: a precursor of exile.

So it comes about Whistleblowers are frequently reviled, vilified, and *ignored* by the outside world : the very people they intended to assist. And the final ignominy : being disowned *by their own families !*

What then is the alternative to Whistleblowing ? Staying silent. So is it ever worth it ? Despite various " Whistleblowing Charters," the answer currently has to be "No." Instead, aim to keep all relevant knowledge and paperwork (anonymity can't be *100%* guaranteed) until you have *already left* the organization ; or until new management is drafted in. Ironically, *official denials* are nearly always more believable - *and believed* - than the Whistleblower's so far unsupported allegation(s)   *FACTOR / RESULT / or RESPONSE*

WILD GOOSE CHASE [SETTING UP TO FAIL] 5

Untold merriment comes from sending the oppressed one on a Wild Goose Chase : a mission impossible, a cul-de-sac, a hiding to nothing. Wild Goose Chases are elaborate practical jokes, if they were not so deadly serious : also a Setting Up To Fail. It is not unknown for an entire offer of employment to be a Wild Goose Chase. Either the job doesn't exist, or has already been filled, or is commission only° with no guarantee that minimum commission could ever be earned. When the Chaser of Wild Geese *gets back* from her fruitless expedition, everyone else is gleeful. After all, they always knew she was a loser. Nor should we forget demoralized,° overworked,° and ground-down cruise staff - *staff on cruises rich people book* - always promised reward, never given it.   *CAUSE / MOTIVATION*

WILFUL BLINDNESS 7
Wilful Blindness is a relatively recent term to describe the herd or silo° instinct that prevails in many organizations - *large and small* - endangering staff, customers and the general public alike. It as if there's going to be a disaster - one that might cost many injuries and deaths, millions of pounds in recalls, or compensation - *which nobody stops.* That *inevitability* is the result of absolutely no one daring to put her head above the parapet, or expose scandal to the press, or alert any so-called "regulator" disinclined to listen.

It emerges, far too late, that everybody *thought* someone else had the matter in hand ; or else the situation was so bald, so astonishing, others *could not have failed* to see what their colleagues° saw. So why wasn't disaster turned back on itself ? Some juniors feared their seniors,° or stood in awe of them. And some seniors° imagined they themselves were simply *too smart* to have waved a model of car or bottle of new fizzy or unsecured ferry or toxic lorry or contaminated batch of food or handsome bribe through. Some big players in the aviation industry now adhere to a "just culture" to counter Wilful Blindness. Every single supplier ; every single operator ; every single mechanic ; every single pilot or stewardess, is charged with *pooling* the discovery, or shortfall,° or risk,° or dishonest practice,° or loophole, that might lead to plane crash - *even where this knowledge is commercially sensitive or might assist a competitor.* FACTOR / ASSOCIATION / MOTIVATION

WILLINGNESS 8
An employee's Willingness is so welcome, *so relatively rare*, that it risks being exploited,° and taken for granted. The more a paid or unpaid worker expresses Willingness to do more, *or to do it in her own time*, the greater the calls on her goodwill... in full knowledge she dare

not refuse, and will not protest.° The Americans even have a saying : "coalition of the willing." Arguably, Willingness only bubbles up to the surface in a workplace if staff are valued,° praised° and properly rewarded.°   *FACTOR / MOTIVATION*

WIMPS [WIMPISHNESS] 7
Some grumps and geeks, chatterboxes and complainants° at work are discounted, ridiculed, as mere Wimps : people unable to stand the heat of the kitchen; people totally unsuited to the ebbs and flows of everyday on the shop floor; unready for the fray; hopeless facing the enemy. Wimpishness is taken as an indicator of weakness.° Sad.   *FACTOR*

WORK RETURNED 8
Work returned to its originator due to omission, suggested improvement, change of specification, whatever, *should* be a routine, and fairly harmless, part of the working day. After all, everyone *wants* the best pack or sale or analysis or court report or update or staff circular that can possibly be obtained. Sadly, however, Work Returned is also a potentially threatening,° indeed menacing, device - especially when there was little or nothing wrong with the first draft or the first specimen ! An *insecure*° employee might need quite a bit of gentle encouragement and reassurance that she has done well so far ; that she could not have known of a different expectation somebody held; or a development nobody had told her about; or a blocked delivery : all arising since the original allocation of work to her. *FACTOR / RESULT*

WORK TO RULE 6
Work to Rule is an alternative to going on strike. For several hours or days or weeks, all employees belonging to a union° or association are

invited to do only what they are contracted to do : no more, no less. In effect, nearly everyone is withdrawing cooperation° : the cooperation that would normally keep the conveyor belt or office or warehouse going. Work to Rule is more effective in a large organization - but even here it attracts bullying.° Individuals are leant on or threatened or blacklisted in order to make them abandon their plan or their sit-in ; in order to get them to do *that little bit extra*, in defiance of their union,° but for the common good, just to fulfil one important order, just to allow scholars back to school, just to give little old ladies their luncheon... . In turn, those who *take pity on* management attract the wrath of their less willing,° or more militant, co-workers !° The whole episode becomes a miasma.   *RESULT*

WORKPLACE COUNSELLORS 6

You have to be a fairly large school, hospital or outfit to afford a Workplace Counsellor. Where one *is* available, her remit should definitely include suspected or potential bullying° on the interface, or on the shop floor. Questions then arise : Should the Counsellor be approached in work time , or after hours ? Should the Counsellor have access to (possibly culpable) line managers ?° Who exactly is the Counsellor answerable to ? How do you prevent an employee developing dependence on her Counsellor ? Many workplaces assume that a foreman or charge hand or overseer or branch manager is *automatically* the Counsellor ! Other organizations say : " Go to Human Resources." Yet others say : "Here is a list of private Counsellors approved and used by us in the past." Counselling under whatever guise must never be *compulsory*. Nor should those who consult a Counsellor be counted as weaker° or more vulnerable° or more idle or more thin-skinned° than their colleagues.° *RESPONSE*

YES-MAN [YES-WOMAN] 7

The colloquial Yes-Man is essential to the smooth-running of an organization. Yes-Men, Yes-Women, are favoured ones° and sycophants : willing° conformists.° Whenever there is a vote, Yes-people can be relied on to vote with the majority. And whenever there is conflict of interest, they will side with the *more* powerful party or with their patron.° Troublesome° employees are automatically dismissed° as the "awkward squad." Significantly, oppressed workers are rarely Yes-men and Yes-Women : rarely so compliant. *RESULT*

YOUR PROBLEM [THAT'S YOUR PROBLEM] ...9

Workplace Oppression is isolating °: never more than when everyone at work withdraws, turning their backs on cooperation.° "Your Problem!" - they say, and leave you to it. And if you sink, hard cheese!
MOTIVATION

ZERO-HOURS' CONTRACTS [& CONTRACTING] 10

The Zero-Hours Contract marks a return to one of the worst aspects of human slavery :° *permanent availability*. And there has been a feast or a riot of Zero-Hours Contracting in the past twenty years.

The idea is that someone contracts to sit by his or her telephone awaiting a call to come in. A succession of weddings, for instance, might demand a caterer 0, 30 or 75 hours in a week. Illness or wellness in a shop might demand of an assistant 0, 25 or 60 hours behind the counter. A sudden rush of Christmas shoppers might lead an all-for-95pence shop to ask for 0, 8, 16, or 29 hours. The poor prospective employee is never " on the books;" nor really off the books either; never legally entitled to jobseekers' allowance, because she is never technically available to work for a different employer ; never able to rest or to go out for the day, in case the phone rings. To make matters worse, if somebody on Zero-Hours *turns down* a shift,° or, worse, goes to work elsewhere, perhaps for a competitor, she will never be called up by Network Rail, the care home° or the pub manager again.

In summary, the Zero-Hours Contract benefits *only* the employer. The pathetically grateful employee is left with sky-high ambition - and down-to-earth again total silence from the only place supplying hope, and bread. Zero-Hours proves *dreadfully* insecure as well serving to massage the Government's joblessness figures. Zero-Hours also entails having a car or taxi one cannot afford, no CV, little or no stability of employment, then lots of unpaid travel° in a minibus when one *does* get "invited" into work.   CAUSE / MOTIVATION

ZERO TOLERANCE 9

Some of the most successful and productive workplaces are those which show Zero Tolerance towards sexism,° homophobia,° obscenity, bad language,° spitting, trashing - and bullying.° Inside these exemplary work settings, it is the bully,° not the oppressed one herself, who is in for the high jump. Managers or co-workers° are instantly interviewed to garner evidence of supervisory bad practice. And there is a presumption that the downtrodden worker is telling the truth. As for the object of complaint,° he is immediately in line for reprimand,° demotion,° relocation,° or dismissal.°....which is how it ought to be : provision of *nowhere to escape to* for those who misuse their position of trust and tarnish their badge of office ; who traduce the stewardship that a County Council, a matron, a head teacher or a factory owner has bestowed upon them.   RESPONSE

ΨΩΨΩΨΩΨΩΨΩ

WHERE TO PROGRESS FROM HERE ?
a ten-point plan

1)   Appoint one single person in every work setting, with responsibility for mapping / reporting upwards any oppressive practice in that office, outlet or outpost ;

2)   Conduct a simple bi-annual audit of what workplace oppression has - or hopefully *has not* - taken place ;

3)   Include a clause in every single acceptance letter of a recruit / new employee that there is Zero Tolerance of bullying ;

4)   With the agreement of an employee under pressure, ask that (s)he consider a Mentor to be a guide round the hurdles of physical and emotional isolation at work ;

5)   Include bullying / harshness Role-plays in every In-Service Training Course - *whether or not* that course is about Oppression;

6)   Arrange at Head Office unannounced inspections with the sole purpose of uncovering any bullying / undue harshness anywhere in that organization. And where that organization is very small, ask an outside friend to pop in at random ;

7)   Let there be no return to work after more than 5 days of Absence without ascertaining whether that employee was away *because of Oppression* ;

8)   Employ only wise and kind foremen / line managers ;

9)   Make plain Human Resources do "want" to hear about bullying and arbitrary injustice ;

10)   Start and end each working day / shift / assignment on a high note....with a bit of positive Feedback mixed in.

ΩΨΩΨΩΨΩΨΩΨΩΨΩ

KEY REPLIES TO A BULLYING MANAGER
==

<< I'm afraid I don't understand....>>

<< I wonder whether you could say that again....>>

<< I'm sorry. I've lost you ! >>

<< What exactly are you trying to say ? >>

<< I wonder if I could just pop to the loo...>>

<< Perhaps we'd be better talking about this another day>>

<< What you're saying sounds irregular to me >>

<< Maybe we've both got the wrong end of the stick >>

<< Let's draw this to a close just for now >>

<< Neither of us appears in the right place to speak of this further to-day >>

<< Nothing's adding up in my book. How about you?>>

<< Let's sleep on it ! >>

<< It's been an unusually fine Spring this year ! >>

<< I'm hearing you.....>>

<< Let's see what happens.......>>

ΩΨΩΨΩΨΩΨΩΨΩ

STILL STANDING AT 5 :
KEY STRATEGIES FOR GETTING THROUGH

** Get to work earlier than the Oppressor

**Stand bolt upright

**Pretend nothing's amiss

**Let the Oppressor speak in front of colleagues or fellow-managers, not to you on your own

**Keep saying : " I'm afraid I must consult --------- first"

**Ask for arbitration/ mediation straightway, always

**Carve out little periods each day : the water cooler, the rest room, the chippie, filing, the car, the archive...where you can chill out

**Treat each day as a story : providing a running commentary to self like an advanced driver might

**Take up your Oppressor's personal space : moving nearer and nearer, drawing up your chair too

**Inhabit your Oppressor's shadow, coming up from behind

**Keep scribbling

**Talk to trusted others - wherever in the workplace they are

**Squeeze your Oppressor in a pincer-movement...so he is being got at, discovered, by both your co-workers and HIS bosses

ΩΨΩΨΩΨΩΨΩΨΩ

PSYCHOLOGIST : OLIVER JAMES' CONSTRUCTION OF <<THE TRIADIC PERSONALITY>> IN RELATION TO CONTROLLING BOSSES

In his book <<OFFICE POLITICS>> summarized in the METRO Newspaper, 4th. February, 2014, James argues that some people with maniacal tendencies, power-crazed, are let loose in the workplace. His 3 manifestations of managerial dysfunction are :

1) << THE PSYCHOPATH >> described as glib, with superficial charm ; grandiose ; can tell lies and con colleagues ; can manipulate; always a lack of remorse or guilt ; also a lack of empathy ; and a total failure to accept responsibility.

2) <<THE MACHIAVEL>>...named after famous politician : Niccolo Machiavelli [1469-1527] : with a great desire and capacity to seek power over others, through manipulation. The Machiavel lacks emotional connection or restraint when dealing with intimates. Quite scheming.

3) <<THE NARCISSIST>>...named after Narcissus : a mythological Greek who fell in love with his own image. The Narcissist has inflated self-esteem. Sees himself cleverer, more attractive, and more compelling than he really is. Often a charming extrovert : uncomfortable with intimacy or commitment.

Oliver James is a reliable guide in this field. His typology might be a trifle artificial ; but he freely concedes all 3 tendencies can exist together or separately in an overbearing manager - and that imperfect managers might not always intend to be as unfeeling as they sometimes appear. Nor does he see his bosses as always to be *dreaded*. Occasionally, poor managers are *comical* figures as well.

ΩΨΩΨΩΨΩΨΩΨΩΨΩ

SELECT BIBLIOGRAPHY
[arranged by title, alphabetically]

Assertiveness at Work: A Practical Guide to Handling Awkward Situations
Ken Back & Kate Back 2005

Be Bulletproof: How to achieve success in tough times at work
James Brooke & Simon Brooke 2012

Beat the Bully: A Guide to Dealing with Adult Bullying
Alex Gadd 2011

Bullied by the Boss: The Essential Guide to Overcoming Workplace Bullying
Eva James 2012

The Bully at Work: What You Can Do
Gary Namie & Ruth Namie 2009

Bully in Sight: How to predict, resist, challenge and combat workplace bullying - Overcoming the silence and denial by which abuse thrives
Tim Field 2012

Bully Blocking at Work: A Self-Help Guide for Employees and Managers
Evelyn Field 2011

Bullying At Work: How to Confront and Overcome It
Andrea Adams 1992

Complete Guide Understanding, Controlling and Stopping Bullies and Bullying at Work: A Complete Guide for Managers, Supervisors and Co-Workers
Margaret Kohut 2008

Controlling People: How to Recognize, Understand and Deal with People Who Try to Control You
Patricia Evans 2003

Dignity at Work: Eliminate Bullying and Create and a Positive Working Environment: Eliminate Bullying and Create a Positive Working Environment
Adult Bullying: Perpetrators and Victims
Peter Randall 2001

Fighting Back: How to Fight Bullying In the Workplace
David Graves 2002

How People Tick: A Guide to Over 50 Types of Difficult People and How to Handle Them
Mike Leibling 2009

How to Use Power Phrases to Say What You Mean, Mean What You Say, & Get What You Want
Meryl Runion 2004

I Thought It Was Just Me [but it isn't...] : Telling the Truth About Perfectionism, Inadequacy and Power
Brene Brown 2008

In Sheep's Clothing: Understanding and Dealing with Manipulative People
George Simon 2010

Managing Workplace Bullying: How to Identify, Respond to and Manage Bullying Behaviour in the Workplace
Aryanne Oade   2009

Nasty Bosses: How to Deal with Them without Stooping to Their Level
Jay Carter   2004

Nasty People
Jay Carter   2003

Office Politics: How to Thrive in a World of Lying, Backstabbing and Dirty Tricks Oliver James   2014

Perfect Phrases for Dealing with Difficult People: Hundreds of Ready-to-Use Phrases for Handling Conflict, Confrontations and Challenging Personalities
Susan Benjamin   2007

Rising Above Bullying: From Despair to Recovery
Rosemary Hayes   2011

Snakes in Suits: When Psychopaths Go to Work
Paul Babiak & Robert D. Hare   2007

Taming the Abrasive Manager: How to End Unnecessary Roughness in the Workplace
Laura Crawshaw   2007

Too Nice for Your Own Good: How to Stop Making 9 Self-Sabotaging Mistakes
Duke Robinson   2000

Water Off a Duck's Back: How to Deal with Frustrating Situations, Awkward, Exasperating and Manipulative People and... Keep Smiling!
Jon Lavelle 2010

When I Say No, I Feel Guilty: How to Cope, Using the Skills of Systematic Assertive Therapy
Manuel Smith 1975

Who's Pulling Your Strings?: How to Break the Cycle of Manipulation and Regain Control of Your Life
Harriet Braiker 2004

Workplace Bullying in the NHS
Jacqueline Randle (Editor) 2006

Your Conversation - or Mine ? 100 Tactics When Talking
Godfrey Holmes 1999

21 Dirty Tricks at Work: How to Win at Office Politics
Mike Phipps & Colin Gautrey 2005

ΩΨΩΨΩΨΩΨΩΨΩΨΩΨΩΨΩ

PRINTED BY RUBICON PRINT & DESIGN LTD.,
BROOMBANK ROAD, SHEEPBRIDGE,
CHESTERFIELD S41 9WJ
TEL. 01246-454525

How to Potty Train a Toddler the Loving Way

Proven Tips for Potty Training Boys and Girls with Amazing Stress-Free Results

Jenny Stapleton

© 2012 Jenny Stapleton

All Rights Reserved. No part of this publication may be reproduced in any form or by any means, including scanning, photocopying, or otherwise without prior written permission of the copyright holder.

Disclaimer and Terms of Use: The Author and Publisher has strived to be as accurate and complete as possible in the creation of this book, notwithstanding the fact that he does not warrant or represent at any time that the contents within are accurate due to the rapidly changing nature of the Internet. While all attempts have been made to verify information provided in this publication, the Author and Publisher assumes no responsibility for errors, omissions, or contrary interpretation of the subject matter herein. Any perceived slights of specific persons, peoples, or organizations are unintentional. In practical advice books, like anything else in life, there are no guarantees of income made. This book is not intended for use as a source of legal, business, accounting or financial advice. All readers are advised to seek services of competent professionals in legal, business, accounting, and finance field.

First Printing, 2012

Printed in the United States of America

Contents

Contents 3

Introduction 5

Equipment 6

At What Age Should You Start Potty Training Your Toddler 7

Communication 9

Showing Interest When Others Use the Bathroom 10

Independence 11

Regular Dry Periods 12

How Long It Takes to Potty Train Your Children 13

How Potty Training a Boy Is Different From a Girl 14

Training for Girls 15

Training for Boys 16

The Different Stages of Potty Training 18

Stage 1 19

Stage 2 20

Stage 3 22

Stage 4 23

How to Do Night-Time Potty Training 24

Age 25

Underwear 26

Encouragement 27

Things to Avoid 28

How to Potty Train Your 1 Year Old 30

How to Potty Train Your 2 Year Old 31

How to Potty Train Your 3 Year Old 33

Potty Training Ideas Not Involving Food or Money as a Reward .. 34

Whether to Use Training Underwear or Regular 36

Traditional Cloth Underwear 37

Cloth Training Pants 38

Disposable Training Pants (Pull-Ups) 39

Whether to Go Back to Diapers (Nappies) If Your Toddler Experiences Accidents 41

How to Deal With Fear 42

How to Deal With Stubbornness 44

How to Deal With Potty Training Regression 46

Conclusion 48

Introduction

Becoming a parent for the first time is one of life's great experiences, nobody really knows what to expect with their first child and there is an overwhelming amount of information and advice on offer.

Your child's first year is very much a learning curve and parenting issues centre on feeding, sleeping and changing diapers but as your baby gets older they reach the toddler age. At this stage your child will probably start to walk and talk and that is when most parents feel that the time has arrived to start potty training.

Potty training is one of those achievements that every parent and child has to endure. Every parent will seek advice on how best to approach the matter but as with most parenting issues the best approach will be the one that suits you and your child.

Most parents eagerly anticipate potty training as a milestone in their child's development - if only because it means an end to changing dirty diapers. There is no right or wrong way to potty train a child and very few parents are prepared for how long it can take. Some children will grasp the process within a few days but many take several months. Both you and your child have a better chance of success if you know the basics before starting any form of training as it's important to keep the child involved and make the process clear to them.

Throughout the training process it is important to remember that there will be setbacks, accidents will happen from time to time but try to remain calm and do not get angry with the child. When accidents occur they should be dealt with calmly with the parent explaining to the child that it does not matter and that next time they need the toilet they try using the potty instead.

Equipment

Your approach to the training will dictate the equipment you need, many parents opt for a slow transitional period where the child uses "pull up" training pants that are similar to diapers and they then move on to cloth training pants when the child starts to grasp the idea.

Obviously the potty is the most important piece of equipment when you start the training and many parents opt for having more than one potty with one located in the bathroom upstairs and the other downstairs in the living room or kitchen.

Toilet seat adaptors are also a good idea as they allow the child to sit on the toilet without falling in. Many children will choose to sit on the toilet after a short period of training as they like to imitate the actions of their parents. The adaptor is also very useful when you are away from the home as it allows the child to use public toilets with the adaptor offering a sense of familiarity.

A footstool is also something that may prove useful when using the toilet as it gives the child stability and somewhere to rest their feet when sat on the toilet.

At What Age Should You Start Potty Training Your Toddler

There is no set age to start potty training your child but most parents decide to start the training process sometime between 18 and 24 months. There is no hard and fast rule about when to start but it's widely accepted that when a child gets to about 18 months it has the necessary physical and expressive skills to grasp the concept of potty training.

Before any form of training starts it's important to assess your child to establish whether he/she is ready for the transition as starting too early can cause frustration and anxiety in the child and will only lengthen the process as the child may develop a fear or stubbornness towards the potty.

Not all children will be ready to start around the age of two, some children might pick it up earlier and others might continue to struggle well into their third or fourth year but it's important that the parents start when they feel that their child is ready. One of the key things when assessing your child's readiness is their ability to communicate. It is essential that your child has the appropriate skills to inform you when he or she needs to go to the toilet so it's never a good idea to start training before your child can talk and walk.

Before you start any kind of training it's always worth making some kind of plan especially if your child is going to be looked after by other people. Decide on a start date, what approach will be taken to underwear and how to handle setbacks, offer praise and decide on what (if any) incentives should be used. Be sure to discuss your plan with anybody else that looks after your child and ensure they stick to the rules as failure to maintain a consistent approach will only result in confusion.

Key factors that should be considered when evaluating your child's readiness for potty training are: communication, an interest when others use the bathroom, independence, and having regular dry periods. Let's take a closer look at these key factors.

Communication

As mentioned, this is an essential ingredient of training as the child must have the ability to understand simple commands and the parents must be able to acknowledge the child's request for the toilet. The majority of children will be talking at the age of two and should be more than capable of asking for the potty, but if the child is less developed in this area then it might be a good idea to wait a while.

Identify key words to use when the child needs to go and stick to them, it's also important to make sure that any other adults looking after your child use these same key words. Many parents opt for the words "wees and poos" as they are short and easy to understand.

Showing Interest When Others Use the Bathroom

It is also important that the child shows an interest and willingness to be trained. Many parents find that their child starts to question what is happening when they see their parents and older brothers and sisters using the toilet. Sometimes this can act as a good platform for introducing the potty.

One of the more popular methods used when introducing the child to potty training involves sitting the child on the potty whilst the parent also sits on the toilet. This works well because most toddlers love to imitate what mum and dad are doing.

Generally, it is also widely accepted that training a child that has an older brother or sister proves to be a quicker and less stressful process than training a first or only child.

Independence

Most children are perfectly capable of walking and sitting before they are two but it is essential that they can do this before training starts. One important part of the training process is the ability to encourage your child to understand that they are free to use the potty independently but if the child does not have the confidence to walk and sit unaided it will only prolong the training process.

In the early stages some parents adopt a technique of allowing their child to run around without a diaper with the potty close at hand. They then promote independence by reminding the child that the potty is nearby should they need to go.

Another less essential part of this area also involves the child's ability to pull their pants or diaper up and down. Parents will probably need to take the lead in this area to begin with, but after a short period of time the child should be doing this for themselves.

Regular Dry Periods

Before making the decision to start potty training it's always worth monitoring the state of your child's diaper to establish how long he/she is holding their urine and stools for. If your child can stay dry for a prolonged period (normally 2-3 hours) then it might be a good time to start. Research has shown that very few children under the age of 18 months are able to take command of their bladder and bowel movements due to their muscles not being fully developed so starting before this age will ultimately cause problems.

Prior to starting the training, pay attention to when your child has bowel movements throughout the day because as a child reaches the toddler age they will become more regular. Note how many times a day this happens and at what times as this will make things easier when training. Many children often have a bowel movement after breakfast and around evening meal time so try using this as a starting point.

How Long It Takes to Potty Train Your Children

The length of time that it takes to potty train a child will vary depending on the individual and the methods adopted by the parents.

Research shows that training your first child tends to take longer than training a child that has an older sibling and on average you should expect the process to take between 3 and 6 months. Many children grasp the idea of using the potty or toilet very quickly but may struggle when staying dry throughout the night so it is not uncommon for parents to continue to use pull up style diapers right through the night to avoid accidents in the bed. If you choose to adopt this method then it is important that the parents offer praise to the child when he or she successfully completes a dry night.

It's inevitable that the child will suffer setbacks throughout the potty training process and both the parents and child will become frustrated when this happens but it is important that the parents stay relaxed and continue to encourage the child in a positive manner.

How Potty Training a Boy Is Different From a Girl

When potty training your toddler you will need to take a slightly different approach depending on their gender. Many experts claim training boys is harder than girls but both genders have their problems.

Both will experience the same feelings and unease when there bladder or bowel is full but boys tend to adapt slower as they have to grasp two methods of using the toilet: standing and sitting which can lead to confusion.

Training for Girls

Girls also have a distinctive advantage when potty training as their brains develop quicker and no matter what their body is telling them it inevitably results in them sitting on the toilet to complete the process. In addition, many children are often looked after by their mother or another female helper and find it easier to copy their actions so they tend to pick up the process quicker. The main issues with training girls stem from using the correct seating position and promoting a correct wiping procedure.

Urine infections can occur with girls during potty training and are often caused when the child is wiped incorrectly. The correct procedure should involve a front to back motion as many infections are caused when the reverse occurs and bacteria from around the child's bottom infects the urinary tract. These infections are not uncommon in young children and research shows that around 8% of girls will suffer from an infection by the time they reach the age of 5.

Once your little girl has grasped the concept of using the potty it's a good idea to try and teach her to wipe independently, if she struggles with the idea of wiping from front to back then encourage her to pat herself dry until she has a better understanding.

Training for Boys

As mentioned, boys tend to adjust slower to the idea of potty training, partly due to their brain development and also because they have to contend with standing and sitting whilst using the toilet. Some boys get confused with the idea of seeing their dad stand over the toilet whilst mum sits.

Most parents avoid using the standing option initially and start them off by sitting to improve confidence and awareness. Eventually most boys will want to copy their dad and stand over the toilet but before that can be achieved it's recommended that parents simply concentrate on getting the child to identify when they need to go and make sure they are content with using the potty or toilet.

Once this has been achieved the next stage should be getting the little boy to stand over the toilet when urinating, most boys will pick this up after watching their dad and many will insist on standing at an early stage because they want to do it the same way as daddy, but it's important that the child is not rushed into it as this can have a negative effect on the any previous success in the training process.

If the little boy shows a willingness to stand, then he will need a non slip stool to stand on and this should be used until he reaches a height that allows him to stand over the toilet safely. One of the key features of standing will be aiming. Don't show frustration if he urinates on the seat or misses the toilet completely and don't be afraid to show him how to point his penis into the toilet to avoid spraying the bathroom.

Some parents decide to have fun with this aspect of training as they feel it promotes faster development. Some suggestions for helping the little boys aim consist of adding shampoo to the toilet bowl that create a bubble effect when urinated on, whereas other fun tasks can involve placing toilet paper or certain types of breakfast cereal into the bowl that will help him concentrate and improve his aim.

The Different Stages of Potty Training

So, having read through this book you will now have a feel of what to expect in terms of when to start and how long it could take, but you may still be unsure of how to approach the training itself.

Once you have ascertained that your child is ready then it's always worth drawing up some kind of plan. Decide on an approach to the training process by discussing ideas with your partner, child minders and health workers and make sure that everyone sticks to the plan when in charge of the child.

The important issues to be covered in the plan are a start date, what underwear should be used, dealing with the inevitable setbacks and what rewards should be offered. It's also worth noting the importance of maintaining the child's sense of routine when deciding on a start date, so try to avoid starting before any major events occur in the youngster's life such as a new baby arriving, moving house, starting nursery or a change in child minder.

Stage 1

After drafting a plan and agreeing on a start date the initial part of the training process should focus on getting the child to understand that going to the toilet in their diaper is not the right thing to do. To do this it is important to introduce the child to the potty and explain to them that this is what they should be using when going to the toilet.

Before commencing any training some parents find that it helps if they empty the contents of their child's diaper into the potty in front of them whilst explaining why they are doing it. A similar technique can also be applied in the early stages whereby the parents sit the child on the potty fully clothed and explain the process to them whilst they use the toilet themselves which also helps the child to overcome any fears that he or she may have of using the potty or toilet. Should the child display any fears of using the potty or toilet then it's important not to rush them into it as it will only prolong the training process and create anxiety within the child when using the potty.

During the early stages of training it is also important to introduce the child to their new underwear. Keep it fun by buying underwear that is brightly colored or has a picture of their favorite character on them as it will help maintain a better level of interest when using them.

Stage 2

Once the child is happy to sit on the potty and starts to accept that filling their diaper is not the right thing to do then it's time to take the next step.

At this stage many parents opt to jump straight out of diapers and into normal underwear during the day and pull-up training pants through the night. Other parents prefer to introduce the change gradually by using pull-up training pants through the day and night. There is no right or wrong way but many experts feel that the modern pull-up pant is too similar to a diaper and can cause delays in the training as the child is able to maintain some level of comfort after filling this type of underwear and thus discourages the child from asking for the toilet.

By now the child should have an understanding of what the potty is used for but may not have grasped the idea that he or she should be using it for themselves. There are several different approaches that can be taken at this stage but most parents tend to build a routine of putting the child on the potty at regular intervals to give them the opportunity to go. If the child had regular toilet habits whilst wearing diapers, then the parents should find it fairly easy to build the potty routine around those habits, for example, placing the child on the potty after meal times and before a bath often works.

In some cases, parents will religiously place their child on the potty every hour and encourage them to go when sat on it. This builds the understanding of what the process is about but it is important not to force the issue by trying to make them go or make them sit there for too long as this can have an adverse effect on the training.

Whatever the decision, the objective is the same, it provides the child with the opportunity to build confidence in using the potty and it allows the parents to lavish praise on their child when he or she gets it right. Praise is an important part of the process but it needs to be done in a balanced way. Too much praise can cause apprehension and a fear of failure in the child, but it is also essential to give praise and maintain a positive approach even when things don't go according to plan.

Throughout this part of the process it is essential that the child remains relaxed and is not made to feel rushed into learning something new. Keep the process fun and allow the child to develop at their own pace. Never punish the child for making a mess or give any indication that he or she has failed in anyway. Remain positive even when clearing up accidents by offering encouragement by telling the child that it's not important and suggest that they use the potty next time.

Your child should now be well on the way to becoming potty trained but it's essential to understand that the process has not been completed. Some parents may get lucky and have a child that adapts well and stays dry through the day and night but most children will still suffer accidents from time to time, especially when sleeping.

Stage 3

The next stage of the process will focus on honing their new skills, promoting independence and addressing the occasional setback.

Some children will pick up potty training within a few days or weeks and will never look back but others will require more time to develop their confidence. An important part of the process will be to encourage the child to use the potty independently and with minimal prompting from the parents. A useful technique when trying to achieve this is to have a potty readily available in whatever room the child is playing in and allow them to use it when they want. It's sometimes a good idea if the parent asks the child to go every once in a while, but eventually he or she will grasp the concept and be able to make their own decision to sit on the potty when the need arises.

To begin with certain aspects of the training, such as wiping and aiming, will require the parent to get involved but at some point the child will want to learn this new skill for themselves. It's important to promote and encourage this independent streak but be prepared for the odd mishap during this transition. Again, it's important to remain positive and to not show any kind of negativity towards the child if an accident occurs.

Setbacks can often occur at this stage because the child gets too confident and thinks that they can hold on for a bit longer. This often occurs when the child is playing and does not want to stop.

Stage 4

The child will now be well on their way to mastering their new skill but the final stage is really about the child acknowledging that it is their job to go to the toilet or at least let someone know that they need to go. Most children adapt very quickly when they receive praise for getting it right so be prepared to continue with that even after they appear to have perfected this skill.

Most parents tend to approach the training with the philosophy of getting the child to stay dry in the day and worry about the night time later. This can work in as much as the child will sometimes accept that having accidents is not the right thing to do and get into a routine of going to the toilet before and after sleeping. Other parents will try to deal with night training at the same time as day training by waking the child at set times in the night to go to the toilet. Whatever method you chose you will need to be prepared for the occasional blip and accept that night-time training is a completely different aspect.

How to Do Night-Time Potty Training

It's likely that your child will grasp daytime toileting long before they remain dry through the night. If your child continues to wet the bed after mastering their skills throughout the day, then don't be concerned that they are regressing in their development as it's perfectly normal. In general, children grasp the idea of bladder control by the time they are 3 but night-time control can take a bit longer. Many children continue to urinate in their sleep up until they are 5 years old and some beyond that.

During the early stages of daytime training it can be useful if you monitor your child's underwear when they wake up to establish whether they frequently urinate through the night. Many children will resist going in the night as a result of the concepts they have learnt via daytime training and this will result in making night-time training much easier.

Key factors when considering your child's readiness for night-time training are discussed next.

Age

There is no definitive time or age to start night-time training. A lot will depend on the child's progress and willingness to learn during the day, but many parents decide to deal with night-time training once their child has shown enough progress during the day.

When your child reaches the age of around 3 or 4 and remains dry and accident free through the day then it might be a good time to try night–time training.

Underwear

Most parents will decide to keep their child in diapers or pull ups for a short time during the night even if their child is fully trained and accident free in the day just to avoid a wet bed, but at some point the child will need to make the transition from protective style underwear to cloth pants.

There is nothing wrong in keeping your child in diapers or pull ups until you feel that the time is right. A good indication of this will be gained when they wake up in the morning and you are able to establish whether their underwear has remained dry through the night.

If, over the course of a week or two the diapers are predominantly dry then consider moving into cloth underpants during the night, but when you chose to do this it is highly advisable to invest in some kind of mattress protector.

Encouragement

It is essential that your child has a toilet break built into their bedtime routine to give them the opportunity to go before they get into bed. Equally, it is important to let the child know that if they require the toilet in the night, they can either get up and go independently or wake the parents to help. The latter option is usually preferred by most parents as it allows the parent to offer immediate praise when the child wakes them and also discourages the child from wandering around in the middle of the night.

Depending on the size of the house and location of the bathroom it is not always a good idea to encourage the child to use the bathroom independently during the night so it may be useful to leave a night light on in the child's room with a potty to hand just in case they need it.

Whatever the parent's decision it is important that the child is encouraged to get up and deal with their need for the toilet as opposed to just wetting the bed. So before putting the child to sleep, reassure them that if they need to go in the night, they should first wake mum or dad.

Things to Avoid

Do not condemn the child when they have accidents during the night; try to praise the child where possible and offer encouragement when things do not go according to plan.

Do not punish the child in any way for wetting the bed; making them sleep in wet sheets or bed clothes will only cause stress and anxiety and delay the training process.

Do not reduce the child's fluid intake before bedtime in the hope that it helps them stay dry. This will only cause health problems and will not work as the bladder tends to adjust to fewer fluids by holding less but cutting out tea, coffee or fizzy drinks before bedtime may help as they can sometimes encourage the child's body to produce more urine.

Try to avoid talking about any problems you are having when around the child as they will pick up on this and it can result in them feeling humiliated and embarrassed which will only cause setbacks.

Avoid waking the child during the night as this will not have the desired effect on the training process. This method might reduce the number of accidents that occur in the night but it will not encourage the child to respond to its body telling them that they need to go. This term is often referred to as "lifting" and has been used as a training technique with limited success. The success can depend on the child but you should always remember three important rules when waking or "lifting." They are:

– To ensure that the child is completely wide awake and aware of what is going on by explaining the process

– If the child is already wet, then it is important that the child is still placed on the toilet and encouraged to go

– That the parents use different timing patterns when waking each night to avoid repetition

It is important for parents to remember that it can take years for them to become consistently dry through the night. Some children continue to have accidents well into their early school years and as a result the parents will need to remain patient as eventually the child will grow out of it.

This situation is not uncommon and it's unlikely that the child will have nothing wrong with them other than the odd child having an overactive bladder or the occasional bladder infection which may cause wetting. Most children that continue to wet the bed between the ages of 5 and 7 have just struggled with bladder control and struggle to identify that their body is telling them that they need to go.

How to Potty Train Your 1 Year Old

The concept of potty training a 1 year old may seem a little strange given everything that you have read so far but it is not an uncommon procedure in certain parts of the world.

Statistics published in the Contemporary Pediatrics magazine shows that more the 50% of children in the world are toilet trained by the time they get to their first birthday. Many of these children come from less developed countries where toilet training is more of a necessity than a convenience as disposable diapers and potties are not available.

Many experts believe that this training process works better when executed in the first six months of a baby's life but it does require a lot of time and effort which is something that is not conducive to the modern parent.

The process basically requires the adult to hold their baby in a seated position with the thighs up against their stomach and then asks the parent to perform hissing and grunting noises to encourage their child to carry out toilet duties. In time the parent will learn their child's habits and the child will learn to perform when put on the toilet or potty, but it takes time and requires a lot of effort but success can result in saving a small fortune in disposable diapers as well as benefiting the environment.

Baby potty training is not a common practice within the UK or U.S. and many health workers will advise against it but it is a useful technique for people that want to get their child potty trained early on because of child-care issues.

Many of the experts that endorse baby potty training also point to the fact that when a child is deemed ready for potty training at the age of around two they also develop other habits and skills than can deter learning – many people describe this age bracket as being "the terrible two's" and at this stage children can sometimes develop tantrums and other kinds of behavioral issues and therefore training at an earlier age can avoid these testing times.

How to Potty Train Your 2 Year Old

There are no set rules about when you should start potty training your child but studies indicate that the national average in the U.S. is about 27 months.

The important thing to remember when starting the training is to take it slowly and ensure that your child is physically and emotionally ready. Most of these attributes will have developed in a 2 year old child and as such most people choose to start the training around this age.

Before any formal training begins encourage the child to show interest in what goes on within the bathroom. Allowing the child into the bathroom when mum or dad are using it may ignite an interest or encourage them to press the flush after you have finished but try to persuade them gradually and don't be too pushy at this stage. From the outset it is important to talk to the child and tell them what is going to happen, use simple words to describe the different toilet actions and make sure that everyone involved uses the same ones.

The next step will be to introduce them to the potty by allowing them to sit on it fully clothed, let them treat it as a new seat or a play thing for a while to overcome any potential phobias they may have. After a short time when the child seems comfortable with it ask if they would like to try using it when going to the toilet. If they are happy too then start introducing it into a routine where the child sits on the potty a couple of times a day.

Even if the child fails to go in the potty it helps to empty the contents of their diaper or underwear into the potty or toilet to help them understand why it is there. Many parents decide to do this as part of the introduction stage and dispose the contents of the child's diaper into the toilet whilst the child is watching. Once this process has started the child should begin to progress with the training and the parents should see signs of development over the course of the coming weeks or months.

Many children will pick it up quickly and are walking around in cloth underpants within weeks, but parents must be prepared for the long haul as the child will inevitably have accidents from time to time.

How to Potty Train Your 3 Year Old

Essentially, training a 3 year old will not be any different from training a 2 year old but it is possible that a child of this age has had previous problems with potty training and the parents have taken a decision to hold off.

If this is the case, then the parents may encounter problems as a result of previous experience and in this instance it is even more important to take things slowly and allow the child to develop in their own time.

Making the child feel guilty or pressuring the child to learn because the parents are trying to hurry the training process along will only cause anxiety in the infant.

Another issue when training your child at this age can occur when your child attends Pre School classes. Many parents decide to send their child to Pre School in preparation for starting normal school and a lack of toilet skills will cause nervousness and concern for both the parents and the child when attending. In cases like this it can often have a good effect and act as a catalyst for the child to start learning after seeing other children demonstrate different toilet habits.

No matter what the situation, it's always worth mentioning any concerns to the Pre School teachers before they start as it's highly likely that they have encountered the problem before with other children.

Potty Training Ideas Not Involving Food or Money as a Reward

Many parents decide to offer incentives and reward their children when potty training as it's generally acknowledged that children tend to respond well to this type of motivation. However, using these tactics can sometimes have an adverse effect especially when using food or money as a form of reward and parents need to be careful as such tactics are best used when the child needs that extra push.

Instead of using money or food to encourage the child there are other more creative ideas that can be implemented which your child may respond to. The key is to keep it interesting so your child associates the success of going to toilet with a fun or exciting reward. At this stage it's worth noting that whatever you choose to reward them with it has to be done almost immediately and needs to be explained.

Some of the more popular ideas for rewards involve stickers and charts with some parents creating charts for their children with a simple aim of giving the child stickers to put on the chart when they have been successful. Other parents choose to go one stage further and have a good and bad chart that also focuses on the unsuccessful attempts, in a similar way stickers can also be rewarded and used to decorate the child's potty when success has been achieved.

Coupons can also be used as an incentive and they can be as creative as you want them to be. The child can be given the opportunity to pick a coupon after a successful trip and the coupon can be for anything you want. Ideas include extra play time with mummy or daddy, additional bed-time stories, blowing bubbles, extra hugs and kisses or more time playing in the park. Whilst this may seem like a very simple idea it does work as it offers variety to the child and does not allow them to get bored with the same routines or rewards.

Rewards should also be kept small, such as coloring pens, Matchbox cars, or stickers. These small gifts or trinkets can often be found in the dollar store. Buying a stamp with an inkpad and stamping your child's hand whenever they successfully go has been found to be popular and so too has the use of temporary tattoos. Magnets can be a great reward and especially magnetic alphabets and numbers. After each successful attempt your child can be rewarded with a new alphabet letter or number and so in that way they are not only learning their toilet training but also their ABC's and 123's. An extremely cheap reward idea is to give your child printable coloring sheets because kids love to color.

These rewards can then be placed somewhere out of reach, but still in eyesight to the child when they are using the potty. This will help the child to develop the idea of goal-setting. These small rewards could also be placed in a box or tin with a lid and calling it a mystery gift box. The child can then put their hand in to find which mystery gift they have chosen.

Another fun and entertaining way to promote success is to create a "potty song" that the parents and child can sing along too when sat on the potty. Whilst this is not a reward as such it will act as an incentive for the child by generating excitement and attachment by regular celebration which is something that toddlers respond well too. Another incentive is to put 2-3 drops of blue food dye into the toilet and watch it turn green when they pee into it.

There are various training methods available that offer no form of reward other than praise from the parents. During the infant years children respond well to praise in all aspects of their life and this can be used to install confidence within the child.

Whether to Use Training Underwear or Regular

There is a wealth of advice and information on what your child should wear for potty training and each option has its strengths and weaknesses, but it's a decision that parents really need to make based on their situation and expectations.

For example, if your child spends a large amount of time in nursery or with child minders, you may feel that "pull up" style training pants are better suited for you or if you are a full time parent with no work commitments, you may be better served just getting your child into normal cloth underwear as soon as possible. Every scenario is different but what follows is a guide to each type of underwear with pro and cons listed.

Traditional Cloth Underwear

The good:

– Fairly cheap to purchase with most baby outlets and supermarkets offering multi packs at an extremely reasonable price

– After purchasing this type of underwear it can be washed and used again until the child grows out of them

– Easy for the child to use when taking them off and putting back on as there are no fastening straps

– Most underwear is made of relatively thin material and does not absorb liquid so if the child does have an accident, they will feel wet and dirty which encourages them to use the potty

– Gives the child the sense of being like the parents as the underwear is similar to what adults wear

The bad:

– When accidents occur it is often necessary to change the child's complete outfit (certainly the bottom half of it)

– Creates more washing

– Can cause problems when travelling out and about as the child has no protection whatsoever

Cloth Training Pants

The good:

– Like the traditional cloth underwear this type of garment can be washed and reused

– Cloth training pants are more expensive than the traditional option, but they are more cost productive than disposable training pants

– Unlike traditional cloth pants this type of underwear does offer some protection against leakage, but the material also gives the child a sense of discomfort when an accident occurs

The bad:

– Material does not offer full protection against accidents, so a change of clothing may be necessary when accidents occur

– Like the normal cloth pants these can create a lot of washing

– Some children will struggle to pull these up and down

Disposable Training Pants (Pull-Ups)

The good:

– Offers excellent protection when accidents occur

– Can be used in a period of transition between diapers and cloth training pants

– Completely Disposable

– Creates no washing/laundry

– Offers protection when out and about and in car

The bad:

– Very expensive in comparison to the other options. A pack of about 20 pull-up pants may only last a couple of weeks

– When you run out you will need to visit the supermarket to buy more

– Can discourage the child from asking for the toilet as this type of pant absorbs wetness and therefore offers a level of comfort when accidents occur

– Looks and feels like a diaper so the child may struggle to differentiate between the two

– Can be difficult to pull up and down

– Does not resemble adult underwear

When selecting the type of underwear to be used it's sometimes a good idea to remain flexible as the child may have a different preference to the parents. Many parents will switch to pull-ups or training pants initially to see how the child adapts and if all goes well they will then switch the child into traditional underwear.

Depending on how you approach the night-time training you may opt to use pull-ups through the night to avoid a wet bed but a lot will depend on the child's development.

Whether to Go Back to Diapers (Nappies) If Your Toddler Experiences Accidents

No matter how quickly and successfully your child adapts to the idea of potty training it's highly likely that he or she will have the occasional accident. Approximately 80% of children experience some kind of setback during the potty training process. These accidents are part and parcel of the training process and should be dealt with in a controlled and calm manner.

Many of these accidents occur when children become so engrossed with what they are doing that they simply forget that they need to go to the toilet or misjudge the situation by thinking they can hold on for longer. These situations will occur from time to time and should be treated as accidents and not major setbacks.

On the other hand your child may really struggle to grasp the concept of using the potty from day one and continues to have accidents on a regular basis. If this occurs and you start to feel frustrated, then don't be afraid to stop the process and take a break for a few days or even a week and give yourself and the child a rest from the training routine.

During this break it will be necessary to put the child back into their diaper for a short time but make sure that it is only for a short period of time. After the break it is important that you explain the process again to your child, tell them that diaper will no longer be used and that they will be expected to use the potty and grown-up pants. It sometimes helps if you take a slightly different approach to the training when this occurs.

Returning to diapers when your child is having regular accidents is not unusual, but it should only be done on a temporary basis.

How to Deal With Fear

Many children can develop fears throughout the training routine and these uncertainties can cause problems throughout the process. A child's fear or concern can relate to a number of issues like:

– Falling into the toilet

– Flushing the toilet

– Fear of failure

– Fear of the potty itself

No matter what the concern it is important to view the situation from the child's point of view as up until this point your child has been happily going about doing their business in a diaper and then having a bit of pamper time when mum or dad changes them. All of a sudden they are being told that this will stop and they are expected to go to toilet on a seat with everyone watching them.

In cases where the potty is thought to be the fear or problem this can cause potty resistance. This is common and can be dealt with by offering the child non-threatening exposure to the potty to allow them to become familiar with it. As previously mentioned, a useful technique in dealing with this phobia is to allow the child to become familiar with the potty prior to starting the training. Encourage the child to sit on the potty fully clothed and incorporate the potty into play time by getting his favorite toy or teddy bear involved.

Fear will need to be tackled as and when it arises and it's important to discuss the problem with the child and make sure that you take their concerns seriously. Make them understand that you are there to help and try to keep them as stress-free and comfortable as you can when training. If the flush causes fear, then try not to use it for a while when the child is around. If the child is concerned about falling off or down the toilet, then reassure them that won't happen if mummy or daddy are there and give them the option of using the potty instead.

Never discard your child's fear as being silly or stupid no matter how trivial it seems and always seek to reassure them that it will be OK.

How to Deal With Stubbornness

Unfortunately the age at which most parents decide that their child is ready to start potty training is the same time they start to develop certain behavioral issues. Whilst these issues are completely normal in a child's development, they can hinder the training process and cause added frustration.

Some children develop stubbornness when lifestyle changes occur or when they are being pushed too fast, so it is important to acknowledge when it starts and address the issue that is causing the problem. If the issue cannot be resolved immediately, then consider holding off or taking a break from the training.

There are many factors that can cause stubbornness whilst training. Sometimes this can stem from when a child suffers a bad experience whilst training or that the parents have decided to start the process too early. Certain children are just strong willed and will be hard to train, so it is essential that the parent identify this and proceed with the training.

Experts believe that there are several reasons why a child would develop stubbornness in training. Some of the more common ones have been listed below:

– Fear of sitting on the potty or toilet

– Scared of the toilet flushing

– Starting the training too early or trying to develop the child too quickly

– Suffering forms of punishment

– Conflicting training methods. This often occurs when being looked after by different people

– Medical conditions such as constipation or urine infections

– Craves attention

If the child persists with their stubbornness, then it's never a good idea to force them to do anything. This will only have a negative effect on the process. Don't be afraid to delay training for a few days or weeks and consider adopting a new strategy to the training regime. Consider introducing rewards like stickers or coupons into the process or just try making it more fun by creating a song.

How to Deal With Potty Training Regression

The word regression is described as a backwards movement or relapse and when training a child you will have to accept that this will occasionally happen. Getting your child to use the potty everyday can be a demanding and lengthy task. Any form of regression can be frustrating for the parents and in some cases this can cause them to revert back to diapers.

Regression often happens when the child suffers some kind of emotional disturbance. It's possible that there has been a recent change in the child's life that might have triggered the setback. Such instances can often occur when:

– Child care arrangements change

– He or she has recently started school or nursery

– A new arrival in the family

– The family is moving home

– Parents splitting up

– Family bereavement

Whatever the reason for the relapse it should be dealt with in the same way as previous accidents. The parents should remain calm and not make a big deal about it, discuss the situation with the child and offer encouragement about getting to the toilet the next time.

Sometimes it helps when parents offer reminders at regular intervals as regression can also be caused by forgetfulness, especially when a child is reluctant to interrupt a play routine or favorite television program. Offer light encouragement towards the child every hour or so to remind the child that the potty is there should they need it. If the child continues to have accidents and ignores the request, then take the child to the potty and encourage them to go in a firm manner and explain to them that they can return to whatever they were doing before once they have been to the toilet.

Complete regression is unlikely but in some cases it will occur. It often occurs when a child undergoes a major change in their life such as moving house or the parents splitting up. If this does happen, then don't be discouraged as these setbacks should be managed with tolerance and understanding and when appropriate the parent should look to implement the techniques previously used.

Conclusion

After reading this book I hope that you will have gained a better grasp of what is involved in potty training a child.

Nobody is claiming that it is easy, but as a parent you will have dealt with the sleepless nights, the feeding and the endless diaper changes so you should be equipped to cope with the next stage in your child's development.

Whilst there is no golden rule to potty training, it's always worth reiterating what has been previously mentioned in this book. The essential points are:

– Ensure that your child is physically and emotionally ready to start learning new skills

– Purchase the appropriate equipment. Potty, toilet seat adaptor and underwear are always a good start

– Draw up a plan and ensure that everyone caring for your child sticks to it

– Introduce the potty gradually and create a routine for using it

– Stop using diapers and switch to training pants as soon as possible

– Keep explaining the procedure to the child and remain positive even when things don't go according to plan

– Encourage independence when the child starts to accept their new skill

– Deal with regression, fear and stubbornness in a calm and controlled manner

And now all that is left for me to say is:

Good 'Potty' Luck